CW00968305

Establishing the Anglo-American Alliance

THE SECOND WORLD WAR DIARIES
OF BRIGADIER VIVIAN DYKES

Also from Brassey's

BAYNES
The Forgotten Victor
General Sir Richard O'Connor Kt, GCB, DSO, MC

DANCHEV
Very Special Relationship
Field Marshal Sir John Dill and the Anglo-American Alliance 1941-44

MEARSHEIMER
Liddell Hart and the Weight of History

MESSENGER
Hitler's Gladiator
The Life and Times of SS-Oberstgruppenfuehrer
and General der Waffen-SS Sepp Dietrich

PERKINS
A Fortunate Soldier

STAHLBERG
Bounden Duty
The Memoirs of a German Officer 1932-1945

Establishing the Anglo-American Alliance

THE SECOND WORLD WAR DIARIES
OF BRIGADIER VIVIAN DYKES

ALEX DANCHEV

BRASSEY'S (UK)

(Member of the Maxwell Pergamon Publishing Corporation)

LONDON · OXFORD · WASHINGTON · NEW YORK
BEIJING · FRANKFURT · SÃO PAULO · SYDNEY · TOKYO · TORONTO

UK (Editorial)	Brassey's (UK) Ltd., 24 Gray's Inn Road, London WC1X 8HR, England
(Orders all except North America)	Brassey's (UK) Ltd., Headington Hill Hall, Oxford OX3 0BW, England
USA (Editorial)	Brassey's (US) Inc., 8000 Westpark Drive, Fourth Floor, McLean, Virginia 22102, USA
(Orders North America)	Brassey's (US) Inc., Front and Brown Streets, Riverside, New Jersey 0075, USA Tel (toll free): 800 257 5755
PEOPLE'S REPUBLIC OF CHINA	Pergamon Press, Room 4037, Qianmen Hotel, Beijing People's Republic of China
FEDERAL REPUBLIC OF GERMANY	Pergamon Press GmbH, Hammerweg 6, D-6242 Kronberg, Federal Republic of Germany
BRAZIL	Pergamon Editora Ltda, Rua Eca de Queiros, 346, CEP 04011, Paraiso, São Paulo, Brazil
AUSTRALIA	Brassey's Australia Pty Ltd., PO Box 544, Potts Point, NSW 2011, Australia
JAPAN	Pergamon Press, 5th Floor, Matsuoka Central Building, 1-7-1 Nishishinjuku, Shinjuku-ku, Tokyo 160, Japan
CANADA	Pergamon Press Canada Ltd., Suite No. 271, 253 College Street, Toronto, Ontario, Canada M5T 1R5

First edition 1990

Library of Congress Cataloging in Publication Data
Dukes, Vivian, 1898–1943
Establishing the Anglo-American alliance: the Second World War diaries of Brigadier Vivian Dykes/ [edited by] Alex Danchev—1st ed.
p. cm.
1. Dykes, Vivian, 1898–1943—Diaries. 2. World War, 1939–1945—Diplomatic history. 3. Great Britain—Military relations—United States. 4. United States—Military relations—Great Britain. 5. World War, 1939–1945—Personal narratives, British. 6. Generals—Great Britain—Diaries. 7. Great Britain. Army—Biography. I. Danchev, Alex. II. Title.
D750.D95 1990 940.54'8141—dc20 89–22279

British Library Cataloguing in Publication Data
Dykes, Vivian
Establishing the Anglo-American alliance: the Second World War diaries of Brigadier Vivian Dykes.
1. Great Britain. Foreign relations with United States. Biographies. 2. United States. Foreign relations with Great Britain. Biographies. I. Title II. Danchev, Alex
327.4'073'092'4
ISBN 0-08-036260-5

Printed in Great Britain by B.P.C.C. Wheatons Ltd. Exeter

In memory of my parents

Contents

ACKNOWLEDGEMENTS   viii

LIST OF PLATES   ix

ABBREVIATIONS AND CODENAMES   x

INTRODUCTION   1

Part I: The Donovan Trip   17
Introduction   19

Diary December 1940 – March 1941   24

Part II: Washington — Organising for War   67
Introduction   69

Diary December 1941 – April 1942   73

Part III: Washington — Finding a Strategy   125
Introduction   127

Diary April 1942 – July 1942   130

Part IV: TORCH — Conception and Birth   169
Introduction   171

Diary July 1942 – November 1942   174

APPENDIX: The Combined Chiefs of Staff Organisation   227

NOTES   228

INDEX   237

Acknowledgements

My primary debt is to Mr Richard Dykes and Mrs Evelyn Armitstead for making available, for the first time, as many of their father's diaries and papers as could be found after an interval of some 40 years. The process was facilitated by the Historical Branch (Army) of the Ministry of Defence. But for the early intervention of Gill Tyler, key documents might never have seen the light of day. For information from those who knew and worked with Dykes, I am especially grateful to Major General W. M. Broomhall; Lord Broughshane (Patrick Davison); the late Captain Lord Coleridge and Lady Coleridge; Lieutenant General Sir Ian Jacob; Miss Joan Mainprice; the late Lieutenant General Sir Harold Redman; Brigadier C. E. F. Turner; Lieutenant General Russell L. Vittrup; and General Albert C. Wedemeyer. I have benefited enormously from Dr Mike Pugh's careful scrutiny of a complete typescript of all the diaries. My greatest debt, however, is a personal and private one.

Extracts from Crown Copyright documents appear by permission of the Controller of Her Majesty's Stationery Office.

Except where otherwise indicated, all photographs are reproduced courtesy of the Dykes family.

List of Plates

1. On commissioning into the Royal Engineers, 1917.

2. The wedding of Dykes and Ada Winifred Smyth at Shortlands Parish Church, Kent, on 8 June 1922.

3. In Shanghai, 1927.

4. Winifred with Richard and Evelyn, 1931.

5. With Winifred outside her family home, Castle Widenham, Castletownroche, County Cork, 1937.

6. With Richard at Castle Widenham, 1937.

7. Consulting map boards on a Staff College exercise, 1939 (Dykes second from right, with hand raised).

8. The Committee of Imperial Defence Secretariat assembled on what Dykes called the 'Jubilee of Sir Maurice Hankey' in April 1937. A keen photographer, Dykes both took the photograph and managed to appear in it himself, popping up at the rear towards the left. The front row, left to right: Admiral Barry Domville, Sir John Chancellor, Hankey, Lawrence Burgis, 'Pug' Ismay. 'Jo' Hollis, a particular friend of Dykes, stands in the second row on the left; Gordon Macready, later Head of the British Army Staff in Washington, third from the left in the back row.

9. The opening session of the Imperial Conference, 14 May 1937. Chamberlain is second from the right. Dykes sits by the curtain at the rear, with Ismay on his right.

10. The Combined Chiefs of Staff in session in Washington, 23 October 1942. Dykes is fourth from the left, with Field Marshal Dill on his right. For the US Joint Chiefs of Staff, Admiral King is second from the right, Admiral Leahy third from the right, General Marshall fifth from the right. (Official US Navy Photograph; Marshall Research Foundation.)

11. Winifred receiving Dykes's posthumous US Distinguished Service Medal.

12. A portrait of 'Beetle' Smith, Dykes's devoted friend and US opposite number in 1942. (Marshall Research Foundation.)

Abbreviations and Codenames

ARCADIA	First Washington Conference (December 1941 – January 1942)
ATS	Auxiliary Territorial Service
BOLERO	Build-up of US forces in Britain for cross-Channel attack
C	Head of Secret Intelligence Service
CAB	Cabinet papers in the Public Record Office
CCS	Combined Chiefs of Staff
CIA	Central Intelligence Agency
CIGS	Chief of the Imperial General Staff
C in C	Commander in Chief
COS	Chiefs of Staff (British)
CPS	Combined Planning Staff
CTP	Cocktail party
DMO	Director of Military Operations (British)
DOTEL	Demi-Official Telegram (War Cabinet Office to JSM)
DSM	Distinguished Service Medal
EXCESS	Plan for convoy of stores from Gibraltar to Egypt (1941)
FO	Foreign Office (British)
GHQ	General Headquarters
GOC in C	General Officer Commanding in Chief
GOK	God only knows
GSO	General Staff Officer
GYMNAST	Plan for Allied invasion of North Africa (later TORCH)
JCS	Joint Chiefs of Staff (American)
JPS	Joint Planning Staff
JSM	British Joint Staff Mission in Washington
LETOD	Demi-Official Telegram (JSM to War Cabinet Offices)
NA	National Archives, Washington, DC
NATO	North Atlantic Treaty Organisation
OSS	Office of Strategic Services (US)
PLOUGH	US-Canadian force trained for operations in Norway
PM	Prime Minister

PRO	Public Record Office, London
RAF	Royal Air Force
RIVIERA	Atlantic Conference (August 1941)
RNVR	Royal Naval Volunteer Reserve
ROUNDUP	Plan for Allied invasion of North West Europe in 1943
SIS	Secret Intelligence Service (British)
SLEDGEHAMMER	Plan for limited invasion of North-West Europe in 1942
SOE	Special Operations Executive
TORCH	Allied invasion of North Africa (November 1942)
WCO	War Cabinet Offices
WO	War Office
WORKSHOP	Plan for landing on Pantelleria Island in 1941

In war, keep your own counsel, preferably in a notebook.

GENERAL SIR IAN HAMILTON

Introduction

Vivian Dykes, like Gwendolen Fairfax in *The Importance of Being Earnest*, never travelled without his diary; not to read something sensational, but to record it. Dykes the diarist travelled hopefully, avid for new experience. Dykes the bureaucrat, steeped in the culture of the Committee of Imperial Defence, noted and adapted what he found. Dykes the mimic registered and observed, wit sharpened. Dykes the diplomat absorbed atmosphere like a sponge. In all these guises, as British secretary to the Combined Chiefs of Staff, he travelled from Washington to Casablanca in January 1943 for the first of the great mid-war conferences between Churchill, the Emperor of the East, and Roosevelt, the Emperor of the West, complete with their retinues. Dykes was considerably elated. The glamour, the excitement, the sheer opulence of the Conference were palpable and seductive. Harold Macmillan, in attendance as Minister Resident in the Mediterranean, and not one to stint himself, marvelled in his own diary that 'the whole thing was free, including the most excellent food and quantities of drink. Even cigarettes, cigars, chewing gum, sweets, of which the Americans are very fond, and soap, shaving soap, and razors – all these were freely distributed.'[1] A visit to Marrakesh conjured up for Dykes the *Arabian Nights*. 'I wanted to wear a turban and those big oriental trousers . . . . I felt like an *Esquire* cartoon', he told one of the Americans.[2]

He was accommodated in a luxurious villa with Brigadier Ian Jacob, a friend and contemporary and fellow member of the close-knit Cabinet Office band of brothers. Together the two men kept the British record of the high-level meetings throughout the Conference. They worked late, breakfasting in their villa and gorging themselves on an inexhaustible supply of fresh oranges. Jacob also kept an illicit diary of his official travels. A bravura passage describes how he and Dykes, whose brilliant mimicry was much appreciated in Whitehall, 'had great fun over the CIGS [Chief of the Imperial General Staff, General Brooke] whose birdlike aspect and fast

1

clipped speech lent themselves to caricature. I have never met a man who so tumbles over himself in speaking. . . . All this, together with his constant habit when talking of shooting his tongue out and round his lips with the speed of a chameleon, made him an easy prey to Dumbie's imitative wit.'[3] Dykes was known as 'Dumbie' after Sir Walter Scott's 'hard-hearted lord of toil', the cantankerous Laird of Dumbiedikes, 'who piqued himself upon the loyalty of his principles "in the worst of times"', and who was himself nicknamed Damn-me-dikes because of his 'transports of violent and profane language'.[4] The sobriquet was a mark of the affection in which he was held by his Cabinet Office colleagues.

The Conference concluded satisfactorily, especially for the British. In Jacob's verdict, 'our ideas . . . prevailed almost throughout'. But this was the last time. 'All of us in keeping score counted Casablanca as lost,' one of the US planning staff remembered, in a revealing turn of phrase. After Casablanca, however, 'we went all the way up'.[5] For the moment the British were buoyant. Following the Allied landings in North Africa in November 1942, the logic of continued Mediterranean operations had proved incontestable. Dykes decided to return to Washington via London, in the company of another friend, Brigadier Guy Stewart, Director of Plans at the War Office. They set off in an aircraft en route through Algiers and Gibraltar. The flight was uneventful until about 7.30 a.m. on 30 January 1943, when an outer starboard engine suddenly caught fire over the British Channel. The pilot switched off the fuel supply to that engine and used the automatic fire extinguisher. The engine continued to blaze. In a couple of minutes it fell out of its bearings and crashed down into the sea, breaking off a piece of the wing as it went. Dykes and Stewart were asleep in the 'bomb bag' in the belly of the plane, a Liberator. The pilot found that he could still fly on three engines. They made landfall in Pembrokeshire. The pilot came down to about 2,000 feet, looking for an aerodrome. Approaching the one at Haverfordwest, the inner starboard engine cut out. The pilot kept both port engines full on and managed to hold more or less straight, hoping to make a forced landing on the aerodrome. But they were losing height too fast. The tail struck a small mound and sheared off. The aircraft bounced on the ground and turned over and over. It did not catch fire, though there were over 1,000 gallons of petrol left. Dykes, still asleep, was killed outright in the crash. He was just 44.[6]

Dykes's death caused consternation in London and Washington.

He was immediately awarded a posthumous US Distinguished Service Medal, a then unprecedented honour for an Englishman. The citation underlined the very real sense of comradeship he had engendered in the US capital. As a British colleague recalled, 'his name was a byword among Americans as the Englishman whom they could all understand and do business with. They hate the man with airs, and Vivian was not the chap for frills of any kind.'[7] For the US military staff, the natural litmus test of a good Briton was how much he understood Americans and how much they understood him. Dykes evidently passed with flying colours on both counts.

> As British Secretary to the Combined Chiefs of Staff he made an outstanding contribution to the Allied cause and the war effort of the United States. His sympathetic understanding of American problems and aims, his broad knowledge and experience of British military and cabinet procedure, and his great organisational ability contributed in an important measure to the expeditious establishment of the Combined Chiefs of Staff on a sound basis.[8]

For Jean Monnet, who worked with Dykes on war production and supply in Washington, and who recognised a kindred spirit, his death was 'a really great loss – he was one of those men not outwardly in the public eye but a quiet powerful force in the actual conduct of the war.'[9]

From the Cabinet Office in London, General Ismay wrote with emotion: 'We have had some bad knocks in the last three and a half years; but it is no exaggeration to say that no single event has cast such a gloom over this office as Vivian's death.' He added, in an unmistakable echo of Dumbiedikes, 'I miss him all the time, and I shall always miss him – particularly when things are going badly, and there's a tough job of work to be done. He was a grand man in a tight place – never flustered, always courageous, absolutely dependable.'[10] Dykes had already achieved an international reputation in military circles. Like Ismay, and like his deputy, Commander Richard Coleridge, he would have been an ideal candidate for the secretariat of NATO – conceivably for Secretary General. Ismay himself thought 'he would have gone right to the very top', a common estimation among those few who knew the scope of his duties. As one who worked with him in the Joint Staff Mission put it:

> In any other profession he would have been CIGS – if I make my Irish self clear – and his sense of humour was second to none. I have certainly never come across a better. It is no hyperbole to say that his death is a very great loss to Anglo–American relations. He was a splendid ambassador as well as a very great staff officer. 'Send no money' he will be saying, but we shall miss him a lot.[11]

Dumbie Dykes was born on 9 December 1898 in Shortlands, Kent, the second son of Alfred Herbert Dykes, a Justice of the Peace.[12] He was educated at Dulwich College (1910–16), where he was a School scholar, an editor of the *Alleynian*, a member of the Shooting VIII, Cadet Officer in the Corps, and Captain of the School. A contemporary was C. S. Forester, creator of the Hornblower stories, whom he was later to meet on a number of occasions in Washington.[13] Dykes won an open scholarship in Classics at Corpus Christi College, Oxford, but chose instead to go to the Royal Military Academy, Woolwich. On 6 June 1917 he was commissioned into the Royal Engineers, specialising first in signals work. Early in 1918 he was sent to France, only to return a few months later, temporarily blinded by mustard gas. After the war he served with the Royal Signals in Ireland, India and Waziristan before returning to England and rejoining the Sappers in 1922. The same year he married Ada Winifred ('W' in the diaries), the younger daughter of Richard Smyth, of Castletownroche, County Cork. A VAD (Voluntary Aid Detachment) nurse in the war, Winifred drove an ambulance during the 'Troubles' in Ireland. She is remembered as a sweet-natured retiring Irishwoman, well suited to her dynamic consort, though sometimes, perhaps, a little shocked. The marriage appears to have been a very happy one. There were three children, two boys and a girl. Tragically, one of the boys died in infancy in 1932 after swallowing a toy: a bitter blow, rarely mentioned.

In 1923 Dykes spent the then customary year at Cambridge, at Caius College, followed by the supplementary course at Chatham. He received an MBE for his work with the British division hurriedly sent to China to combat any Japanese threat to the International Settlement at Shanghai (1926–28). He was a popular and successful Adjutant of the Royal Engineers' 1st Division at Aldershot (1929–31), a posting which led to his nomination to the Staff College, Camberley, in 1932. As with so many officers of promise, the two years Dykes spent at Camberley proved to have a determining influence on his future. There was a high-calibre Directing Staff, including Colonel 'Jumbo' Wilson, the Chief Instructor, and a brilliant pipe-smoking Wing Commander, Jack Slessor, who both rose to five-star rank. For Dykes, however, the key connection was none other than the revered Commandant, the future Field Marshal Sir John Dill, then a Major General. Over the next decade Dill often relied on the judgements of character and ability he formed as Commandant of the Staff College during the period 1931–34, and required a good deal of contrary evidence to change his mind. Significantly, with Dykes he was much impressed. At the end of the course in December 1933 came the final interview. Dyke's diary breathes a sigh of relief: 'Got a first-class chit, for which many thanks.'[14]

Dykes also had a first-class interpretership in Italian. Soon after leaving Camberley he went to the War Office in the Italian section of Military Intelligence (1934–35). This led directly to the first unusual twist in his career. He was recruited into the inner sanctum of British defence policy making: the secretariat of the Committee of Imperial Defence, governed by the magisterial figure of Sir Maurice Hankey, with Ismay, another influential patron, already functioning smoothly at the heart of the machine as Hankey's deputy. Dykes became secretary of the Overseas Defence Committee (1935–38), the body responsible for reviewing the defence schemes of the whole colonial Empire and coordinating advice to colonial governments on all aspects of preparations for war. Competitive rearmament and mounting international tension lent an increasing urgency to highly demanding work.

It was immediately clear that Dykes was in his element. Jacob remembered his 'wonderful knack of spreading good humour and willing cooperation'. Military and civilian colleagues alike came to him for advice and enouragement. 'His particular capacity for friendship, his vivacity, and his exceptional powers of humorous expression in speech and writing' were all given full rein.[15] He was twice promoted, and awarded the CBE. There followed an interlude as Instructor at the senior wing of the Staff College at Minley. On the outbreak of war in September 1939, he was immediately recalled by Ismay to what was now the War Cabinet Office (1939–40). In July 1940, eager for command of troops, he took over 26 Field Company, Royal Engineers, reforming after their virtual destruction in France. Four months later he returned again to the War Office, first in Military Operations and then as Director of Plans (1940–41) for Dill, now CIGS.

It was from the War Office in December 1940 that Dykes's career was given a second twist. He was selected for a mission as improbable as it was important: to escort the legendary Colonel 'Wild Bill' Donovan, soon to become head of the Office of Strategic Services (forerunner of the CIA) and effective coordinator of US intelligence, on a fact-finding tour of the Mediterranean, at American request. Together Donovan and Dykes visited Spain, Portugal, Greece,

Bulgaria, Yugoslavia, Albania, Turkey, Palestine, Iraq and Egypt. Donovan opened doors. They spoke to kings and prime ministers, generals and diplomats. They examined the political and military situation throughout the region. They were away from December 1940 until March 1941. The detailed diary kept by Dykes of the whole 'Donovan Trip' forms the first part of this book.

In August 1941, as Director of Plans, he took part in the historic 'Atlantic Conference' between Churchill and Roosevelt in Argentia Bay, off Newfoundland, at which the Atlantic Charter was drawn up and some further halting steps taken towards Anglo-American military coordination. Among the staff, discussion centred on the production and supply of war *matériel*, the issue uppermost in American minds at a time when they had not yet formally declared themselves. Dill led for the British; General George C. Marshall, the US Army Chief of Staff, led for the Americans. It was the first meeting of these two men, who discovered an affinity of outlook and temperament out of which grew, with remarkable speed, a personal relationship underpinning the whole war-time Anglo-American alliance.[16] Dykes led the ensuing informal staff talks in London. He emphasised to the Americans three points which had resonance for the future strategic debate. The first was the necessity for flexibility in strategy. The second was British interest in a land offensive in Europe in general and North Africa in particular – but also the enormous difficulties of landing large forces on the Continent. The third was a question: whether the Americans were still interested, as they had appeared to be at the Atlantic Conference, in possible operations in North Africa.[17] The response was studiously non-committal.

These experiences were a prelude to his last and most important duty. On 12 December 1941, five days after Pearl Harbor had precipitated American entry into the war, the Prime Minister set off once again to confer with the President, this time in Washington, accompanied by a sizeable entourage. Dykes was never permanently to return to England. The Conference, codenamed ARCADIA, announced the birth of the Combined Chiefs of Staff organisation, a fretwork of 'combined' Anglo-American committees, each with a specialist function (planning, intelligence, transport), with permanent headquarters in Washington. All the committees were responsible ultimately to the Combined Chiefs of Staff themselves, that is, to the US Joint Chiefs of Staff and British Chiefs of Staff together. Because the whole organisation was based in the United States, however, the British Chiefs of Staff needed full-time representation in that country. A powerful team was assembled for this purpose. At its head was Field Marshal Sir John Dill, recently 'retired' as CIGS in favour of his friend and protégé General Sir Alan Brooke (later Field Marshal Lord Alanbrooke), who now rose again, phoenix-like, in Washington. Dill became senior British member of the Combined Chiefs of Staff and head of the British Joint Staff Mission – and against all expectation, the most influential foreigner resident in Washington during the pivotal years of the war. Inevitably, a combined secretariat was also required for the new organisation. The two men selected to found and build this vital link were Brigadier General Walter Bedell Smith, US Army, and Brigadier Vivian Dykes.

The pairing was a brilliant success. The earliest intimation of any problem would often come through this channel, exchanged officially or unofficially through the medium of the Combined Secretariat, which evolved a distinctive blend of commonality and camaraderie at the very epicentre of Anglo-American decision making. Dykes and Bedell Smith swiftly established one of the keynote relationships of the military alliance. They worked together with the greatest informality, regularly dashing into each other's offices to pool information, or simply to gossip – 'What's the matter with Uncle Ernie today?' (The rebarbative Admiral Ernest J. King, US Chief of Naval Operations.) In the event of any delay they became adept at 'putting the heat' on the Combined Chiefs by manipulating the agenda of the weekly meetings. They regularly 'fixed up' the minutes, with a degree of secretarial licence.

> After a meeting the secretaries would get together and write it up. Bedell said that one of them would take one thing one guy had said and write it up in draft, and then he would pass it over to the other guy. Once Dykes passed over something to him . . . Bedell read it over and said, 'This sounds just fine; it's wonderful. There isn't but one thing wrong with it.' Dykes said 'What's that?' Bedell said, 'Hell, that isn't what he said.' Dykes said, 'I know damn well it isn't, but it's what he should have said.'[19]

As rendered by one schooled in the ways of the War Cabinet Office,

> And so when the great ones repair to their dinner
> The secretary stays getting thinner and thinner
> Wracking his brains to record and report
> What he thinks they will think that they ought to have thought.[20]

Above all, Dykes and Bedell Smith became friends. 'I have told you, I think, how very fond I was of Vivian,' wrote Bedell Smith to

Winifred on receiving word of Dykes's death. 'Next to yourself and the children, I really think no one feels his loss more deeply than I do.'[21] It was a startling admission. The ulcerous 'Beetle' Smith was an intimidating character, not given to any declaration of emotion other than chronic bad temper. Tough, profane, intolerant, largely self-educated – reputed to have started his career selling newspapers in the streets – but also loyal and discreet, he was a formidable operator whose continuity of service in sensitive positions of government was matched only by the two officers with whom he was most closely associated, Generals Marshall and Eisenhower. He is probably best known for his peerless performance as Chief of Staff to Eisenhower in Europe (1943–45), an achievement inseparable almost from Eisenhower's own, as the latter fully acknowledged.[22] His post-war track record gives some indication of his extreme dependability. First he succeeded Averell Harriman as Ambassador to the Soviet Union (1946–49). He was then Commanding General, 1st Army (1949–50); a reforming Director of Central Intelligence (1950–53) for President Truman; and a trusted Under Secretary of State (1953–54) for President Eisenhower. He died in 1961, the recipient of four Distinguished Service Medals, recognised by the *cognoscenti* as a great chief of staff and the most effective director the CIA has ever had, yet substantially unknown, then and since.[23]

Dykes appealed to Bedell Smith because of his trenchancy, his lack of 'frills', his despatch, his vitality, most of all, perhaps, for his sense of humour. 'I am fortunate in having a *first-class* American opposite number,' Dykes wrote home to his sister, 'who laughs at the same things I do!'[24] The relationship shadowed and reinforced that of their respective masters. Bedell Smith was one of the original 'Marshall men', hand-picked by Marshall himself as worthy of the trust he was to bestow. He had been noticed at the Infantry School at Fort Benning, Georgia, as early as 1931, when Marshall was Assistant Commandant there – an interesting parallel with Dykes, in that sense a 'Dill man' of long standing. On his appointment as Army Chief of Staff in 1939, Marshall brought Bedell Smith to Washington to serve as Assistant Secretary, later Secretary, of the War Department General Staff. Bedell Smith too had entered the inner sanctum. His first loyalty, forged during this period, was not to Eisenhower, but to Marshall (and it was to Marshall again, as Secretary of State, that he reported from Moscow in the frigid years after the war). For his part, Dykes felt some exasperation with Dill (pungently expressed in the diary) during their early days in

Washington, but grew to admire him professionally without ever becoming close to him personally. By mid 1942, they were working together on the basis of complete trust. In July of that year Dykes was sent to London as Dill's *alter ego* to brief the British Chiefs of Staff and monitor their talks with the visiting Americans. Whilst there he defended Dill vigorously from Cabinet Office criticism – a notable example of personal loyalty in view of Dykes's own affiliation.[25]

With the creation of the Combined Chiefs of Staff, Bedell Smith, like Dykes, became 'a power in the land'.[26] In each case, this status was to a degree supranational. Dykes could be used as a conduit to London, and consulted almost as a member of his own staff by Marshall; Bedell Smith likewise by Dill. Both men sometimes refereed disputes in the new organisation. Each was prepared to criticise his own side for being unreasonable. Dykes therefore laid himself open to the charge of being too 'American-minded', just as Dill was accused of becoming 'increasingly Americanised' or even 'going native'.[27] In fact Dykes frequently confided to his diary an impatience with the Americans worthy of the most recalcitrant Briton – worthy even of that incurably impatient diarist, Brooke. Becoming too American-minded, and vice versa, was a risk intrinsic to genuine Anglo-American combination, and very often a stick used to beat its most successful exponents. Dykes certainly strove for an 'ambidextrous' outlook, in Eisenhower's phrase; but he did not neglect British interests.[28] As he himself argued in an important paper, in October 1942, 'from a purely national point of view, our greatest triumph has been to secure American agreement to the whole system of combined organisations. The position of the Americans would be far more authoritative without them, since they could then act as despotically as they wished, and we should be compelled to follow their lead with little or no chance of influencing their decisions in any way.'

> There are very few things which we are in a position to give the United States; but we are dependent on them for a great many things. Our only hope of influencing the US Chiefs of Staff is to work through the combined organisations. These may not work as objectively as was hoped when they were first set up; but they do at least give us the constitutional *right* to discuss our needs on equal terms, instead of receiving gratefully such crumbs as may be left from the rich man's table.[29]

This paper was addressed to the Chiefs of Staff in London, in part to secure greater recognition for the British Joint Staff Mission (JSM) in Washington. 'Only if the Americans feel that they have in the Mission an authoritative body with whom they can deal on equal terms will they be prepared to listen to the Mission's views and be influenced by them.' Thus the perennial problem of the JSM. 'We simply hold no cards at all,' lamented Dykes on another occasion, 'yet London expects us to work miracles. It is a hard life.' It was indeed. Dykes not only serviced the Combined Chiefs of Staff committee, but was also senior secretary of the JSM, and in effect chief of staff to Dill.[30] Although the final responsibility was Dill's, it fell to Dykes and his secretariat to run the Mission from day to day, and to coordinate its various elements.

A nucleus British Military Mission had been established in Washington after the secret, exploratory, American–British (ABC) Conversations of January–March 1941, when Dykes was escorting Colonel Donovan round the Mediterranean. In June 1941 the first batch of officers were reinforced by several dozen 'Military Advisers to the British Supply Council in the United States', a time-honoured and rather threadbare cover. The Mission became a joint one in embryo, with a small delegation from each service: the British Admiralty Delegation, headed by Admiral Sir Charles 'Tiny' Little; the British Army Staff, headed by Lieutenant General Sir Colville 'Chicken' Wemyss; and the RAF Delegation, headed by Air Marshal (later 'Bomber') Harris.[31] As the senior of the three, Admiral Little took charge of the Mission as a whole. Contact with the US services in these pre-Pearl Harbor days was clandestine, unorganised, and sporadic at best, even after the Atlantic Conference. As the Army Staff planner wrote regretfully to Dykes at the War Office, 'There is no disguising the fact that at present the [US] War Department is not forthcoming so far as planning is concerned; they avoid consulting us if they can and *never* invite us to any of their meetings.'[32]

In October 1941 the JSM comprised some 200 military personnel. Their directive from the Chiefs of Staff appeared straightforward enough:

1. To interpret Chiefs of Staff views to the US Chiefs of Staff.
2. To maintain the contact initiated during the Staff [ABC] Conversations and keep American–British plans up-to-date.
3. To maintain constant touch with the plans, operations, intelligence and communications branches of the American Service Departments and pass information freely to the Chiefs of Staff and Service Departments in London.[33]

One year later the difficulty inherent in the JSM's position, 'like a grist between two very large millstones', had emerged with frustrating clarity, writ large in Dykes's diary throughout 1942. Even running the Mission was no small matter. Interpreting Britain to America had become the business of a prodigious war-time 'Washington Whitehall' of over 9,000 people. The JSM itself had ballooned to almost 3,000. There were some 800 in the British Admiralty Delegation, 1,200 in the British Army Staff, 650 in the RAF Delegation, 100 central staff. The JSM was by far the largest single mission in Washington. Army Staff numbers alone exceeded all save the British Supply Mission (1,800), and quite eclipsed the 1,000 personnel directly tied to the British Embassy.[34]

With so many British representatives in Washington the possibilities for rivalry, or merely chaos, seemed endless. Territorial disputes had been a persistent feature of the previous war, epitomised by a seething hostility between the Ambassador and the head of what was then the British War Mission. Eventually the fantastic position of Ambassador Extraordinary and High Commissioner on Special Mission to the US had been created to bring the two opposing camps under a single authority. No such measures were necessary in Dykes's time. Lord Halifax, the Ambassador, 'the father and mother of all the British missions', had no effective writ, but something akin to a right of veto over missions independently operated and run. He took the trouble to convene a weekly meeting at the Embassy of all the heads – 'rather a waste of time,' Halifax observed in his lordly way, 'but the kind of waste of time that is worth it.' Unlike their predecessors, Dill and Halifax apparently liked and respected each other; as the latter noted, they had 'a great deal of background together that one hardly shares with anyone else'.[35] From the outset the military mission 'worked in' with its civilian counterparts. The initiative was taken by Dykes's congenial deputy, Commander Richard (later Captain Lord) Coleridge, a distant relation of the poet, and Deputy Secretary of the JSM throughout the war, later a natural choice as Executive Secretary of NATO (1952–70). With regard to the Embassy, Coleridge reported, 'we, the secretariat, are on the best possible terms with them and we have free run of all their files, see all their telegrams, and I personally daily discuss matters of joint interest with the Head of Chancery.'[36] Dykes ensured a similar rapport with the secretariat of the important British Supply Council. Coordination at this level was further improved in December 1942, at Dykes's instigation, with the successful innovation of a 'joint' civil secretariat on the JSM model, based at the Embassy and headed by Derick Hoyer Millar, an experienced diplomat well versed in the combined committee system.[37]

The lifeblood of the JSM was its transatlantic communications with London. For Dykes and the secretariat this meant an almost incessant traffic in telegrams. In Washington they were usually working against the clock, in more ways than one, as he explained to his sister. 'One of our troubles is the time factor – when it is evening here, it is midnight in London and tomorrow morning in Java.' Hence 'Signals arrive earlier than they are sent off – but time works *against* the ones we send out – so we are *always* pushed'.[38] The secretariat developed their own special channel. Jacob remembered: 'We kept up a stream of telegrams in each direction on a level below the COS [Chiefs of Staff] channel and were able thus to get the background and to keep Dykes informed of impending matters and of the thinking in London.' These were the DOTELs (demi-official telegrams) and LETODs (DOTEL reversed), supplemented occasionally by other informal telegrams. Through them came advance warning to London of important US negotiating positions, an early example being the 'Marshall Memorandum' of 2 April 1942, the paper which consolidated all previous American thinking on the feasibility of cross-Channel operations in 1942 or 1943. The Memorandum was taken to London by Marshall himself on 8 April. 'Glanced at unofficially' by Dykes, courtesy of Bedell Smith, on 4 April, the burden of it reached the War Cabinet Office by the early hours of the following morning. But the system had not yet been perfected. The wording of the telegram was somewhat ambiguous; uncertainty surrounds the exact use made of it in London, though it did receive an exceptionally wide distribution; and no one from the JSM privy to the Memorandum went to London to elucidate.[39] Future specimens would be fuller, clearer, subjected to the most rigorous scrutiny, and if the occasion merited, reinforced by a personal visit. The April telegram was a prototype, an indicator of what could be done. 'Whatever happens,' Dykes's successor was implored, 'don't stop sending the LETODs . . . they are absolutely invaluable. Judicious use of these may easily save the Empire!'[40] In general the series was useful precisely because of its tightly restricted distribution. LETODs did not go outside the War Cabinet Office unless it was considered appropriate to disseminate, unofficially, a particular morsel. DOTELs were received by Dykes or his deputy and sometimes shared in whole or in part only with Dill and the heads of the service delegations. Particular care was taken to ensure that none of these telegrams ever reached the desk of the Prime Minister. On one occasion an injudiciously explicit summary of a Churchill–Roosevelt exchange was sent to Dykes in more official series. It was spotted by Churchill and promptly expunged from the record.[41] The lesson was clear: it should have gone by DOTEL.

The other elements in the JSM communicated with their parent bodies in London in comparable, if less exuberant, fashion. The Planning Staff, for example, opened a similar demi-official series of telegrams to which they too became addicted. Additionally, in February 1942 Dykes began weekly conversations, usually with Jacob, by radio-telephone. This medium was plagued by reception difficulties and, unlike the telegrams, considered totally insecure. Dykes invented some irreverent but not entirely inappropriate codenames for the members of the Combined Chiefs of Staff, among them Tom Mix (General Marshall), Captain Kettle (Admiral King), Tugboat Annie (Admiral Stark), Colonel Shrapnel (General Brooke) and The Whale (Admiral Pound).[42] The aliases achieved a certain currency on both sides of the Atlantic, and conversation at least served to raise morale. Telephonic communications were improved only after Dykes's death. In July 1943 the new 'x-system' radio-telephone was installed in the US War Department building in Washington and in the headquarters of the US forces in London, with an extension to Churchill's underground Cabinet War Rooms. Secure speech was now possible. For the British, however, the combined facility remained insecure in one important respect – it was controlled and operated by the Americans.[43]

Vivian Dykes's diary testifies to the compelling ambiguity at the heart of the Anglo-American special relationship. It was a relationship at once intimate and injurious, remarkably close and yet particularly strained. The ties were special indeed, but the cousins were also rivals. One form of rivalry, and a certain condescension, was evident in the RAF Delegation's interpretation of its role in Washington, 'to guide the young, inexperienced, self-conscious and rapidly expanding service of a foreign nation and, simultaneously, to draw off a proportion of the aircraft, supplies and equipment which that nation needs for itself'.[44] The Combined Chiefs of Staff organisation was an inspired attempt to resolve the more fundamental rivalry suggested by Churchill's hopeful invocation of 'righteous comradeship'. No longer was Britain 'a client receiving help from a generous patron'. The two nations were now equal partners, he averred, 'fighting for life side by side'.[45]

Dykes was fortunate in experiencing and recording the closest approximation to full partnership ever achieved in Anglo-American relations. Their needs matched; their contributions, if not exactly equal, were vital and complementary. For a long moment, London and Washington were totally interdependent, and they knew it. Dykes's own part in this was a significant one. He was instrumental in making the Joint Staff Mission indispensable to the functioning of the war-time alliance. In tandem with Bedell Smith, he was the architect of an effectual and harmonious secretariat for the whole combined organisation, without which it would have been difficult to operate at all. He was a great exemplar: the mould set by Dykes and Bedell Smith was never completely broken. British secretaries especially continued to have privileged access to Marshall. The ethos of the combined secretariat remained substantially unchanged. As late as the Cairo Conference of November–December 1943, a tyro American member was smoothly inducted into the system by one of Dykes's successors, Brigadier Arthur Cornwall-Jones:

C.J. explained that although our governments had different axes to grind and that our first loyalties were to our own Chiefs of Staff, there were times when, to expedite matters, as secretaries we should be frank with each other, always understanding that any confidential matters would be kept strictly between ourselves.

I sensed that this was not an invitation to spill our positions right and left but a sincere effort to aid our committees in achieving their common goals . . . As secretaries we could figure out some way to break an impasse and get our committees together . . . suggest a certain course of action which would prejudice neither side and indulge in private gratification as we watched negotiations end in agreement.

'Of course,' he added shrewdly, 'this worked only when both sides were after the same objective but were stymied because of some personal misunderstandings or suspicions of each other's motives.'[46]

Even in 1942, suspicions were rife. Each partner feared dispossession by the other. Moreover, as Dykes was quick to appreciate, the balance of power was tilting ominously towards Washington. Churchillian rhetoric notwithstanding, genuine equality was a chimera. The diary records in graphic detail the vicissitudes of Britain's inexorable supersession. Increasingly, frustratingly, it was the United States that ran the show. Even Dill, who established the most special relationship of all, could grow 'very tired of begging from the Americans', as he was wont to say on such occasions. 'Individually, they are charming and kindness itself, but to get all we want out of them is not easy.'[47] It has been well observed that allies are the most aggravating of people. The facility of Anglo-American communication, a crucial advantage, carries one penalty: a corresponding facility of aggravation. Dykes's diary provides an unrivalled account of the way in which, despite the unsparing aggravation of coalition warfare, the Anglo-American alliance was made to work.

It is widely held that those who keep diaries expect someone to read them, sooner or later. In the nature of the case, this is especially true of the diary kept consciously or unconsciously for an 'apologetic' or 'confessional' purpose, as many are.[48] The famous Alanbrooke diaries, ostensibly intended only for his wife, had an indisputably apologetic purpose, one the diarist perhaps half-concealed from himself.[49] General Sir Ian Hamilton decided quite deliberately to keep a Gallipoli diary for the same purpose, remarking candidly that 'the tendency of every diary is towards self-justification and complaint'.[50] The Dykes diaries are certainly full of complaint, particularly in the latter half of 1942 when Dykes is obviously very weary, but they are notably free from self-justification. Dykes was unlikely to be seduced by the apologetic or the confessional. He was a plain man. Instead, he kept a diary to chronicle what he saw. Scribbled nightly, the very process of 'reckoning up the day's business' may have been a comfort in itself.[51]

Interestingly, Dykes actually encouraged someone to read at least part of his diary soon after the events it described, so soon that it was still a highly sensitive document – one aspect of military diary-keeping that is often ignored, not least by the many military diarists. On his return to England in March 1941, Dykes set about 'cleaning up' his Donovan Trip manuscript (kept in a shorthand notebook). He expanded some sections, corrected points of detail, moderated the comments on certain personalities, and excised a number of references to the Secret Intelligence Service and 'C' (its head), though not to other intelligence matters. The revised version he had typed and a copy sent to Donovan himself: '*strictly private* between you and me'.[52] Another copy was given to Ian Jacob; it is possible that this version had some limited circulation within the War Cabinet Office. The version now published retains the expanded sections but reinstates the original comments on personalities, and all references to the SIS, cryptic as they are.

Dykes does not appear to have resumed his diary until he left London in December 1941. He had no opportunity to make revisions of any kind to his Washington diaries. Two of the inevitable shorthand notebooks were found, unread and still secret, in the offices of what is now the British Defence Staff in Washington, some forty years after they had been written. Others were in the hands of his family. They are published here in full, save only for the English countryman's obsession with the weather (a short bulletin ending almost every entry), some domestic detail of similarly ephemeral interest, and the odd indecipherable word of his execrable handwriting. Also published are a number of his letters, where they shed further light on important issues raised in the diary; these are interspersed throughout the text and documented in the notes at the end of the book. The headings to each entry have been standardised and a few obvious misprints corrected. Editorial interpolations in diary or letter are marked with square brackets.

Part I: The Donovan Trip
December 1940 – March 1941

Introduction

In late December 1940 British Ambassadors throughout the Mediterranean area were alerted by the Foreign Office to expect an important visitor:

> Colonel Donovan, who is visiting this country as an observer for President Roosevelt, with whom he has great influence, is leaving on a six weeks' tour of the Mediterranean in the course of which he proposes to visit Gibraltar, Malta, Egypt, Palestine and Greece. His object is to study and report to the President on our strategical situation in the Mediterranean but his terms of reference are very wide. The Prime Minister has directed that every facility should be afforded to Colonel Donovan, who has been taken fully into our confidence.[1]

Donovan was bear-led round the Mediterranean by Lieutenant Colonel Vivian Dykes, 'the best man in the Cabinet Secretariat'.[2] In the event, they travelled further and faster than even Donovan had envisaged. After leaving London on 26 December they went to Gibraltar, Malta, Cairo; from Cairo to the Western Desert battlefield in Libya; on to Athens, Sofia, Belgrade; back through Greece and the Albanian front; on again to Istanbul, Ankara, Nicosia, Jerusalem, Cairo, Baghdad, Cairo once more; returning via Malta, Gibraltar, Madrid and Lisbon to London, on 3 March 1941. Donovan's unbeatable Anglo-American credentials gave access everywhere except Vichy France-controlled North Africa and Syria, and to everyone except General Franco in Spain, who was 'too busy', and General Weygand in North Africa, who was effectively quarantined at German insistence. Donovan did see King Farouk of Egypt, King George and Prime Ministers Metaxas and (later) Korizis of Greece, King Boris of Bulgaria, Prince Regent Paul of Yugoslavia, the Mufti of Jerusalem, and Foreign Minister Suner of Spain. He also conferred at length with all the senior British military figures in the region, including Admirals Cunningham and Somerville, Generals Wavell and Wilson, Air Marshals Longmore and Tedder – not to mention the Foreign Secretary Anthony Eden (with whom Dykes provoked a tremendous argument) and the CIGS General

19

Dill, on the intractable problem of whether or not to give military aid to Greece.[3]

Colonel William J. Donovan's nickname was said to derive from a laconic retort from the ranks to his offensive ardour: 'We ain't as wild as you, Bill.'[4] Wild Bill was a legendary war hero, a successful New York lawyer, a former Assistant Attorney General (1924–29) disappointed in further political advancement, an imaginative, perhaps over-imaginative, publicist, preoccupied most recently with the dreadful danger of Nazi fifth-column infiltration and the wonderfully intriguing possibilities of 'shadow warfare' to combat this threat and many others. He was of internationalist persuasion, but Irish-American, Republican, and anti-New Deal to boot. He was not on the face of it a credible vehicle for furthering the cause of Anglo-American solidarity in complex and sensitive international diplomacy. There were, however, distinct advantages to his involvement at this critical juncture of the war. He enjoyed the personal friendship and sponsorship of the influential owner of the *Chicago Daily News*, fellow Republican Frank Knox, recently created Secretary of the Navy in President Roosevelt's carefully calculated shift towards a bipartisan administration. He had long-standing connections and a certain temperamental compatibility with the President himself. He had undertaken an earlier fact-finding mission to England in July 1940, if not at direct Presidential request, then at least with Roosevelt's knowledge and approval. He had succeeded in cultivating an unusual range of high-ievel British contacts (though not at this stage the Prime Minister), including one of especial relevance to his own concerns, the idiosyncratic Director of Naval Intelligence, Admiral Godfrey. He was sufficiently well-liked for a hint to be dropped that he would be a very acceptable replacement for the defeatist Ambassador Kennedy.[5] Most important, he was a true believer. At a time of considerable scepticism on both counts, Donovan had no doubt that Britain would survive and that America should help. He also felt that he personally could make a difference. And he could be remarkably convincing. The charmed reaction of the quizzical US Ambassador in Athens, Lincoln MacVeagh, suggests the impression he made. Donovan had just flown in from Egypt in mid-January 1941:

> He is representing the Secretary of the Navy, unofficially, and is observing and talking with all and sundry, especially in the Near East and Mediterranean, with an idea of finding out what is being prepared here and how we can help, and incidentally also to carry assurances that the United States means

business. This last should be helpful to the British in the Balkans . . . The Colonel, despite his nickname of 'Wild Bill', is a man of well ponderated judgement, of considerable intelligence, wide interests, and pleasant and rather restful manners! . . . He is the only American to have won the Congressional Medal [of Honour], the DSC and the DSM. A stunning record. Yet, since he is getting a bit stout, one might think him a mere *bon papa*, if it weren't for those bright blue eyes![6]

Everywhere he went, Donovan's message was the same. The Americans were solidly behind the British war effort. Those who resisted the Germans would gain favour and perhaps assistance. Those who collaborated, or merely procrastinated, would receive neither aid nor comfort from the United States. It was a futile attempt to stiffen the resolve of the Balkan states in particular. Donovan was not convincing enough for such pitiable figures as Paul of Yugoslavia, said by Churchill to be 'like a man in a cage with a tiger, hoping not to provoke him while steadily dinner-time approaches'.[7] The Bulgarians, too, felt that their only option was to play for time. Foreign Minister Popoff told Donovan a story to illustrate the point:

A prominent criminal in Turkey was about to be hanged in the presence of a large crowd, including the Sultan and the Grand Vizier, when he pointed to a camel behind the Sultan's throne and made signs that he wished to speak. On being interrogated, he said that if his execution were postponed he would solemnly undertake to teach the camel how to speak. He was told that he would be given a year, but if the camel could not speak at the end of that time, he would not only be executed but also painfully tortured.

When his friends asked him how he proposed to fulfil his promise he replied: 'I have at least got a year's grace. During that time who knows what may happen? The Sultan may die – or the camel – or I may die myself.'[8]

For those in the cage with the tiger, Donovan's message was apt to seem fanciful, if not fraudulent. They could not afford to play the Anglo-American game of truth, dare or promise. 'You big nations are hard,' Paul told the US Ambassador in Belgrade. 'You talk of our honour but you are far away.'[9]

Donovan was more successful in his fact-finding and reporting, and in reinforcing British policy. Without question, the British high command were exceptionally open with him – no doubt hoping for something in return – and one of the chief interests of Dykes's diary is its remarkably detailed account of the strategic thinking of the commanders on the spot. Among others, Wavell on the whole Middle East, Marshall-Cornwall on Turkey and the Balkans, Wilson on the Western Desert, Cunningham on the Mediterranean, all offer comprehensive surveys of their domains.[10] In addition, Dykes recorded – and actively helped to influence – the development of

Donovan's own thinking, fully reported to Secretary Knox in Washington, and shared with a select circle around the president, including his 'best friend' and closest adviser, Harry Hopkins.[11] For his part, Dykes reported direct to the CIGS, carefully including copies of Donovan's despatches as well. Not for nothing was Dykes trained in the Committee of Imperial Defence. Several of these reports are included in the text of the diary.[12]

A high point of the trip was Donovan's intersection in Cairo with Eden and Dill, also touring the Mediterranean, for a somewhat similar purpose. The diary adds some new detail to our knowledge of the various points of view. Discussion centred on whether to aid Greece or Turkey. Donovan argued strongly for Greece, 'who is now fighting hard'. There was a political imperative, but also a moral obligation. 'Britain has kept her in the fight and discouraged her from coming to terms.'[13] The ill-fated decision for military operations in Greece was finally taken in London a few days later. Donovan's influence on that decision has been the subject of much wild speculation. Churchill, Eden and Dill all adduced Donovan's arguments in support of their own;[14] but probably the most that can be said is that his influence was indirect. Dykes plausibly believed that Donovan was much more successful in stiffening the resolve of Dill, in particular, then he had been with the recalcitrant Balkan royalty.[15]

The one genuinely secret aspect of a surprisingly public mission was Donovan's voracious interest in British intelligence organisation. References to the shadow world of subversion and counter-intelligence activities form a fascinating sub-text of Dykes's diary of the trip. A good many of those encountered *en route* belonged to that world. Wavell's Director of Military Intelligence, Brigadier Shearer, revealed some of his facilities for the interception, decryption and analysis of enemy wireless traffic, though no mention was made to Donovan of 'the Ultra secret', intelligence from the German Enigma coding machines.[16] Less conspicuously, there were the ubiquitous Passport Control Officers;[17] Air Attachés or Assistant Air Attachés, notably the garrulous Forbes in Athens;[18] Liaison Officers like the young Patrick Leigh Fermor in Albania, who later organised the resistance on Crete, and later still became an acclaimed travel writer.[19] It is, in fact, a curiously literary cast. Freya Stark, already a well-known explorer and writer on Arabia, is discovered working on Arabic propaganda in Cairo. The bibulous Commander Fleming, of the Director of Naval Intelligence's office, with whom Dykes shared a car on the way from Gibraltar to Madrid, turns out to be the creator of James Bond.[20]

Donovan put the information he gathered on the trip to good use. His own stature was immensely enhanced. He had seen more of the war than anyone else in Washington. It had been a great adventure. (Dykes too had enjoyed himself enormously.) As the Secretary of the Treasury, Henry Morgenthau, put it, entranced:

> He has been for a week actually up in the trenches up in Albania. He was down in Libya when they took the last town, whatever the last town was. He was with Wavell for over a week. He was with Eden in Cairo. He has been twice in England. He has been in Spain and he has been in Portugal. I think he knows more about the situation than anybody I have talked to by about a thousand per cent. And he is not discouraged.[21]

On the contrary, he had returned with a new idea. He was undeniably impressed with the benefits of Anglo-American intelligence cooperation. But above all he was fired with the need for the better coordination of American intelligence: the need, in other words, for some kind of central intelligence agency.[22]

Diary
26 December 1940 – 3 March 1941

Thursday 26 December 1940   **London**

I picked up Donovan at Claridges soon after 10.00 and we left on the 10.30 to Plymouth from Paddington. Gort [Inspector General to the Forces] and Dill [Chief of the Imperial General Staff – CIGS][23] came to see Donovan off which he seemed to appreciate very much. On the way Donovan told me of his visit to Mussolini in 1935 in which he succeeded in obtaining an invitation to visit Abyssinia and Libya in order that he could see for himself the great improvement in the Italian forces since the last war. He had told Mussolini that from what he had seen at that time he did not think much of them as soldiers. While in Libya he had spent about three weeks with [General] Badoglio [Commander in Chief] and formed a very good impression of the Italian training and administration. Their regular troops and Askaris had fought well, but the Blackshirt troops had been of poor quality.[24]

Friday 27 December 1940   **Plymouth**

The Navy had arranged a round of visits to various Naval establishments to fill in the day. At 4.30 p.m. we arrived at Egg Buckland to see the combined operations room which is located in an old fort. [Admiral] Dunbar-Nasmyth showed us round and explained the way [Atlantic] convoys are worked in through the western passages. All convoys now converge through the channel between North-West Ireland and Scotland. We had succeeded in pushing enemy submarines west but they were now attacking ships on the surface very much further out in the Atlantic. To meet this new menace we require more destroyers and air reconnaissance from bases further to the westward. It was not sufficient to have destroyers with greater endurance, a larger number were required to maintain a shuttle service. If we had air bases in the West of Ireland we should be able to keep the enemy submarines submerged and prevent them attacking convoys on the surface as they now did.

At tea Donovan put over the American point of view and very interestingly. He urged the necessity for cutting out false sentiment and for both sides looking at the matter from the standpoint of mutual self-interest only. The

24

violently pro-English American was liable to be one of this country's worst friends in America. Donovan explained America's difficulty in pressing Ireland on the subject of the bases until America herself was properly in the war. She would be asking Ireland to do something which she herself was not prepared yet to do. De Valera's [Head of the Irish Government] latest appeal for arms may possibly give an opening for America to offer to send them and convoy them over with her own ships, but only in return for the use of Irish bases.

Saturday 28 – Monday 30 December 1940   *Plymouth*

[Further delayed by impossible flying weather.]

Tuesday 31 December 1940   *Plymouth–Gibraltar*

Weather over the Bay [of Biscay] was bad for about six hours, but we had an excellent breakfast at 9.00 a.m.[25] and arrived at Gibraltar in perfect weather at 11.00. Group Captain Rogers and the Governor's ADC met us and we went straight up to Government House. After lunch we set off for a tour of the defences with [General] Mason-Macfarlane [Deputy Governor and General Officer Commanding]. At dinner Brigadier Torr (Military Attaché, Madrid) was confident that Spain would resist a German invasion directed against Gibraltar, but we should foster this spirit of resistance by not making too much fuss over the Spanish occupation of Tangier and using the weapon of blockade with discretion against Spain. He urged Donovan to visit Madrid on his way home from the Middle East.

Wednesday 1 – Saturday 4 January 1941   *Gibraltar*

[Delayed again by bad weather.]

Sunday 5 January 1941   *Malta*

Quare and Forbes saw us off at 6.30 a.m. We took off at 7.00 and arrived at Malta at 3.30 without incident, though it was a very bumpy voyage which I did not enjoy very much. General Dobbie, the Governor, met us with Air Commodore Maynard [Air Officer Commanding]. After tea I had a long talk with Dobbie to whom I tried to give the atmosphere at home. He asked me about Operation WORKSHOP [a landing on the Italian island of Pantelleria, between Sicily and Tunisia] and I gave him what information I could about the PM's predilections. He was naturally very interested as, if it came off, he might have to supply garrison troops for the islands.

Monday 6 January 1941   *Malta*

In the morning we went down to War Headquarters. Saw General Scobell [General Officer Commanding] – not so vigorous as Mason-Mac at Gib – and the system of tunnelled dug-outs which have been made in this area. . .

The American Consul, Henry, with his wife and daughter were up for dinner. She is British from County Cork – a dull lot, I thought. Fyers [the Governor's military assistant] told me after dinner that it had been a very great disappointment in the Island that Dobbie had received no recognition in the New Year's Honours for all his good work there. There is apparently considerable intrigue against the Dobbies on the part of Mabel Strickland and the Bonham-Carters, who still seem to consider that they have a connection with the Island on the ground that Dobbie is only acting Governor. He asked me to put in a word for him [Dobbie] with the CIGS and to get it through to Lord Lloyd [Secretary of State for the Colonies] also. On the wireless we got news of the capture of Bardia [Libya] with 30,000 prisoners and heard the summary of President Roosevelt's speech to Congress, which certainly sounds most forthcoming.

Tuesday 7 January 1941   *Malta–Cairo*

Dobbie saw us off from Luca aerodrome at 8.15 a.m. in a Wellington bomber in which we made a good journey to Heliopolis [near Cairo]. It was very cold at first and rather bumpy and a Wellington is not well designed for carrying extra passengers. Once we got above the clouds into the sun, however, it got a bit warmer. We made a landfall on the North African coast about Mersa Matruh and followed the coast all the way in, arriving at 3.30. Air Marshal Longmore [Air Officer Commanding in Chief, Middle East] met us at the aerodrome and we went straight to the British Embassy, where the Lampsons received us very hospitably [Ambassador Sir Miles Lampson, later Lord Killearn]. The Associated Press had somehow or other got wind of our arrival and was in to see Donovan almost at once.

At dinner in the evening there were present besides the Lampsons and ourselves – Prince Ali Khan (son of the Aga Khan, now in a yeomanry regiment after leaving the Foreign Legion) and his wife (she was a Guinness), and ['Chips'] Channon (Parliamentary Private Secretary to R. A. Butler, Junior Minister for Foreign Affairs), a typical Mayfair bullshitter.[26] Lady Lampson is very pleasant too – small, petite, and shows her Italian origin, I think! The atmosphere a bit too hothouse for my liking. Channon was going on to Belgrade [Yugoslavia] to stay with his old friend the Regent [Prince Paul].

Wednesday 8 January 1941   *Cairo*

We went round to see General Wavell [Commander in Chief, Middle East] and Longmore at 9.35 a.m. Wavell gave a very interesting general survey of the position in his area, describing the boundaries of his command and Long-more's. The Middle East has naturally a close liaison with India and with South Africa. Smuts [Prime Minister of South Africa] is much interested from the political point of view in obtaining early success in East Africa. At the start of the war our position in the Middle East had been weak and the policy had been not to annoy the Italians, even though the French encircled them in Tunis and Djibouti [North-East Africa]. After the French collapse the position naturally deteriorated and we could only do our best with the limited air forces, until reinforcements of troops arrived in mid-September [1940]. By November our defensive position was reasonably secure and the next stage was to work up for an offensive, which had been launched early in December. There seemed a good prospect of being able to get right through to Benghazi [Libya] as the Italians had by now lost nearly all their guns in North Africa. The only limiting factor was the difficulty of supply of the forward troops. The clearance of the North African coast would be of great assistance to the Navy, but no useful purpose would probably be served by going further west than Benghazi until and unless General Weygand [French Governor General in Algeria] was prepared to come in with us.

The next task would be to clear East Africa and thus reduce the commit-ments of the RAF. Campaigning in this area was limited by the climate, the rains starting in March. For an offensive from Kenya very large quantities of motor transport would be required, but General Cunningham [General Officer Commanding East African Forces] was pushing forward to the line Kismaayu–El Waji [Somalia]. The revolt in Abyssinia was being steadily fostered, and there were two Indian divisions and the Sudan Defence Force now on the Sudan border. Kassala [Sudan] should be retaken soon.

Palestine had been comparatively quiet since the outbreak of war. The position in Syria was difficult. The senior French officers were pro-Vichy – otherwise the junior officers and the majority of the Army would probably have thrown in their lot with us. General Catroux [Commissioner for Moslem Affairs in the National Liberation Committee, later Commander of the Free French in Syria] thought they would never come in now, and is all for taking every opportunity for having a dig at them. Wavell however feared that this might weaken control in Syria to such an extent that it might cause an internal upheaval; in which case we might be faced with the necessity for intervening – otherwise the Turks might step in. If the Turks came in on our side, we might in any case have to demand right of transit over the Syrian railways. As for Turkey, the Tripartite plans which had been worked out before the collapse of France were all now a dead letter. They had been based on the hypothesis of a friendly Italy, and Turkey now wanted to start fresh conversations. General Marshall-Cornwall [General Officer Commanding British Troops Egypt] was shortly going to Turkey for that purpose. The Government in Iraq was disloyal and reinsuring with the Axis. The Prime Minister, Ghaidani, who had taken office after the resignation of Nuri was very troublesome. The Italian Legation was still in Baghdad, a focus of enemy activity. The Mufti of Jerusalem was also there. We want to get rid of Ghaidani, but have at present no force with which to back up our demands. Wavell nevertheless was not seriously perturbed – we have always the threat of long-range bombers operating from Egypt if things get too bad. Our principal interests in Iraq are: (a) South Persian oil (b) deny [to the Germans] Mosul oil (c) the desert route from Baghdad [Iraq] to Haifa [Palestine, now Israel], though now that the Red Sea was open to traffic the latter was of less importance. It might be wise to assert our rights by opening up the desert route. A new route through Basra [Iraq], Kuwait and Amman [Jordan] was now under consideration. The attitude of Ibn Saud [ruler of Saudi Arabia] was quite satisfactory.

The war in Greece had brought new commitments for us. The Greeks were crying out for more aircraft, but the aerodromes were so bad that we could not operate more than we have already sent even if we could spare them. It was therefore uneconomical to send additional air forces; if the test was to be the number of Italian aircraft destroyed, it was much easier to do this in Egypt than in Greece. If we had to send troops to the Balkans we should want to liquidate the Dodecanese [Islands] first. Morale in the Islands was low already, but one complication lay in the rival claims of the Greeks and Turks to these Islands. If Yugoslavia was drawn in too, there would be fresh demands from them for aircraft, anti-aircraft and anti-tank guns. To meet possible contingencies in this area, schemes of aerodrome construction and improvement of ports and roads in Turkey were being pressed on. It would however always be difficult to operate in the Balkans against Germany since she possessed the advantage of interior lines.

In Egypt, the King and Ali Maher had been in touch with the Axis in order to reinsure themselves, and Ali Maher had had to be removed by representations on our part. The political situation was now fairly satisfactory. Speaking of German intentions, Wavell thought that they would try to keep the Balkans quiet and consolidate in the south-east, thus avoiding operations on two fronts. They had put in strong defences in Romania to protect their oil and were using Bulgaria as a buffer state. As regards Italy it was rumoured that 300 aircraft had been sent there by Germany, but we did not know whether the crews had been sent with them. They might be only to make good the heavy damage which had been done to the Italian Air Force in the course of our operations in North Africa.

After leaving Wavell, Donovan called on the American Minister Bert Fish. In the afternoon we saw General Hutchinson [Deputy Quartermaster General], who gave us a survey of the logistic position. Supplies for the Middle East come from the UK, India and Australia. The ports in use are Suez, Port Said and Alexandria [all in Egypt], though Alexandria is primarily a naval base. These base ports have had to be largely developed, especially Suez. To supplement them, wharves have been made in the Suez Canal. The use of the [South African] Cape route instead of the direct route through the Mediterranean means the employment of five times the amount of shipping for the same load delivered. For every division (which may be calculated as 14,000 men), 13,000 corps, base and line of communication troops are required. A large amount of local labour has been taken up and also brought in from Cyprus, India, Palestine, and the Seychelles. A considerable proportion of these labour units are armed and disciplined. The use of prisoners of war for labour is not considered economical in view of the large numbers of guards which would be required to look after them if employed in small packets.

The Egyptian railways were not under British control and not very efficiently run; a great deal of tact had to be used with the Egyptian officials. Inland water transport was being used to supplement the railways. Maintenance to the Western Desert was by rail to Mersa Matruh and thence by motor transport anything up to 400 miles. Recent operations had taken up all the motor transport available in the Middle East. Of the Italian lorries captured only 80 or 90 had been serviceable, all the remainder needing repair of spare parts. The Greeks were howling for some of these Italian lorries as their further advance [north] depended on obtaining more transport.

We next saw General Marshall-Cornwall. He thinks the Turks are absolutely reliable as they hate the Germans. He agrees with Wavell that the Germans will not want to drive down through the Balkans, and thinks that the German troops in Bulgaria are primarily there for the anti-aircraft defence of the Romanian oilfields. Germany is probably ready to throw Italy overboard, giving Northern Albania to Yugoslavia and Southern Albania to the Greeks at the price of a settlement. She would then occupy Northern Italy, leaving Southern Italy as a no-man's land. He doubts whether Germany will move down into Spain and Portugal now, as she has missed her best opportunity in the autumn. Nevertheless such a move would undoubtedly be the worst thing that could happen to us. Marshall-Cornwall thinks that we should strive to bring in the Yugoslavs and the Turks on our side and go in through Salonika [Greece], thus forming a wide front for attack on Germany on the south-east; this is the only way we can get at her.

Our next call was on Brigadier Shearer [Wavell's trusted Director of Military Intelligence; formerly Managing Director of Fortnum and Mason]. He reported that the Fascist troops had fought no better than the Regulars, and there was a general feeling among the Italian prisoners of jealousy and suspicion of the Fascisti. All were loyal to the King and, so far, to Mussolini himself, but morale was definitely poor. They felt that Italy would lose whatever happened. The Italian generals were very poor stuff indeed. So far we have destroyed eight Italian divisions in all.

At dinner there was Freya Stark [the intrepid traveller and writer] who is doing Arabic propaganda.[27] She stressed the need for a good 'ground' backing for the BBC broadcasts, which are in themselves very useful. Mrs Hore-Ruthven, who lives with her, was also there, and Air Marshal Longmore. Lampson told me that the Egyptian courts had practically suspended gold payments for Suez Canal dues, which was naturally very much to our advantage.

Thursday 9 January 1941   *Cairo*

We set off at 9.00 a.m. to look at some of the Base installations and then motored out to Suez, about 80 miles, and looked over the port and quays. The average time for a ship to unload is 10 to 15 days. Port facilities are bad, there being no shore cranes at all; one quay is unpaved, and they have only just managed to finish a transit shed. There were 20-odd ships in harbour, unloading or waiting for berths. A troop train was waiting to move off, containing drafts *en route* for the Sudan.

I got [Brigadiers] Jock Whiteley and Dudley Clarke [on Wavell's headquarters staff] to dine with Donovan at the Continental [Hotel], and we had a great discussion on Germany's probable intentions and what we should do to counter them. We all agreed that Germany should have gone for Spain in the autumn, and will probably occupy at least part of Italy. Jock is all for attacking Romanian oil by air, especially if and when a German invasion attempt on the UK has failed. Dudley Clarke is inclined to expect a fairly rapid crack of German morale, but this Donovan doubts.

Friday 10 January 1941   *Cairo*

Donovan went out early with Shearer to see some of his Intelligence establishments ('Y' and 'M'), with which he was very much impressed. I fixed up details for our visit to the Western Desert. In the afternoon Lieutenant Colonel Bagnold told us all about the Long-Distance Desert Patrols and something of their work.[28] Patrols of 10 trucks contain two officers and 30 other ranks and are self-contained for 1,500 miles. Three patrols have already been formed, and three more are to be raised. Their first role had been reconnaissance, but later they had taken on raids on Italian dumps and supply routes and undertaken the dissemination of propaganda among the Arabs in the desert. The Wops have been completely surprised by the appearance of these patrols in places where they had never expected them. Unlike the Commandos, the patrols were all drawn from the same unit, and the type of man preferred was the fellow who owned his own car in peace-time. . .

In the evening we went round to Headquarters, British Troops Egypt, and saw Galloway [Brigadier General Staff], who told us something of the operations in the Western Desert. We dined with Longmore at Air House. Among the others: Tedder [Longmore's deputy] and Elmhirst (Air Member of the British Mission to Turkey). I had an interesting talk with Tedder after dinner on Beaverbrook [then Minister for Aircraft Production] and his little ways and the development of the RAF generally. He strikes me as a first-class fellow.

Saturday 11 January 1941   *Cairo–Western Desert*

We got off from Heliopolis at 9.30 a.m. with Longmore and Whiteley in a Lockheed, arriving at Sollum at 12.00. General ['Jumbo'] Wilson [General Officer Commanding in Chief, Egypt] met us. Air Commodore Collishaw showed us his Air Operations Room located in the old Egyptian barracks, or rather what was left of them after the bombardment. From there we went on by car to Advanced Headquarters, British Troops Egypt, at Capuzzo, where they are very uncomfortably lodged in a tent. After lunch General Wilson took us for a conducted tour of the Bardia battlefield. We started on the west side, at the point where the Australian Division breached the perimeter with an infantry assault one hour before dawn. Their sappers had blown a gap in the wire with Bangalore torpedoes and they had then made a small bridgehead to cover the filling-up of the anti-tank ditch. The 'I' [infantry] tanks had then gone through and moved down along the perimeter systematically knocking out all the Italian guns. The Italian dispositions were very unskilfully made, consisting of a very widely-extended outer perimeter which was completely unsupported from the inner defences. Neither line of defences had any depth at all. Nevertheless, the assault had been carried out with great skill, as it is perfect machine-gun country. The point of assault was very cleverly chosen so as to give the maximum observation for our own troops, with some defilade fire [positions] on both flanks and for the forming up position. I suspect that Jumbo Wilson with his extraordinary eye for country had had a good deal to do with the choice.

The Italian strong-point at the point of assault was very solidly constructed with covered trenches, but all their weapons were poorly protected. The natural result had been that the garrison had been more keen to stay in their underground protection than to come out into the open and man their weapons. The 'I' tanks had apparently stood up to field-gun fire extra-ordinarily well.

We next went over the eastern side of the perimeter and looked at some of the Italian battery positions in a wadi which had held out for a long time. There were some pretty ancient weapons there, including six-inch guns without any buffers. The gunners' bivouacs were very bad considering the time they had been there. They had been living in low sangars [look-out posts] about three feet six inches high, with groundsheets rigged up to give some cover. All over the place were masses of equipment and troops' letters. I read several of these and was interested to see that among a couple of dozen there was no sign of the 'dynamic spirit of Fascism' – they were all rather pathetic ones which seemed to show that the heart of the Italian people was not in this war at all.

From there we moved to Headquarters, 16 Infantry Brigade (Brigadier

Lomax) who are clearing the battlefield. They had fixed themselves up very comfortably in an Italian Headquarters in a deep wadi, but had had a lot of cleaning to do before the place was habitable. All over the battlefield there are motor vehicles and guns of all sorts, but the Australians had done a great deal of damage to these by souvenir-hunting; most of the dial sights and instruments had been taken off and broken. Lack of salvage and repair units was a great handicap to the recovery of all this equipment which is so badly needed for the Greeks and other allies. Before leaving Bardia we had a look at the harbour which is very small, with no facilities at all except one tiny jetty which has been badly knocked about by our bombardment. The crane at the end of it is somewhere at the bottom of the sea, and there are several small ships sunk in the harbour itself. There was a very good repair shop left by the Italians alongside the harbour, but the approaches down from the escarpment are very steep and winding. The port will be of very little use for maintenance purposes.

From Bardia we motored up to Headquarters, 13 Corps (General O'Connor), which we reached at 6.00 p.m. The surface of the road was breaking up pretty badly in places, as there is only a thin tarmac carpet over dry stone road metal. All our motor transport was moving at about 50 miles per hour, either on the road or across the desert, which is neither good for the road nor the vehicles – but distances are so great that if they don't move fast they would never complete their journeys. 13 Corps HQ was established in a few huts left by the Italians near a landing-ground, supplemented with bivouacs. The wide dispersion in all our camps is very noticeable. We found General O'Connor in very good form. His ADC, Bailey, runs a very good show there. He was running a hotel in Cyprus before the war and raised the first Cyprus Mule Corps. In the Mess we met General Tilly (2nd Armoured Division), who looked a very sick man; Harding [Brigadier General Staff]; Gill (Commander Royal Artillery); and Fellers (US Military Attaché). We found a corner in one of the huts for the night and bedded down quite comfortably there. Water is pretty scarce and rather salt and was doled out in cupfuls.

Sunday 12 January 1941   *Western Desert–Cairo*

We left a bad dust-storm which got steadily worse as we reached HQ, 6th Australian Division (General MacKay), south-west of Tobruk. There we sat in on a conference with General O'Connor at which the preliminaries for the attack on Tobruk were being made. The principal points touched on in this conference were: need for more 4.5-inch guns, with the necessary range to reach Tobruk; leaflets to be dropped as soon as possible in Tobruk, calling on the troops to surrender; General O'Connor's offer of a Machine-Gun Battalion warmly accepted; distinguishing pennants for captured Italian tanks which were to be used by our own troops; need for more air photographs to improve our information of Italian dispositions; proposal that the Australians should undertake full responsibility for the advanced base at Tobruk when captured;

need for some form of trailer to carry the 'I' tanks from point to point as they wear themselves out in travelling long distances over the desert. We heard that the total casualties in the assault on Bardia had been under 500, including the 100 killed.

The dust-storm was too bad to look at any of the other Australian units or headquarters, so we left at 11.15 with visibility down to a few yards. On arriving at Sollum at 2.10 we found that it would not be possible to take off until later, when it was hoped that the dust would have decreased a little. To fill in time we went down to have a look at Sollum Harbour with Wilson and Longmore. . . All over the place there were swarms and swarms of Italian prisoners. Like a litter of pigs, the healthy ones got to the outside where the food and air was; I think some of the ones in the middle of the jam must have been having a rather uncomfortable time. These crowds of prisoners are a great feature all through the Western Desert. You see a column of 2,000 or 3,000 marching along from one camp to the next, most of them with their little handbags packed, and one British soldier at the head and one at the tail of the column. 'Join the Italian army and see the British Empire' is the motto.

We got off finally at 4.00 p.m. in Longmore's Lockheed and arrived at Heliopolis at 5.50. Jumbo Wilson came with us. It was very pleasant to get a good bath and to remove some of the sand. I found myself bitten quite a lot by desert fleas which swarm in many of the Italian positions. Donovan dined with Wavell that night.

Monday 13 January 1941   *Cairo*

Wavell went off to Greece in the morning for consultations there. Longmore promised to take us there next day with him when he went over. News came in that Operation EXCESS [a convoy of stores from Gibraltar to Egypt] had caught it hot from dive-bombers (German) when passing through the Mediterranean, with the loss of the *Southampton* sunk and one destroyer and the *Illustrious* badly damaged. Donovan saw General Catroux for a short time before going to a private showing of a newsreel in one of the cinemas (the Bardia picture disappointingly short).

We lunched with Michael Wright and his wife at the Mahommed Ali Club.[29] He is First Secretary in the Embassy and knew Donovan well in Washington some years ago; very smooth and a great admirer of Eden, whose Private Secretary he was for some time. He is very critical of Chamberlain and Baldwin, but I suspect he was a great supporter of disarmament [i.e. appeasement] in his time. Mrs Wright is a very nice woman. In the afternoon I drafted a cable to the CIGS [Dill] giving Donovan's impressions of the Western Desert operations and got it sent off, after showing it to Jock Whiteley and Arthur Smith [Wavell's Chief of Staff].

Donovan seems much impressed by our achievements in the whole Mediterranean with limited resources. After visiting the Western Desert he stresses our mistake from the US point of view on dwelling too much on the readiness of the Italians to surrender. We should emphasise the skill needed to break the powerful Italian defences and the strength of Italian resistance until the front was broken. On wider issues he is convinced of the need for the Americans to win over Weygand since only in North Africa could they find room for an adequate base of operations in the European theatre. This would give them a self-contained area and he is set against their forces being mixed up with ours.[30]

A big dinner party at the Embassy for Lady Lampson's birthday. I was put between Princess Ali Khan – quite pleasant and reasonably genuine – and Mrs Shone, wife of the Minister in the Embassy, an affected and unduly sophisticated female. A dance afterwards. Much society froth there. Donovan performed in great style, as he said he wanted a good spot of exercise!

Tuesday 14 January 1941   *Cairo–Alexandria*

Donovan saw Catroux after breakfast, who left him a memorandum on his views.[31] Then we had an hour with Dudley Clarke on the Commandos, started after Dunkirk to regain the offensive spirit . . . We left on the 4.45 p.m. train for Alexandria and put up at the Cecil Hotel. We had dinner with Longmore and Admiral Cunningham [Commander in Chief, Mediterranean].[32]

Wednesday 15 January 1941   *Alexandria–Athens*

We got off from Alexandria harbour in the Sunderland at 8.00 a.m. with Longmore, Curtis (his PA) and Guy Burton (Middle East Liaison Officer). Very soon the weather got bad and we had a very bumpy trip to Athens. Over Crete the flying was particularly bad and we were unable to land there as had been intended. By the time we landed at Athens a good many of the passengers including myself had had enough and one or two had definitely passed out. I thought Longmore had a very faraway look in his eye.

We lunched at the Grand Bretagne Hotel, a big place which has been taken over by the Greek Government as their own General Headquarters and the HQ of the British Mission. After lunch we went up to the Legation where the Palairets gave us a very warm welcome [Ambassador Sir Michael Palairet]. Donovan stayed with them and I was billeted out with Wace (of Pembroke [College, Cambridge]), an archaeologist who was head of the British school in Athens for many years and is now working in the Passport Control Office. Harold Caccia is First Secretary (very good)[33] and Jasper Blunt, Military Attaché. During the afternoon I went down to Mission Headquarters and made contact with ['Guido'] Salisbury-Jones[34] and General Heywood [member and head of the British Military Mission in Athens].

At dinner at the Legation there were present – Wavell who is staying in the place, Longmore, Curtis, Anne [Miss] Palairet, Lord and Lady Dunsany, Donovan and myself. Dunsany is Byron Professor of English Literature at Athens University this year and is delivering a course of lectures; a funny old boy who looks like a goat and lives quite in a world of his own. Dinner was a very pleasant simple affair, rather a change from Cairo. When I got back I had a long talk with Wace who told me of all the difficulties they are having with Jewish refugees and other would-be illegal immigrants to Palestine. Guts much upset by the journey, but held out OK.[35]

Thursday 16 January 1941   *Athens*

After breakfast got the form from Caccia and Heywood on the discussions with the Greeks the previous day about the furnishing of British troops to help them. The Greeks would not have any formed units from us, nor would they allow us to send anything to Salonika. They fear acceptance of troops might precipitate German action against them and ask only for material, quite regardless of the fact that their men are untrained in its use. [Prime Minister] Metaxas said that the Yugoslavs had hinted that they would disclaim all responsibility if the Greeks accepted help from us. Heywood gave us a very good disquisition on the general situation in the Balkans and the possibilities of German action.[36]

Donovan and I paid a very short visit to the Acropolis before we went to lunch at the US Legation. Donovan had a good long talk with the King after lunch. In the afternoon we went out with MacVeagh [US Ambassador] to the site of the Battle of Marathon, a fascinating little bit of flat land between the mountains and the sea. On the top of the mound which was the burial place of the Athenian dead, MacVeagh explained the battle very well.[37]

In the evening Donovan saw Papagos [Commander-in-Chief] and Metaxas. He told me he had impressed on them that the US would see the Allies through; the debates in Congress on the Lease and Loan Bill are only concerned with the form in which executive authority is to be exercised and not on the principle of giving aid to Britain. From Papagos he got a list of the principal needs of the Greeks and undertook to send a cable to Colonel Knox pressing for them to be supplied.

Metaxas fears that to anticipate Britain's strengthening her foothold here Germany may attempt to seize Salonika and that this Yugoslavia and Bulgaria may not resist, and British force is not yet sufficient. General Wavell asked me to say that he has drawn, and is drawing, heavily on his resources to aid her but due to existing commitments and limitations of shipping cannot at this moment do more.

Metaxas says that the name of President Roosevelt exercises great influence throughout the Balkans and that anything which would stress his interest and assurance of support in maintaining the frontier of Greece would vitalise the resistance to and probably prevent any German attempt.

More particularly there is a need of shoes, uniforms, 1½-ton Ford trucks, burros [donkeys], mountain guns and ammunition and aircraft. If we could provide these it would give renewed confidence to the Greeks and would aid greatly in maintaining this position not only as a line of resistance but as a line of departure.[38]

Donovan dined with Princess Aspasia [of Greece; mother-in-law of Peter II, King of Yugoslavia from March 1941]. On his return he saw Wavell and told him of his interviews with Papagos and Metaxas. I dined with Salisbury-Jones who was feeling a bit despondent. Age has not increased his stability. He feels Weygand's collapse very badly as he was a very great personal friend of his. He was very sad at having been pulled out of a staff job with a division on the Eritrean Front [Ethiopia].

Friday 17 January 1941   Athens

In the morning we heard that Papagos had rather changed his attitude during the night (as a result of his talk with Donovan?) and was now more disposed to favour acceptance of our offer of troops. He had had an interview with Wavell early in the morning before Wavell left.

We went down to see Ranking [British Military Mission] in the morning and he told us something of the administrative difficulties. Mountain artillery with ammunition is one of the chief needs and the War Office can only offer mortars. The Greeks have insufficient shell-making capacity. The clothing situation is bad and new classes cannot be called up owing to the difficulty of fitting them out. The Greeks are prepared to take our battle-dress, but they have not enough transport to get boots and clothes through to the troops in the front line who are in desperate need of them. Their transport maintenance organisation is almost non-existent and they have 40 or 50 different types in use. 200 British lorries have fortunately just arrived in with the convoy that came through on an Operation EXCESS. These may ease the situation a bit and there are more lorries due in from Egypt shortly. 400 more have been promised from the UK. As a result of insufficient transport, rations are only delivered to the front line about once in three days and then in short measure. There is a large accumulation of stuff at the railhead which cannot be got forward. The Greeks want 12,000 mules. 700 are coming from Cyprus, and Palestine is being 'tapped' for more. Medical equipment is very short, but equipment for a 1,200 bed general hospital is en route from the UK and a similar quantity has been asked for again by the Greeks. They also asked us for five field ambulances without transport and one with transport (all without personnel). The Greeks have apparently no idea at all of doing any salvage [from the enemy] which they think is rather infra dig. . . .

At 11.00 p.m., after discussion with Palairet and Heywood, Donovan agreed to go straight on to Sofia in the hope that he would be able to put some stiffening into the Bulgars.

Saturday 18 January 1941   Athens–Salonika

Legg (the Air Attaché) got on to the Greeks first thing in the morning to fix up for our air transport to Salonika. When I had got this settled I saw Salisbury-Jones and told him what had been said to me about the unfortunate effect on the Greeks of the high standard of living of the British Mission in Athens, at a time when their people were having such a very bad time at the front. Guido was most sympathetic and told me he had felt just the same thing. After buying a felt hat (known in Greek as a 'republica') on which our Greek driver took great pride in getting me a 10% rake-off, I changed into mufti and got packed up ready for our journey into the Balkans. Donovan attended a press lunch at the American Legation and we managed to get away from there at 2.20 p.m. for the aerodrome. We took off in an Anson piloted by the Greeks at 3.15. There seemed to be a good deal of string tying up the inside of it, but we had quite a good flight. The going was pretty bumpy at times but by this time I was becoming acclimatised.

We landed at Salonika at 5.15 just before sunset at an aerodrome on the east side of the town on which a good deal of improvement work was being carried out. It was bitterly cold when we got out of the aircraft. The Cavass [armed attendant] from the Consulate met us there – Abdil, an Albanian – a fine-looking old boy with big moustaches, an astrakhan hat and a double-breasted khaki greatcoat. After paying our respects to the Station Commander we set off in a very moth-eaten taxi which landed us finally at the British Consulate. Laurie, the Vice-Consul, was very doubtful indeed about the possibility of making the journey to Sofia by car. Quite apart from the state of the roads, it was almost impossible to obtain a reliable car, all having been commandeered by the Army. He got on to the American Express agent for us to fix up our tickets and we went on from the Consulate to the house of the agent. We found this in a small back street and succeeded in winkling the agent out from the bosom of a very numerous family and taking him along to the hotel which was grandly named 'Luxe Palace'. Here we found the American Consul, Johnston, and the Vice-Consul, Gullion. . . .

The hotel was all wrapped up in dust sheets and seemed to be doing very little trade. My bed had a longitudinal crevasse down the middle of it but I slept very soundly on one half.

Sunday 19 January 1941   *Salonika–Nish*

We had to turn out early at 5.00 to catch the train. Gullion and the faithful Abdil turned up to see us off, but on reaching the station we found the train would not get away before 8.00. We adjourned to the cafe opposite the station, a grubby little place where I had a minute cup of chocolate – I could have done with a dozen of them. I bought some rings of bread covered with sesame seeds to supplement the rations which Lady Palairet had given us. Gullion also provided us with some food as it would not be possible to get anything on the train. After a further wait in the Station Master's office we finally got off at 8.00. The train was freezing cold but after a bit it warmed up. The line passes up the flat Vardar plain over which there were big flocks of geese flying. At every wayside station we stopped to drop off trucks as it was a mixed passenger and goods train. The guard, Pollay by name, had served with the British Army in Constantinople from 1918 to 1923 and spoke English with a grand London accent. Like all Greeks he expressed the national determination to fight Italy to the last. About 12.00 we arrived at the frontier station where we had to change trains as the Greeks will not allow their rolling stock out of the country.

On getting out to see our bags through the customs we could get a look at some of our travelling companions. One of them was a German diplomat who looked very much like a fat toad with a shaven head and many rings of flesh over the back of his collar. He was highly indignant because he had had to carry some of his stuff to the Customs Office and had not been attended to first in spite of having a diplomatic passport. The Customs Officer was unsympathetic and told him that most people on the train seemed to have diplomatic passports. The Yugoslavs do not seem to like the Germans very much. Another party consisted of a French diplomat complete with wife, two children and a maid. There was also an American-Greek who greeted Donovan profusely as a fellow countryman, an oily looking ruffian wearing spats and a fur collar with plenty of gold in his teeth. He looked as though he was going on business in a good many shady enterprises from drug trafficking to espionage as well as his ostensible business of making contracts for copper.

One of the two porters on the station was exactly like an amiable chimpanzee – quite the grubbiest person I have seen for some time – in a pair of home-spun jodhpur pants that must have belonged originally to someone half his size. The dress of the peasants on the station was quite different from that worn in Greece. They go in for high furry hats and flat turkish slippers with rather baggy oriental-type trousers.

To save our food we went out to the little town to get something to eat in the only restaurant in the place. It was pretty grubby and the maid of the French diplomat was highly disgusted at the tablecloth on her table which certainly might have been there since the last war by the look of it. Our Greek-American friend interpreted impartially for ourselves, the German, and the Vichy Frenchmen. The town itself looked like a cross between a village in France and one in Connemara [Ireland]. There seemed to be plenty of troops about, presumably those manning the frontier defences of Yugoslavia, or else Customs' guards. The troops looked very good material, a fine infantry type with good uniforms.

The train for Nish got away punctually at 3.30. The line passes through a defile in the hills with the road running close alongside it. The bridges and culverts on the road looked substantial but the road itself did not appear to be up to much heavy traffic. At Skopje, Lawrence, our Vice-Consul, joined the train. Departure was delayed for some minutes owing to a furious row which broke out in the next carriage over reserved seats. All the passengers in the train filled up the corridor outside our carriage to see the fun and it sounded as if knives would be drawn at any moment. The lady in the case made an impassioned address to an admiring crowd on the platform. A policeman who came along to try and settle the fuss got a button pulled off his coat, but, at last, everyone concerned got completely hoarse from shouting and the racket died down and the train went off. Lawrence told us that sentiment in that part of Yugoslavia is still strongly Macedonian and that the population have no very solid national feeling. Generally speaking however they dislike the Germans intensely and are all for resisting them if it comes to the point of an invasion.

Monday 20 January 1941   *Nish–Sofia*

We reached Nish at 1.00 a.m., where we had to change again. We adjourned to the station cafe and knocked back some beer, bread, cheese, salami and fruit and then waited there till 5.20 a.m. when the Sofia train came in. It was at least fairly warm in the place as there was a good stove in the middle. I got a good sleep sitting up at the table. Fortunately Donovan was awake when the train came in and roused me. We were lucky to get a carriage to ourselves on the train and so could get some more sleep in the morning. When daylight came we found ourselves moving through a fairly narrow valley between the mountains. We reached the Bulgarian frontier about 9.00 and went on through the Dragoman Pass. Here the road looks good with a lot of new work on retaining walls culverts and bridges. Sofia itself lies in a flat plain which was covered at that time in snow. A thaw however had set in and the snow was clearing off fairly fast.

At the station the American Minister, Earle, met us with Millard (First Secretary) and Barber (Second Secretary). They took us to the Bulgarie Hotel where rooms had been booked for us by our respective Legations – a huge modern steam-heated affair opposite the Palace. It smelled like all other cosmopolitan hotels and was infested with Germans. After a bath and a shave I went round to our Legation and reported to Rendel. He had to go off to lunch at the US Legation with Donovan, but I stayed. Alick Ross came in after lunch and we had a long talk about the situation. He certainly knows his stuff as Military Attaché but has not changed a bit since 1934.[39] He is far too much worried by the fact that he is still only a Lieutenant Colonel and lower in rank than all the other Military Attachés in the place. Rendel arrived back about 4.00 with Donovan and gave him a long disquisition on the present situation. The general opinion in the Legation is certainly that there is no chance of Bulgaria resisting Germany in any way. Rendel made a good deal of the uncompromising attitude of Yugoslavia towards Bulgaria.

In the evening we went to a small stand-up supper party at the US Minister's house at which there were present Rendel, Ross, Millard, Barber, and the Greek Minister Pipinelis. The latter seems a very good fellow and certainly most stout-hearted. Earle looks a sick man who is not very effective. He seems to spend a good deal of his time collecting antiques and dancing girls. Alick Ross held forth to Donovan at considerable length on the military situation. The Greek Minister sheered off and lost interest as soon as Rendel mentioned the desirability for Bulgaria of a port in the Aegean!

Tuesday 21 January 1941   *Sofia*

Donovan saw Popoff (Bulgarian Foreign Minister) at 11.00 and talked very straight to him.[40] He met the Prime Minister and the Minister for War at lunch. I spent the morning giving Alick Ross and Crawford, the Air Attaché, the picture at home and in the Western Desert. They were hungry for news. . .
.

Wednesday 22 January 1941   *Sofia–Belgrade*

Donovan was out early to see the Military Cadet School and then went on for his crucial interview with King Boris.[41]

I spent the morning chasing round for our tickets and my passport which was lost for some time between our Legation and the Turkish in the hands of their slowest moving passenger. At 12.00 Rendel showed me a telegram from Cairo urging Donovan to return as quickly as possible and see Weygand. I promised to discuss the matter with him during our journey to Belgrade. After collecting our baggage and paying the bills at the hotel I got down to the station. Donovan arrived with Earle shortly before the train left. There was a swarm of newspaper men waiting to see him off. He had just had time after his interview with the King to dictate a record and have a few words with Rendel. I went off to collect some food for the journey and when I returned I found him looking as worried as I have ever seen him. He asked me whether I had got his wallet with his passport and money in it. He had not got it on him and we made a frantic search through all his bags and belongings in the train while someone went off to the Legation to see whether he had dropped it there after returning from the Palace. All searchings were in vain, however, and we had to go off without it at 2.00. The Police were to be warned at the frontier to square things with the Yugoslav officials and let him through without a passport. Donovan told me all about his interview with the King to whom he certainly spoke most frankly. We continued our discussions on the Balkan situation as a whole, which we had started on the journey from Salonika to Sofia.

We got through the frontier with no trouble at all. In fact, it was easier than when Donovan had a passport as we were invited in for coffee with the police. He has become a very well-known person since Earle launched him as a public figure in the Balkan press, which Donovan says he did in the best American political party style. We had a very comfortable journey in a *wagon-lit*, arriving at Belgrade at 10.00 p.m. where Donovan was immediately set upon by a crowd of press men and photographers. I made an unobserved get-away by the other door of the carriage having spotted the Legation messenger Oakley, who took charge of my bags. Donovan was staying with Lane, the US Minister.

Thursday 23 January 1941   *Belgrade*

I got off a telegram to Wavell in the morning saying that Donovan wanted to complete his tour as planned but would be willing to cut it if it was considered essential. He had various interviews and lunched with Prince Paul. He had a short time with Macek, Leader of the Croation Peasant Party, who did his usual trick of removing his collar and tie before receiving him, to emphasise his peasant sympathies! Donovan described Prince Paul as a Serb with an Eton and Oxford veneer, which might influence him strongly to do what he felt was the correct thing by English standards.[42]

It was obvious that if we were to get back to Greece to do a tour round the Albanian front, we should have to fly back to do it in the time. Rankin, the commercial secretary in the US Legation, undertook to find out what could be done about flying down to Salonika where we might be picked up by a Greek plane if necessary. At 5.00 p.m. he told me that it would be very difficult to arrange and he had therefore booked sleeping berths on the railway instead. However, Macdonald (Air Attaché) said that there should be no difficulty about getting a civil aircraft. As the American Minister wished his people to fix it all up I had to leave it to them, but asked Donovan to make sure and try to get something out of the Yugoslav air people when he saw them next day. I had spent most of the day with Macdonald, Dew (First Secretary), and Garron (Second Secretary) giving them news from home and collecting information. Turned in early with rather a sore throat.

Friday 24 January 1941   *Belgrade*

Donovan had interviews with the Minister of War, Chief of Staff, Minister of Marine, and Head of the Air Force and visited the aerodrome. Simović [Air Force] impressed him very favourably and the Yugoslav Air Force though small seemed very efficient indeed. Simović is all out to fight the Germans at the first possible opportunity; he is said to be going to succeed the present Minister for Air very shortly.

I lunched at the American Minister's house and met Mr Lane and Colonel Fortier, the Military Attaché [encountered again in Washington]. Fortier comes from Louisiana and is a curious chap – I am afraid I found him an awful bore. Dined at the Lanes' with Donovan and [Ronald] Campbell [Minister in Belgrade, later in Washington] as the other guest.[43] Mrs Lane is a very good soul who lent me a sweater and also produced some flea powder in case we needed it in Albania. Fortier brought round his valise for Donovan. My throat was no better when I went to bed, in spite of a visit to a doctor in a clinic opposite our Legation who said that it only needed a gargle.

Saturday 25 January 1941   *Belgrade–Koritza*

We turned out early and reached the airport at 6.40 a.m. The Yugoslav civil air line produced free of charge for Donovan a very nice Lockheed 14 in which we took off at 7.00. Donovan told me that the German Air Attaché had also offered to fly him down to Salonika but he had politely declined. . .

We reached Bilisht, a village just on the [Albanian] frontier soon after dark. Here the British Liaison Officer with the Northern Army, [Patrick] Leigh Fermor,[44] met us – rather a precious youth who did not appeal to Donovan much, but quite helpful. He took us in to see General Pitsichas, the Army Commander, who was established in a small Albanian house. We found the old boy sitting in his bedroom in a woolly bed jacket and carpet slippers, getting through some of his correspondence. His daughter was apparently acting as A.D.C., Camp Commandant and general factotum – a very sensible arrangement and certainly most economical. The General is a dignified old man who apologised very charmingly for his domestic surroundings and offered us cups of coffee. From him we went on to see his Chief of Staff in the Headquarters itself, Colonel Georgoulis. He impressed me very favourably and gave us a masterly explanation in French of the opening phases of the war. I should judge he must have been a teacher at their Staff College by the way he put it over. The small size of the staff in the Headquarters was most noticeable, though admittedly no administrative work is done at the Army Headquarters. His staff, however, seemed to be no bigger than that of a Brigade Headquarters in the British Army.

We reached Koritza about 8.00 p.m. and Leigh Fermor very kindly put me up in his room in the only hotel in the place. By this time I realised that I had quite a high temperature and was quite unable to swallow. The hotel was extremely squalid but at least seemed free from livestock. I turned in in my overcoat with all the blankets I could find on top of me to get warm, and Leigh Fermor found a young Greek doctor, Kitsos, to have a look at me. He produced some prontosil, captured from the Italians, to treat my throat and his orderly gave me a good hard massage. He made it quite clear that I should not be able to travel next day. Donovan had dinner with the Governor of Koritza and stayed the night with him.

Sunday 26 January 1941   *Koritza*

I stayed in bed all day sweating out my fever.

Monday 27 January 1941   *Koritza–Jannina*

My temperature was a good deal less in the morning so we set off at 8.00 for Jannina, Donovan having arranged to take the Greek doctor through with us to Athens. . .

We reached Jannina about 4.00 and Kitsos got me put up in a room in the hotel which is used at the Greek G.H.Q. – very clean and comfortable, and a great improvement on Koritza, presumably because it is a Greek town. He produced some soup for me from the hospital and 'yaoghte', a sour curd stuff, not very palatable. All the party dropped in during the evening at intervals to see my progress and pass the time of day. Donovan arrived about 8.00 having had a long day tramping about the front line and being bombed into the bargain. He told the Greeks on this occasion that it was quite like being in London.

Tuesday 28 January 1941   *Jannina–Athens*

My temperature was down to normal so Donovan determined to get right through to Athens in one day if possible. We set off at 8.30 along the road which follows the River Louros for a considerable distance through a very fine gorge. Progress was not very fast as we were meeting strings of lorries, mostly new British ones, the sight of which cheered our Greeks very much. Shortly after we had stopped to change a wheel, a lunatic in a ten ton truck doing about forty miles an hour rammed us on a corner, but fortunately did no more damage than crumple up the near-side wing and some of the body work. We passed through Arta which is in the centre of a very attractive orange-growing area. There is a wonderful hump-backed bridge over the river here. From Arta the road passes all along the coast to Karvasseras and Agrinion, the surface being fairly good. A very narrow gorge, like the Cheddar Gorge on a large scale, leads down to the coastal plain at Missolonghi.

The prefect of the district met us at the boundary of his territory and we went on through a village which was all beflagged in honour of Donovan's passage and full of cheering people, to find a huge reception for us at Missolonghi. Here the square was packed with people and with the Greek equivalent of the Boy Scouts and Girl Guides and the Town Band turned out to welcome us. We advanced through a very enthusiastic crowd to the Town Hall where after looking at some of the Byron relics and pictures, we sat down to a considerable luncheon washed down with anisette and very resinous Greek wine, which tastes like turpentine. During lunch we got through to the Legation at Athens to warn them that we should be arriving soon after midnight, the intention being to cross the Gulf of Corinth by ferry and take the shorter road to Athens along the northern coast of the Peloponnesus. After lunch we visited the Memorial Cemetery and saw the tomb of Byron and the memorial to the American Volunteers in the Greek War of Independence on which Donovan laid a wreath. Donovan and I were informed that we were both made honorary citizens of Missolonghi. My legs just held out through this palaver and I was very glad to get into the car again about 2.30.

On reaching Naupaktos, it was found that the sea was too rough for the ferry, so we went on by a newly made road, well graded but very winding, over the high mountains to Amphissa passing through Lidorikion. This was a terrific drive, in the course of which we met a huge R.A.F. wireless lorry and trailer going in the opposite direction from Larissa to Jannina. It had failed to get over the Pindus Mountains, which is the direct road. It was dark long before we reached Amphissa where we stopped for an omelette and some macaroni in a cafe. I slept most of the way in from Amphissa to Athens, roused only to change into one of the other cars when mine broke down. We finally reached the Legation at Athens at 2.30 a.m. where we found some very welcome supper waiting for us. I had certainly had enough and was very glad indeed to crawl into bed at Wace's house at 3.00 where his two faithful maids Marika and Ephgenia were still awake and cheerful.

Wednesday 29 January 1941   *Athens*

Papachelas came round about 9.45 with the news that Metaxas had died during the night. Great consternation in Athens. Donovan saw Admiral Turle, Heywood and D'Albiac and gave them his impressions of Bulgaria and Yugoslavia before going to see Apostoleides, the Minister of Finance, at 12.45. In the evening he saw Korizis, the new Prime Minister; and the King. He described Korizis as having an intelligent head, honest eyes, but a bad stomach and seemed to doubt whether he would have sufficient forceful personality to deal with opposition politicians who had been kept under during the Metaxas regime. I fixed up with Forbes the arrangements to fly us to Istanbul on the following afternoon. I dined at home with Wace who told me a lot of interesting stuff about his travels in Northern Greece and Albania. He had spent a lot of time with the Vlachs, who are of Romanian origin and migrate regularly every year from the plains to the hills in the summer.

Thursday 30 January 1941   *Athens*

We went down early to see Heywood who told us a good deal about Weygand. Weygand is said to be the natural son of Maximilian; he joined Foch as his chief of staff when the Ninth Army was formed and stayed with him throughout the rest of the war. In 1934 he retired and came very much under the influence of his wife's friends who are of the extreme right party; he himself is an ardent Catholic. At this time he became obsessed with the danger of communism and took up very keenly some of the youth movements, including La Rocque's. In 1938 he had a serious illness, but after being operated on seemed to recover very well and showed himself very fit during a tour in England with a party of reserve officers in 1939. On that occasion he had spoken very prophetically about the coming war in a lecture at Chatham House [the Institute of International Affairs]. Heywood gave Donovan a copy of a paper which he had written in August 1940 on the prospects of further resistance by the French. Salisbury-Jones told us that Weygand's strategic conception for the Balkans had always been to hold defensively with the Yugoslav and Romanian armies a line from the mouth of the Danube through the Transylvanian Alps, the Iron Gates and Belgrade, pivoting through several alternative positions in the mountains to the Adriatic coast. The Allies would come in through Salonika which would be a base for a possible eventual offensive.

Donovan called in to see [US Ambassador] MacVeagh at 12.50 and I could not get him away before 1.20, so we did not reach the aerodrome at Menidi till 2.00. The weather was not at all good and Forbes decided that it was too late to make the attempt so we had to return. I had a long talk with Forbes who is very dissatisfied like everyone else with our 'C' and 'D' organisation in the Balkans. D's Romanian plots have been a complete fiasco.[45]

Friday 31 January 1941   *Athens–Istanbul*

We left from Menidi at 11.00 in Forbes' Percival Gull and had a rather bumpy passage to Istanbul which we reached about 2.35. Lady Palairet had packed us up an excellent lunch for the journey. She is a very nice woman, very simple and quite the best type. The atmosphere in the Legation is excellent. Palairet, if not a flier, is a sterling fellow. The whole of the Maritza over which we passed was covered with enormous floods. Commander Tuggle (US Naval Attaché) met us and after dropping some papers at the British Embassy we went on to the American Embassy, where the Consul and Richardson, the Commercial Secretary, produced a meal for us. Marshall-Cornwall, Elmhirst and Allan Arnold arrived almost immediately and Marshall-Cornwall gave Donovan the gist of their recent conversations with the Turks. Arnold gave me a few sidelines on the obstinacy and childishness of the Turks and their wasteful misuse of the technical equipment which we provide. No one who was not a star performer in the Turkish War of Independence counts at all and most of these are now getting on in years. The Turks had apparently been all out to divide up Syria with us and had had to be boomed off that rather firmly.

About 6.00 p.m. we crossed the Bosphorus in the American Embassy launch and caught the train for Ankara. The American Embassy had managed to square the Turks to put on an extra coach as there had been no room in the train. Tuggle and Richardson came along with us. The former was carrying a bag through to Egypt.

Saturday 1 February 1941   *Ankara*

The train was unexpectedly punctual at Ankara where Donovan was met by the American Ambassador MacMurray and a Turkish Foreign Office man. Douglas Brown and Johnson (Royal Marines) also slept there to meet me and took me up to Arnold's house which is opposite the American Embassy. I went up to see [Ambassador] Knatchbull-Hugessen in the British Embassy and had a long talk with him before going out to lunch at a restaurant in the town.

Knatchbull-Hugessen came over to see MacMurray and Donovan in the afternoon and told us of the many attempts we had made to bring about the formation of a united Balkan front. Prospects at the present time were a little more promising and the Turks had assured him categorically that they would fight in the event of any aggression against Bulgaria or Greece including Salonika. The only doubtful point was their reaction to infiltration by the

Germans – how far would they let them go? They had made it quite clear that the Bulgarians would have to resist actively before any move was made to support them. Knatchbull-Hugessen had just had instructions to deliver to the [Turkish] President a personal message from the Prime Minister offering the Turks ten squadrons of aircraft and a hundred anti-aircraft guns. He thought that there was perhaps a shade of odds against the Germans coming down into Salonika in March, but only just a shade. Donovan told him of his idea that the United States should try and take the lead now in getting Bulgaria, Turkey and Yugoslavia together to form a Balkan front. . . .

Sunday 2 February 1941   Ankara

At the Embassy next morning Douglas Brown showed me a report from Arnold, obtained from Romanian sources, that a motorised German division had started moving into Bulgaria from Dobrudja by train on 28 January at ten trains per day. They had had no confirmation of this report however.

After dinner at the American Embassy Knatchbull-Hugessen told me that the Turks had turned down the idea of ten squadrons and one hundred anti-aircraft guns as hopelessly inadequate againt the probable scale of attack. He thought it unfortunate that he had received such rigid instructions and felt that it would have been much better to allow him to use this offer as a bargaining counter as and when a suitable occasion arose. I explained the direct action methods employed by the Prime Minister.

Monday 3 February 1941   Ankara

In the Embassy next morning I heard they had some confirmation of German troop moves from Dobrudja. The Ambassador told me that he had seen Sarajoglu [Turkish Minister of Foreign Affairs] the previous afternoon on the subject of the offer of guns and aircraft and he had told him that he thought it very probable that the President would agree to our putting in as much as we liked in the way of material and even of instructors in plain clothes, but they would not accept actual formations and units. The Turks said they wanted at least 35 squadrons of fighters. I told him something of the numbers of fighters we had for the whole of the air defence of Great Britain and pointed out that a very small number of fighters made day bombing almost impossible. He said he had begged Sarajoglu not to give any absolutely flat refusal to our offer. He was having a further interview with him that morning, and the full text of the Prime Minister's message was being telegraphed to the President who was at Erzerum. (Later in the day he told me that he had now been instructed to get to the President somehow and hand him the message personally; he doubted if that would be possible even if it was desirable.)

In the evening I helped Donovan produce a brief appreciation giving his impressions of the Balkans up to date and what should be done:

The central fact throughout the Middle East is the belief that Germany must invade and hold the British Isles in order to win a decisive victory. As a corollary of that belief is the opinion that the action of the Axis in this theatre is governed by two princples. First, as an offensive principle, not only to destroy England's position here but by denying to her shipping the use of the Mediterranean to soften Britain's resistance by strangling her commerce. Second, as a defensive move, to protect Germany's supply and transport of oil, food and raw materials in southeastern Europe, to anticipate and prevent England's gaining any foothold on this part of the Continent, and in the event of her failure to attack Britain or failure in the attack itself to seize and hold all of the countries of the European Continent, at least to the Turkish line, as elements of trade at the peace table.

Governed by these two principles, Germany has or is setting up certain options, any one or any group of which she may exercise in a given eventuality. But the universal opinion here is that all these projects are but part of one unified plan and subject to the military principle that Germany will try to fight only on one front and do her utmost to prevent the Balkans being used as a battleground. These options include:

(1) joinder of attack with Italy from Albania against Greece (which is generally doubted unless she can reach Salonika in no other way)
(2) penetration through Bulgaria to seize Salonika and thus prevent the establishment of a continuous Balkan front for which the possession of Salonika is essential
(3) attack on the Ukraine (the general opinion being that this will come only after a decision in England)
(4) attack across the Dardanelles into Anatolia either as a way of defeating Turkey, the strongest potential ally of Britain in the Near East, or as a means of achieving complete encirclement of Russia (the Turks fear this but the British doubt it)
(5) invasion of Spain to establish bases from which to intensify the attack on British trade and deny the use of Gibraltar harbour to the British (this is more and more doubted in this section of the world because it is believed Spain would refuse)
(6) the possibility of an attack on North Africa as a result of the seizure of bases in France by Germany.

Any attack on the Suez Canal now seems out of the question in view of Italy's breakdown. It is the question of penetration through Bulgaria that now engages the attention of Britain and her Allies here.

Yugoslavia would certainly resist if invaded and would not grant passage to German troops. What she would do in the event of an invasion of Bulgaria is as yet uncertain.

Turkey will fight if Bulgaria is attacked and resists, and also if Greece is attacked or Salonika is definitely threatened by way of Bulgaria. The question is what degree of infiltration through Bulgaria with Bulgaria's consent Turkey will be prepared to put up with. It must depend on the size and nature of the forces which Germany puts into Bulgaria. Turkey is not ready for an offensive though if she were supplied with modern equipment she would not hesitate. She believes as do the other Balkan States where I have been that Britain must defeat Germany in the Balkans. This could be achieved in conjunction with those Balkan states not yet occupied by Germany. In Greece, Yugoslavia and Turkey I found many Government officials who were still hopeful of such a union being realised to meet the present situation. Suspicions of Bulgaria form the obstacle to a union of those states. What is needed is some outside impulse from a nation that has no interest. England's part would be to furnish the technical services like anti-tank, anti-aircraft, armoured and aviation units. Britain and Turkey have entered into an understanding as to bases, supplies, etc. The Turks feel that nothing should be precipitated, that time should be given to prepare and that the Allies could not be ready for an offensive before 1942. They believe that such a movement if it had initial success might well draw Russian support.

Summarised, the Balkan situation would appear to be that Germany does not wish to disturb the Balkans, but that she is now obliged to put a vertebra into Italy. She is applying political pressure on Bulgaria which, combined with military threats, may force Bulgaria to yield free passage to German forces; she is seeking to deny Salonika to England and perhaps to seize it herself as flank protection in case she decides to attack through Thrace.

England refuses to be diverted from Egypt and the Sudan. She hopes to liquidate there within the next two months. She is prepared to assist Greece further in the event of German attack and she has worked out a general agreement with Turkey who is standing firm with her. It is believed here that if the attack against Britain is to come at all it will come not later than May but perhaps in April. It is felt that if Germany is defeated there the German General Staff would probably advise holding all the countries now under German control and proposing peace at once. But the factor of Hitler's ambition is thrown in and there remains a possibility of his wildly striking out in more than one direction.[46]

Just before leaving to catch the train at about 10.30 an agitated Secretary came over from the French Embassy to say that instructions had been received from Vichy to say that Donovan would not be allowed to enter Syria. The Germans evidently dislike the very strong line he has been taking on our behalf in the Balkans recently. A telegram had also been received from Washington in the American Embassy to say that the US Minister in North Africa had been told by Weygand's staff that a visit by Donovan at the present moment would be inopportune and undesirable.

Tuesday 4 February 1941   *Ankara–Cyprus*

Travelling with us on the train were Tuggle, Dundas (British Council) and Kermich (in business in Istanbul, and going to Alexandria on work connected with the Ministry of Shipping). Tuggle is a most amusing bird, if not blessed with overmuch grey matter. The remaining passengers on the train were a pretty cosmopolitan lot: two or three Germans; a Russian courier; an Argentine of sorts with a Polish wife who according to Tuggle ran a big espionage racket; several Turks, all clutching portfolios; and two very highly coloured young ladies travelling with a couple of sallow looking gentlemen. We had some argument as to the nationality of the more highly coloured of the two ladies and whether the colour of her titian red hair came out of a bottle or not. Tuggle expressed the opinion that the question could not be settled without a more careful examination than we could make at the time, but stuck to his view that she was Hungarian and not Turkish.

We reached Adana at 3.30 and found Forbes waiting there with his aeroplane, and Wolfson, Naval Intelligence Officer at Istanbul, who was hoping to get a lift through to Palestine with me. They had not heard that Donovan would not be allowed to travel through Syria as originally intended. Forbes had flown from Istanbul that morning. Owing to Donovan's unexpected appearance, poor Wolfson had to be left behind.

The approach to the aerodrome looked pretty unpromising but there were paved runways so we had no difficulty in getting off about 4.00 after a little preliminary trouble with water in the petrol. Forbes was still wearing his civilian suit with an RAF overcoat and cap, which he apparently always wears for these sort of journeys in and out of neutral countries. He seems to be pretty well known in all the aerodromes in the eastern Mediterranean. We flew over Tarsus and along the coast to the westward for some distance. The coastal plain looks rich country with many traces of old disused irrigation ditches. Passing in over Cyprus from the eastern end we landed at Nicosia at 5.30, where the Governor's A.D.C. met us and took us all to Government House for the night.

Battershill, the Governor, and Lady B. gave us a very warm welcome, although they had not expected Donovan at all. The new Government House is very attractively built in replacement of the one that was burnt down some years ago. The whole scheme of decoration is carried out in local material and fabric. Three of the ground floor partition walls, complete with their doors, can be wound up into hollow walls on the floor above so as to provide large rooms for official receptions etc. They move up very smoothly and quietly, and Battershill told me that a predecessor had the shock of his life one night when dining there to find that the wall behind him had suddenly disappeared during dinner. He refused to touch another drop all evening.

Wednesday 5 February 1941   *Cyprus–Jerusalem*

. . . Donovan put up with Wadsworth, while Forbes and I went to the King David Hotel [Jerusalem]. I went up to see MacMichael, the High Commissioner, in the afternoon and had a talk with him, sitting out on the terrace of Government House which overlooks the Mount of Olives. Just in front of it is a very pretty little garden full of lavender and rosemary which were all in flower. MacMichael told me that General Catroux had recently been in Jerusalem and was expecting great things of Donovan's visit to Weygand. I am afraid he will be much disappointed that the visit is off. Donovan arrived with Wadsworth a little later to tea. Wadsworth pressed very hard for him to stay on an extra day in order that he might get some idea of the Jew–Arab problem in Palestine and thus be in a position to deal with the inevitable pressure from the minorities in America. Accordingly when I went down to Headquarters in the evening I got through to Wavell on the telephone to ask him if he felt there was any desperate urgency about our return, particularly in view of what had happened over Donovan's exclusion from Syria. Wavell agreed readily: the original hurry back telegram was all balls really! I then saw General Neame and told him something of our tour through the Balkans. I also fixed up for him to see Donovan next morning, and succeeded in getting off a telegram to the CIGS giving the principal points of Donovan's visits:

> At conclusion of Donovan's tour through the Balkans which became more than exploratory mission originally intended I report the following points which may not already have been covered by H.M. representatives.
>
> Donovan spoke most straightforwardly to persons interviewed with no longwinded finessing. This method and fact that he has no official status but is private citizen of opposition party seemed to strengthen his position greatly. He left no doubt in Balkan capitals of unanimity of American people and made clear that U.S.A. is absolutely with us in this vital theatre. In all cases American diplomatic representatives were associated with him in his interviews and his position was thus given official sanction. There has been no blowback from Washington and Donovan is satisfied that his very strong line has full blessing of State Department.

I was much in American Legations during the tour and saw many of their confidential papers. I was struck by tonic effect of Donovan on U.S. representatives. He urged on them that in a theatre which may well be decisive it was their duty not to continue their present attitude of onlookers but to supplement material aid now being furnished by U.S.A. with open and active moral support of Allied cause. This would fulfil spirit of President's speech. In particular he urged need for furthering formation of united Balkan front and suggested that U.S. Government should be pressed to take initiative as an outside disinterested power or at least that all U.S. representatives in Balkans and Turkey should meet and consult with a view to concerted action locally.

American sources confirm that Donovan's visit has seriously disturbed Germans. Von Papen [German Ambassador] complained to American First Secretary Ankara of Donovan attempting to persuade King Boris to adopt hostile attitude towards Axis.[47]

Forbes and I went to dinner at Wadworth's who had invited most of the Executive Council to meet Donovan. I sat between the Chief Justice and Engert, American Consul General at Beyrouth [Beirut]. Engert is a very good fellow indeed, of Jewish origin I should say, but very alive and very pro-British in his attitude. He confirmed that Donovan's exclusion from Syria had been done on the direct orders of Vichy, doubtless on German pressure. Dentz, the French High Commissioner, had been very much upset by the order as he had arranged a dinner party for Donovan. He had sent a staff officer to the frontier to meet Donovan and had been prepared on his own responsibility to have him escorted through the country.

Thursday 6 February 1941   Jerusalem

We went along to see General Neame at 10.00 for a talk on the defence problems of Palestine. Donovan told Neame that he felt the Turks had now assumed in their own minds the responsibility of being 'guardians of the gate' into Asia. In this they had probably been influenced first by British successes in Libya, and second by the President's very strong speech to Congress. Neame said that the situation in Syria had improved since Dentz had succeeded Puyaux as High Commissioner. The French forces in the Colony had recently been reorganised, and they probably now consisted of one division, one armoured brigade, and internal security troops equivalent to one division in strength. The air forces were not at all numerous but had also been recently reorganised. He went on to give us a description of the general defence plan for the northern frontier of Palestine, which was designed against the possibility of enemy forces in Syria moving down against Egypt. . . .

Friday 7 February 1941   Jerusalem–Cairo

Neame had arranged to show Donovan the Palestinian Training Depot on his way out to the airport, so the party assembled at the King David Hotel at 9.30. The Hotel is used as Headquarters as well as in its ordinary function as an hotel, two floors being taken over by the military. There seemed rather a lot of odd fish passing through the place, but I suppose they have taken adequate security measures. It is certainly very expensive – I paid a bill of over four pounds for two days only. . . .

We left Kantara about 6.15 and arrived at the Embassy in Cairo three hours later. There the Lampsons received us like long lost sheep. Staying in the place were Channon (alas!) and Charles Wood (son of Lord Halifax) who seems quite a pleasant fellow for a young Member of Parliament. News had been received that Benghazi had fallen.

Saturday 8 February 1941   *Cairo*

After a lie-in till about 9.00 we went round to see Wavell and Longmore, to whom Donovan gave his impression of the Balkan situation. He put over very well his idea of looking at the Mediterranean not as an east–west corridor, but as a no man's land between two opposing fronts. The north–south conception seemed to strike Wavell very forcibly, and he was clearly impressed by Donovan's insistence on the need for keeping a foothold in the Balkans. Donovan was gratified to receive a well-deserved telegram of appreciation from the PM.[48]

After lunch we drafted with Lampson a telegram to Madrid asking for advice as to the desirability of a visit there by Donovan on his way home. Donovan did not wish to risk a further rebuff, at the instance of Germany, from the Spaniards. The American Ambassador at Madrid had only been able to say in response to a question through American channels that he had no suggestion to make at all!

At 3.00 Donovan talked of his Balkan tour to a small meeting consisting of Arthur Smith, Jock Whitley, Shearer, Cawthorne, Drummond, Wigglesworth [all on Wavell's staff], and Norman (R.N.). They were all extremely interested and cross-examined him fairly closely. I got the latest news from Jock after the meeting. They were having a lot of trouble with magnetic mines in the Canal; five ships had been sunk and all traffic was stopped. All the ports except Alexandria on the North African coast were also closed by mines, and there were now eighty ships collected at Suez awaiting discharge. The shipping situation was so bad that a promising landing operation on the Eritrea coast to cut out Massawah had had to be abandoned. Preparations for the capture of the Dodecanese were going forward but the Glen Ships with the landing craft had to go round by the long sea route as they had missed the Mediterranean convoy through waiting for Operation WORKSHOP, which never came off.[49] Heavy demands were being made on the available infantry for Canal-watching (three battalions), escorts for prisoners of war (three battalions) and Malta (two battalions). However, it would be possible to reduce Cyrenaica to a 'care and maintenance' basis very soon and operations in Abyssinia were progressing well.

Before dinner I called in for a short time on Charles Turner and Russell [staff officers in the Headquarters] and learnt something of the transportation situation from them. We dined alone with Lady Lampson and took her on with the Michael Wrights to see 'The Man I Married', a very good anti-Nazi film. Michael Wright undertook to fix us up to get places in the flying-boat leaving Lagos on 15 February.

Sunday 9 February 1941   Cairo–Alexandria

At 9.30 we left Heliopolis with Longmore and Curtis and flew to Alexandria where Admiral Cunningham met us at Dekhelia aerodrome. We went on to HMS *Warspite*, the Flagship, where Donovan discussed the general Mediterranean situation with Cunningham and Longmore:

> Admiral Cunningham said that the main function of the Fleet in the Mediterranean was to open and maintain the line of communication through it. The Dodecanese were now one of the chief danger points since they were being used by the Germans for refuelling aircraft which laid magnetic mines in the Suez Canal. Every effort was being made to stop anything getting into the Dodecanese, but the Fleet could not keep out submarines or big load-carrying aircraft. There were probably about sixty Italian submarines operating in the Mediterranean now but no German ones as far as was known. The Italians seemed to have been stimulated to some extent in their activities by the Germans recently.
>
> We had practically cleaned up the Mediterranean once of the Italians but now we had to start and do it over again in respect of the Germans, but Admiral Cunningham believed that we could achieve this. The worst patch was the narrows between Sicily and the coastline of Africa. Even now, however, we could get cruisers through. He was waiting for *Formidable* to arrive through the Canal where her passage had been delayed by recent mining – a new menace in this part of the world of which there was little local experience. Once the *Formidable* had arrived he was confident that he could take the Fleet through Mediterranean again.[50]

We came ashore after lunch, passing through the Fleet in harbour on the way. They looked very sea-stained but eminently serviceable. We passed close to *Valiant*, *Eagle*, *Coventry*, *Colombo* and *Perth*, which was in dry dock with suspected damage to her bottom, a suspicion which fortunately proved unfounded. We got away from Dekhelia Aerodrome at 3.00 and made the journey back to Heliopolis in just under the hour. Jock Whiteley and Norman, who had been down to Alexandria for a conference with the Navy, arrived almost at the same time as we did.

I dined with Jock that night and discussed things in general with him. The principal points he made were:

(i) The need for keeping the balance between the three Services in the Middle East. The Navy is now the bottle-neck, as there are insufficient escorts available to compete with maintenance along the North African coast, Aegean convoys and operations against the Dodecanese. Shipping as a whole is pretty tight, particularly cased petrol ships, of which three have been lost recently, and small craft.

(ii) Lack of equipment and reserves. Formations recently engaged only need replenishment to be fighting fit again, but the Home [Command] policy seems to be send out complete new units and formations. For example, 7 Royal Tank Regiment ('I' Tanks) have half their tanks written off and the remainder needing extensive repairs – but the personnel is still fit to fight. 7th Armoured Brigade tanks all require overhaul, but distances involved in getting them back are huge. Meanwhile their personnel must wait about with nothing to do. Jock felt it would have been far better to have sent reinforcement of tanks and a few men rather than the complete 2nd Armoured Division. Reinforcements of men are needed but only as drafts, since many battalions are much below strength.

(iii) Building up a Middle East reserve. When Libya and Italian East Africa have been liquidated, which should be very soon, there will be in the Middle East three Australian divisions, one New Zealand division, two Indian divisions, one British division, two armoured divisions, and one cavalry division. In addition, Smuts will probably allow the two South African divisions to come up to Egypt, another Indian division is promised from India, and a further Australian division is promised for the summer. This will give us a total of eleven infantry divisions, two armoured and one cavalry division, but these will not all be fully equipped. There is no object in sending more divisions from Home until all these divisions have received their full scale of equipment.

Both of us were dog-tired, and we fell asleep talking to one another for about half-an-hour!

Donovan dined with Longmore, Menzies (the Australian Prime Minister) being also there. Donovan described him briefly as 'a good politician'. Menzies is staying in the Embassy with Shedden [Secretary to the Australian War Cabinet] and his Private Secretary, Tritton. Shedden seems to have even less sense of humour than he had in 1937 and buttonholed me after tea (after deigning to recognise me) for one of his usual boring monologues on the basis of Australian defence policy. Their party had returned from the Western Desert that afternoon.

Forbes told us all about the rather peculiar job he had been on just before he took us to Turkey. He had picked up a lot of information about it from the Poles in Jerusalem while he had been staying there. It certainly sounds like the very best Phillips Oppenheim [i.e. spy] stuff. Donovan wanted to get exact details in writing so that he could perhaps speak to 'C' but I jibbed – too dangerous for Forbes.

Monday 10 February 1941   *Cairo*

After a talk with Brigadier Pollock on the air defence of the Suez Canal, Donovan went on to see Wavell, who was apparently most cordial and told him that he had given them all a great mental stimulus in G.H.Q. by his fresh way of looking at the problem. Meanwhile I was fixing up with Parcelle a programme for a visit to the Eritrean front, Takoradi and Accra, connecting at Lagos with the flying-boat which was due to leave there on 17 February. After Donovan had left Wavell I was sent for, and Wavell asked me if Donovan would be willing to go to Baghdad and talk to the Iraqis in the same firm way as he had spoken in the Balkans. I said I thought he would if Wavell really wanted him to go. I just had time to lay off the Eritrean visit, warn the Chancery to get Iraqi visas and get Donovan's consent to the trip before we went off to lunch at the Mahommed Ali Club with Shearer.

At lunch there were present beside ourselves and Shearer, Tedder, Arthur Smith and Bousfield (Naval Intelligence at Alexandria). Shearer was rather against Donovan going to Spain on his way home as he felt that it would be better to leave the Spaniards alone and not embarrass them in any way. We had much discussion on a thesis put forward by Shearer that all Government servants should be at one month's notice only and that security of tenure militated against efficiency. The general feeling of the party was against the proposal! There was also some discussion on the need for a propaganda slogan for the Allies which might be a counter to the 'New Order' which the Germans make so much of. Arthur Smith urged that it should have a Christian or religious foundation.

Donovan saw the Egyptian Prime Minister and General Catroux during the afternoon. I rang up Wadsworth at Jerusalem at Donovan's request to tell him of the proposed trip to Baghdad and got over from the American Legation two relevant despatches from their man in Baghdad which he wanted Donovan to read. At tea Menzies rather pompously enquired as to Donovan's exact status. I think he feels his own nose rather out of joint. Donovan's attitude can best be summed up by his remark to me when I told him that there might be some difficulty in our getting places on the flying-boat as Menzies and party would also be travelling in it. He said: 'Get this straight – we can't be euchred out of our seats by any goddamn Prime Minister – we have got work to do and we are in a hurry.'[51]

Cawthorne came over after tea to give Donovan some information on the Iraq–Palestine complex and various personalities in Iraq. Meanwhile I fixed up aircraft for the journey to Baghdad and for the further trip southward to connect with the flying-boat. Tedder as usual was most helpful. He is determined that Donovan shall see the aircraft erection depot at Takoradi. Before dinner I called in at the Headquarters to see about various papers Donovan wanted concerning the operations in the Western Desert.

Tuesday 11 February 1941   *Cairo–Baghdad*

We got off from Heliopolis Aerodrome at 9.05 [and] reached Baghdad at 1.45, three-quarters of an hour before we were expected. . . .

Wednesday 12 February 1941   *Baghdad*

Donovan saw the Prime Minister, Taha, and the Minister of Foreign Affairs and the Regent in the morning; and spoke very straightly to them on America's attitude, which I am sure must have had a salutary effect. I spent a couple of hours walking through the bazaar. They do very beautiful silversmith work in Baghdad. The coppersmiths' bazaar is interesting – all in a narrow covered-in street, very much like a scene from 'Chu Chin Chow'. It is extraordinary what good work can be produced with very primitive tools.

When I got to the American Legation about 6.00 I found Donovan and the Minister closeted with the Mufti. They came out after about twenty minutes having told him just where he got off. That night Donovan dined with the Minister of Foreign Affairs, other members of the party being the American and British Ministers, the Turkish Minister, and the Prime Minister, who had apparently recovered from the shock he had in his interview with Donovan in the morning, and was quite affable. . . .

Thursday 13 February 1941   Baghdad–Cairo

. . . On arrival at Heliopolis soon after at 11.00 we found that the message giving our estimated time of arrival had not yet been received, so we had to wait some time to get a car into the Embassy. We went straight over to see Wavell, to whom Donovan gave an account of his talks in Baghdad. The only people he had not seen were the 'Golden Square', i.e. the four turbulent spirits in the Army who had probably intentionally avoided meeting him. We had heard on our arrival that Eden [Foreign Secretary] and Dill were on their way out for conversations with Greece and Turkey, and Wavell supported the view of the Ambassador that Donovan should postpone his departure until he had seen them. Lampson told me privately that the decision had been taken not to advance beyond Cyrenaica [to Tripolitania] at present. News in from the Far East looked bad. It seemed as if Japan were 'turning on the heat' under the instructions of Germany. A reply had come in from Madrid from [Ambassador] Sam Hoare about Donovan's proposed visit to Spain; he is all for it, and hopes Donovan will go to Portugal as well.

Friday 14 February 1941   Cairo

An easy day – almost the first we had had since leaving England. I started work in the morning on our Mediterranean appreciation.

Saturday 15 February 1941   Cairo

Donovan gave a lunch party at the Petit Coin de France for the Michael Wrights. Erskine, who had just given up command of the 2nd Scots Guards to get a brigade, came along too. He was at Camberley with me in the Junior Division. After lunch we all went to have a walk around the Cairo Zoo which is a pleasant place and nicely kept. The number of lions had been reduced recently from eight to two owing to the King having taken it into his head to have a little lion shooting! The shovel-bill bird, an absurd looking creature, performed for our benefit, snapping his great beak like a machine-gun.

In the evening I got some more done on the Mediterranean appreciation. Heywood came in before dinner and Donovan told him about his talks with the Turks. Heywood was very emphatic as to the necessity of hanging on to Greece and keeping a foothold there even if the recent meeting between Mussolini and Franco did presage a peace move. If the Germans once got into Greece we should have lost our control over the Eastern Mediterranean and should not be able to get reinforcements into Turkey. The Germans would have air bases in

Southern Italy, Northern Greece and the Dodecanese. Heywood thought that at least half the Greek nation would be eager to continue the struggle even against Germany, but King George is not taking a strong line and the new Prime Minister, Korizis, is not a powerful personality. He has not called in any of the opposition party to strengthen his Cabinet, and Heywood fears the possibility of political discords in the country. A meeting with the King had been arranged recently at the Palairets' with Heywood, Turle, and D'Albiac, at which they had impressed on him the danger of taking no precautions against Germany. This had apparently had some effect as Heywood had been sent for shortly after by Papagos to talk the question over. Donovan impressed on Heywood how useful MacVeagh might be in influencing the King. He fears that Heywood will not take a strong enough line with King George.

Sunday 16 February 1941   Cairo

In the afternoon Donovan and I discussed my first draft of the Mediterranean appreciation at considerable length. He felt it so essential to form a Balkan front and retain a foothold there that he got Lampson to send a telegram to Eden suggesting that the President should be approached to act as a mediator and that simultaneously the British Ministers in the Balkans should be moved to hint to the Governments to which they were accredited that they should approach the President also to accept this role. He thought that the President would be willing to act in this way if he were asked.

Monday 17 February 1941   Cairo

I got the appreciation into type in the morning while Donovan went to see Prince Mahomed Ali, uncle of the present King. In the afternoon we went to see Marshall-Cornwall who said he was not discouraged by the result of the recent Turkish conversations, although G.H.Q. were disappointed that he had not been able to bring them into the war on our side straight away. The Prime Minister's offer of aircraft and anti-aircraft guns came very inopportunely after Marshall-Cornwall himself had been able to promise nothing. The Turks had at once jumped to the conclusion that it was simply a matter of haggling, and that they had only to open their mouths a bit wider to get a better bargain. They were sticking out for 1,300 aircraft. It had been most noticeable on the tour through Thrace and the Dardanelles however that the Turkish press and people were extremely friendly towards the Allies. But the Turkish General Staff had taken the line of asking what we wanted them to attack if they went to war, what exactly were our plans and what support we would send them. These were difficult questions to answer. Marshall-Cornwall did not think the Germans would go for Salonika until we made the first move. She wanted to keep Turkey out of the war if possible and her penetration into Bulgaria was probably largely defensive in case we attacked the Romanian oil from the air.

His own view therefore was that it would be better *not* to go into Greece yet but to take the risk of Germany forestalling us there.

We gave him our draft appreciation to read. His chief comments were that he doubted whether Germany would drive on through Anatolia if she got as far as the Straits. Her object in seizing the Straits would be rather to use this as the lever for bringing pressure to bear on Russia. There was, however, always the danger that Russia and Germany might get together and carve up Turkey between them. As regards Greece he thought that the chief danger was that if no final success came within two or three months, politicians of the Opposition would work up a peace move, and there might not be sufficient resolution in the Government to withstand this.

Tuesday 18 February 1941   *Cairo*

Donovan started work on the draft appreciation, redrafting it in his own words, in the morning, while I visited Dudley Clarke who was in hospital with jaundice, which seems to be rather a common complaint in these parts. I also tackled Newport of British Airways on the prospects of our getting home. It transpired that by flying east-about we could reach San Francisco by 12 March, travelling via New Zealand and across the Pacific. At that time we were beginning to feel that it was important for Donovan to reach America with as little delay as possible otherwise much of what he had collected in the Balkans would be stale news by the time he got back. All depended on whether it was thought essential for him to see the Prime Minister in London before he returned. There was still no news of the arrival of Eden and Dill.

We lunched with Fellers (American Military Attaché), the others of the party being Colonel Browers (American Army Observer in Egypt) and the Yugoslav Minister. The latter talked at great length of the imperative necessity of bringing in Russia on our side if we were ever to win the war. She would have to be bought probably by the grant of a warm water port. He was naturally in favour of keeping the war out of the Balkans if possible, but thought that Bulgaria could only be brought into a United Balkan front if she were given by Greece a corridor in Eastern Thrace. He had a lot to say about how maladroit we had been in our handling of Russia in the past. Donovan pinned him very firmly down at this point and asked him what he would do *now*. All he could recommend was the despatch of an intimate political friend of Churchill's to Moscow to replace Cripps as Ambassador, since Cripps, in Russian eyes, does not truly represent the present British Government. There was not much of immediate practical value in all that he said, and he was really more interesting in describing his experiences as a cavalry captain in the retreat of the Serbian Army in the last war.

The rest of the day we spent on the Mediterranean appreciation and I did some indexing of all our various memoranda. A telegram came in from Belgrade saying that the President had stiffened Prince Paul against the

German temptation of an agreement by offering full support to Yugoslavia under the Lease and Loan Bill. Donovan was much encouraged to see that his representations are apparently bearing some fruit.

I had a long talk with O'Connor after dinner. He had not changed a bit since I first knew him some years ago as a GSO2. He does not like [General] Haining [then Vice-CIGS] at all and told me he was a fearful intriguer in Palestine against Macmichael. He is a great friend of [General] Giffard – there are considerable resemblances in character between them.

Wednesday 19 February 1941   Cairo

In the evening I took the final draft of the appreciation to Wavell and Longmore, who both gave it their blessing. Donovan was very anxious not to send anything back of which they might disapprove or which might be embarrassing to them. Wavell showed me a paper from which it was clear that he had made up his mind to leap in as soon as possible at Salonika, fearing otherwise that we should be forestalled. He showed the same paper to Donovan, who dined with him alone that night. I think his judgement had been considerably influenced by Donovan's advocacy, as it was a very finely balanced question to decide.

At 11.20 p.m. Eden arrived in the Embassy. They had had a very bad passage indeed to Gibraltar, in the course of which the pilot had confronted them with the choice of being drowned or interned in Spain. However, they had told him to stuff on and had just arrived in Gibraltar with about half-an-hour's petrol in hand. After waiting three days owing to bad weather they had come straight through to Cairo with only an hour or two's stop at Malta and Crete.

Thursday 20 February 1941   Cairo

Donovan was out making various calls during the morning while I made a précis of his final draft of his appreciation. The full text was telegraphed by the American Legation to Washington:

Delays in travel necessitate telegraphic instead of personal report as hoped. I consider present moment offers vital opportunity for decisive action by President in offering services for promotion of Balkan front. Speedy action is essential. Only if Balkan front is formed can American munitions aid Balkan States, and German move south-eastward be stopped. Without it British may find it impossible to pass to offensive later. I am encouraged to suggest this move by President's recent telegram to Prince Paul and confirmed by admiration of magnificent British achievements in this theatre with very limited means.

Reasons for my proposal are as follows: Mediterranean should be viewed not as line of communication east–west but as no man's land between European line held mainly by enemy, and African line much of which is held by British. Great Britain holds a salient in Greece and must now plan advance northward against enemy line. Task will be difficult till Mediterranean can be cleared. This can only be done from inside where Great Britain is on exterior lines, but Mediterranean once cleared will provide lateral communications and put Britain on interior lines. Essential for this purpose that Great Britain should retain foothold in the Balkans. For this shipping and naval escorts are vital, also aircraft and ammunition for Balkan States.

Analysis of German activities indicated two main lines of policy: (i) offensive to destroy Britain, (ii) defensive to deny British any starting point for counter attack and to protect territory vital to German supplies. German action is carefully coordinated throughout the world. For example, Japan may be induced to strike in Far East simultaneously with German action in Europe.

German offensive against Britain may continue only in form of submarine and air attacks on shipping, industry, etc., or may be supplemented by direct invasion attempt. Balkan General Staffs all think invasion certain.

As part of offensive Germany will probably try to seal up Mediterranean by: (i) mining Suez Canal, (ii) possibly advancing into Spain and denying Gibraltar. Counter measures to (i) are being taken by British. Germany is already taking over from Italy task of air attack on shipping in Mediterranean. Nevertheless Malta is still used as repair base and Commander in Chief, Mediterranean, is confident he will still be able to take Fleet through the narrows with air support from carriers. Possible that Germany may seize Balearic Islands as a step to French North Africa as a base for attack on Gibraltar; but this would be hazardous operation for her. Despatch of German armoured formations to Libya is reported. If Germany could obtain French bases in North Africa, British task of clearing Mediterranean would be most difficult.

In Balkans Germany is doing all possible to disintegrate potential resistance. She wants peace there to keep undisturbed her food and oil supplies. Germany probably acquiesced in Italian invasion of Greece hoping she would reach Salonika from the west and thus avoid need for Germany to disturb the Balkans seriously by a move from the north. Her penetration of Bulgaria is doubtless largely dictated by considerations of defence of Romanian oil-fields against British air attack. Germany will stay ready to strike and forestall Britain in Salonika which she herself may need in connection with more extended operations. Events may thus force her to move on Salonika either from Albania in support of Italy, or from the north through Bulgaria.

If Germany gives up idea of invasion of England she might continue present blockade and go nap on overrunning all Balkans and Turkey before British aid could be effective. Success there would complete encirclement of Russia, seriously threaten British security in Near and Middle East and enable Romanian and Russian oil to go round by sea to Adriatic. German occupation of Balkans would make British reinforcement of Turkey much more difficult. Russia's fear of encirclement may bring her in on Allies' side.

Assuming all German plans aim at destruction of England it is not enough for England to liquidate Italy in Africa, securing herself in Pacific by naval arrangements in U.S.A. and beat off attack in British Isles. Germany might then consolidate her gains in Europe and could come to peace table with most of Europe under her domination and prestige of having successfully withstood democracies of the world. Blockade and air attack will not complete her defeat. Her armies must somewhere be beaten when on the defensive and Balkans offer perhaps the only place for this. To enable Britain to retain her foothold all Balkan countries must be brought into one front with Britain who would supply mainly technical services and troops. Britain needs American aid to achieve this end.[52]

Meanwhile, Eden and Dill were discussing with Wavell and Longmore what our policy should be regarding the despatch of British forces to the Balkans. In the evening Donovan had a long talk with Dill about Balkan policy. I have no doubt he put a good deal of stiffening into Dill in the course of it. There were more conferences in the evening, attended by Marshall-Cornwall and Heywood and a good many of the staff. Questions discussed and Donovan's answers may be summarised as follows:

1. If the Greeks would not willingly permit the British to put troops into the Salonika area, what line should the British take?

The British should make up their own minds as to the course which was best for their ultimate good. If, bearing in mind all the risks run from not being fully prepared, they decide that it is best to go into Salonika, let them tell the Greeks so quite plainly and act accordingly. If it is in British interests, it must ultimately be in the interest also of the Greeks.

It is quite certain that Germany will never tolerate Great Britain getting on to the Continent, either now or in the future. Therefore it is best to leap in now while the going is good.

2. If British resources are insufficient to help both Turkey *and* Greece (and bearing in mind the long accepted policy of making the support of Turkey a first charge on British resources) should British support *now* be given primarily to Greece or to Turkey?

To Greece, who is now fighting hard. Britain has kept her in the fight and discouraged her from coming to terms. Whatever might be the advantages of giving all aid to Turkey, Britain has a *moral* obligation to Greece. This policy would be sound *psychologically* for its effect on Germany, and on opinion in U.S.A. Even Turkey would be impressed by this unselfish action. Militarily there might be some risk of a complete débâcle, if Greece collapsed completely; but it must not be forgotten that Turkey would indirectly obtain a certain advantage from British support of Greece.

3. Turkey's military preparations and rearmament are still incomplete. She might collapse under a German attack. Would it be better in these circumstances to get Turkey in as an ally or leave her neutral?

Get her in as an ally now, if possible. One never knows what German pressure and penetration may achieve. Turkish opinion is basically loyal to the British alliance and they take pride in being the 'defenders of the gate'. Cash in now on this sentiment and it might bring in Yugoslavia and even have some effect on Bulgaria.

There should however be no attempt at *bargaining* with Turkey – inform them quite simply that 'we are going to the aid of Greece our ally; in doing so our right flank will be left exposed: your assistance to us as allies in covering this exposed flank will be very welcome'.[53]

The net result was the despatch of a telegram to Athens offering to meet and discuss in great secrecy before Eden and Dill went to Turkey.

Eden and Dill were both in to dinner and I got involved in a great argument with the former on the subject of Government policy before the war. Eden inveighed against Chatfield and Chamberlain as appeasers and argued that we should have fought Germany over the Rhineland, and Italy in 1935. I took the line that we should not have got our people to face war at that time, and that this was largely the fault of the left intellectuals and the League of Nations Union racket. It was rather pleasant to have the opportunity of a real go at the Foreign Secretary on even terms, and I made the most of it. We did not get up from dinner until nearly midnight. After dinner there was the usual whispering in corners on high policy until about 2.15 a.m.

Friday 21 February 1941   *Cairo*

Lampson told me that at the meeting on the previous evening the military argument had been that the Turks would be a liability and it would be best to keep them neutral for the present. On political grounds he strongly disagreed with this point of view as it would destroy any chance of a united Balkan front.

Donovan had a good talk with Eden after lunch and seemed gratified to find that his ideas were accepted, particularly the north–south conception of the Mediterranean. The Greeks had sent an immediate reply accepting the invitation to a conference. Donovan sent a message to the President, at Eden's request, on the need for shipping from the USA:

1. However situation in South-Eastern Europe may develop, it is clear that any British effort in this part of the world must place an additional heavy strain on their already severely limited shipping resources.
2. There is no shipping available locally in the Middle East, and requirements can only be met by using ships of convoys from England as they arrive. This means of course corresponding delays in arrival of later urgent supplies.
3. Anything that the United States can do to make neutral or other shipping available soon would be a major contribution to British war effort.[54]

In the evening we went round G.H.Q. saying good-bye to all. We also had a talk with Major General Tomlinson on the medical situation in the Western Desert and anti-malaria preparations for the Balkans. Eden had sent off a very laudatory message to the Prime Minister about Donovan, which I think is very well deserved. Only Dixon [Eden's Private Secretary] besides ourselves was in for dinner with the Lampsons.

Saturday 22 February 1941   Cairo–Alexandria

... Wright and Coates, Wavell's ADC, came to see us off by the 4.30 train from Cairo for Alexandria. We had a pleasant journey down in a Pullman though it was very hot. We got some dinner on the train and put up for the night at the Cecil Hotel.

Sunday 23 February 1941   Alexandria–Malta

Ground mist delayed our start till 8.45 when we took off in a Sunderland flying-boat, our fellow passengers being Admiral Lyster (Rear Admiral Aircraft) and one or two naval officers. Cunningham down to see Donovan off. We had a good journey to Malta and came down in St Paul's Bay at 4.30. . . .

Monday 24 February 1941   Malta–Gibraltar

A local gale had blown itself out by the time we took off at 1.45 in a Sunderland, and the first part of the journey was not too bad. Very soon, however, we ran into a forty m.p.h. head wind and it seemed as if we would never reach Gibraltar. The pilot was obviously getting rather worried – counting lifebelts! – and by the time we finally came down at Gibraltar at 3.30 we had only fifteen minutes' petrol left. Fortunately he was able to get down in the harbour and not on the east side of the Rock as he feared at one time he would have to do. We had all had quite enough by the time we came ashore where Quare was waiting to receive us. The sight of his cheerful face on the landing stage was a very pleasant one.

After lunch and a bath in Government House, Donovan had a cyst inside his eye-lid opened up by the eye specialist. It had been troubling him for a day or two. He stayed in bed for the rest of the evening as his eye was rather painful. At dinner there were the Governor, Captain and Mrs Hillgarth (Naval Attaché, Madrid), and daughter; Commander [Ian] Fleming, Secretary to the Director of Naval Intelligence;[55] Brigadier Parminter, Inglis, Quare and Forbes. Hillgarth told me that Sam Hoare is doing very well indeed in Madrid.

Tuesday 25 February 1941   *Gibraltar–Madrid*

Quare had made excellent arrangements for our journey to Madrid and at 7.10 we got off in two cars. . . I sat with Ian Fleming much of the way. He is a brother of Peter Fleming [writer, adventurer, aide to Wavell] and was on Reuter's staff before the war. He told me some interesting experiences as a Reuter's man and was a bit inclined to knock it back too much. He agrees 'C' and S.O.2 are a pretty fair crash-out.[56] According to him Mason Macfarlane is intriguing hard against the Governor – as I suspected.

On arrival in Madrid we went into the American Embassy where Donovan was to stay, to make our number with Weddell, the American Ambassador, and then went on to our own Embassy. Sam Hoare seemed very pleased that Donovan had agreed to come to Spain. I put up for the night with the Torrs. Torr [Military Attaché] seemed rather overwrought and had been badly shaken by the pessimism of Dill whom he had seen at Gibraltar. I had to spend a good deal of time restoring morale.

Wednesday 26 February 1941   *Madrid*

Donovan came round with Weddell to see Sam Hoare at 10.00. Hoare gave him a very good picture of the situation and emphasised the need for joint action by us and America to give economic assistance to Spain, if we were to undermine German influence. He also pressed Donovan to go to Lisbon as soon as possible and see Salazar. Donovan took both points very well and promised to act. From there we went on to Wyatt, the Naval Attaché, who seems a live wire but rather a blow-hard. The Americans had apparently done nothing much about fixing up appointments for Donovan and it was clear that we should have to stay on for another day or two instead of getting off next day as we had hoped. The Sunderland was being held at Gibraltar for us as Donovan did not wish to risk delay in returning to England from Lisbon on the civil airline.

We dined with the Hoares, the only others present being Mr and Mrs Weddell and Yencken [Minister at the Embassy]. Weddell is very pleasant but strikes me as quite ineffective. Mrs Weddell, who is extremely wealthy, is a very warm-hearted person and very anti-German. She does a great deal of philanthropic work and is not afraid of tackling the Spanish authorities to get some improvement in the conditions of the thousands of prisoners still held ever since the end of the Civil War. I was told that there are nearly half a million people still in gaol.

During the day Donovan saw the Greek and Turkish Ministers; Pereira, the Portuguese Ambassador; and General Astray, Head of the 'Mutilados', a battered old warrior with one arm and one eye who is all for keeping the Germans out of Spain, but has not now a great deal of authority. Pereira told him that anti-German feeling was growing in the country, but that the danger was that the Germans might use the food shortage to precipitate internal unrest and take this as an excuse for coming into the country.

Thursday 27 February 1941   Madrid

I went round with Donovan at 10.00 to Wyatt's office where he saw one of the leading lights in the White Russian Movement. Torr arrived soon after and we had some discussion on the best way of obtaining an interview with Franco for Donovan. Wyatt was being very tortuous about it all, but Donovan suggested that Wyatt should go round to Vigon [Air Minister] a little before he himself arrived and impress on him that Donovan was a man who could help Spain in the matter of economic aid and that it would, therefore, be in his country's interest for him to see Franco. This line of approach was agreed. Donovan had an hour-and-a-half with Vigon and gave him his usual line with necessary additions to suit the circumstances. After that he saw Moreno, Minister of Marine, and Moreu, Chief of the Naval Staff. . . .

Friday 28 February 1941   Madrid

The Americans had been trying all this time to fix up for Donovan to go and see Salazar at Lisbon, but we could get nothing through from there about permission for Wyatt to fly us down. It began to look as if it would not be possible to do it. I told Sam Hoare that I did not think that Donovan was very keen to go down to see Salazar before the new American Minister, Bert Fish, arrived in Lisbon, but Hoare was very keen for him to go so that he could reinforce his own arguments on the subject of economic assistance to Spain, in the light of a talk with Salazar. Torr told me in great confidence that Hoare had learnt from Pereira that Salazar was to meet Franco for personal discussions very shortly – hence the great desirability of Donovan seeing Salazar at once and not waiting to do so on his return from London to America. When Hoare told Donovan of the forthcoming meeting Donovan agreed to wait and go to Lisbon. I got busy fixing up for the journey by train in case the air journey proved impossible.

We then had a talk with Eccles, the Ministry of Economic Warfare expert in these parts who had come up from Morocco. He is very disturbed by German infiltration in North Africa. Murphy the American Consul General there apparently thinks that if we let imports into North Africa, Weygand will surely come in on our side alright in the end, but Eccles takes the line that we ought only to let stuff in if we get a *quid pro quo* from the French. This should be the exclusion of Germans and the restoration of British Consuls. He does not support the Prime Minister's policy of saying to the French in North Africa 'join de Gaulle or starve'. He thinks that Petain now would be ready to take a risk and is all for staging an incident directed against the Germans in North Africa. The snag to this is that, as Sam Hoare pointed out, an upset in North Africa would disturb Spain badly and perhaps lead to our undoing. Eccles is a pretty bright fellow, quite young, who had made a considerable fortune in business. He is one of the directors of Rio Tinto [Zinc Company], so knows Spain well.

Saturday 1 March 1941   Madrid–Lisbon–Gibraltar

After leaving Donovan at the American Legation [in Lisbon] I went on to our Embassy and after some trouble managed to get on to the Ambassador by telephone and tell him of Donovan's arrival and immediately impending departure. He was only mildly interested having expected us the previous day – Madrid had not warned them of the change of date. So I left him to it and went round to Walsh, Passport Control Officer, to send off two cables for Donovan and get a little money to buy a picnic lunch for myself and Donovan. I should have expected the Ambassador to want to see Donovan after his interview, but his attitude confirms what Hoare told me of him. . . .

Sunday 2 March 1941   Gibraltar

I went round to see Plowden in the morning and get off another cable for Donovan concerning his date of arrival. His partners were anxiously awaiting him to argue a big case before the Supreme Court. Admiral Somerville came in during the afternoon, in excellent form as usual. He agrees with Liddell and Eccles that the blockade should be elastic and used as a means of getting what we want in North Africa and not merely as a negative weapon. Donovan had another small cyst cut out of his eye in the evening. Eccles and Donovan discussed the economic situation of French North Africa at considerable length.

Monday 3 March 1941   London

We had quite a smooth trip and sighted the Scilly Islands about 8.00 a.m., passing over an outward-bound convoy about the same time. Plymouth was reached at 9.00, and after breakfast in the R.A.F. Mess at Mount Batten we flew up to Hendon in a Lockheed arriving there at 12.00. Donovan went off to Claridges with General Scanlan (American Military Attaché), and I reported in at the Cabinet Offices. Lunched with Ian [Brigadier Jacob];[57] saw Pug

[General Ismay][58] very briefly; saw the DMO [Director of Military Operations – General Kennedy][59] in the evening; also the *Chicago Daily News* man about publicity.

Caught the 7.34 p.m. to Camberley. Winnie met me in a taxi after some telephoning. *Lovely* to be home again!

Part II: Washington – Organising for War December 1941 – April 1942

Introduction

Soon after the United States entered the war a notice began to appear in every Washington office. In great big one foot high letters, it read:

TIME IS SHORT

'Don't ask us where we're going,' the saying went, 'get out of the way and let us get there.' Washington was in a frenzy of unreadiness. 'The Nazis couldn't invade this town,' remarked a cabby. 'Not in the rush hour.'[1] When Churchill and his entourage arrived for the Conference inappropriately code-named ARCADIA on 22 December 1941, the United States had been at war for just two weeks. Within the Administration the chaos was indescribable. The machinery for coping with this unaccustomed state of affairs was completely lacking. There was neither the experience nor the predisposition to create it. The Army and the Navy had a long history, proudly nurtured, of mutual suspicion and rivalry. Even the broad-minded Henry Stimson, Secretary of War, could blame 'the peculiar psychology of the Navy Department, which frequently seemed to retire from the realm of logic into a dim religious world in which Neptune was God, Mahan his prophet, and the United States Navy the one true church'.[2] Communication between the newly created Joint Chiefs of Staff and the President was uncertain and *ad hoc*, frequently dependent on the good offices of Harry Hopkins, Roosevelt's semi-permanent house guest and special adviser. 'The whole organisation from a war point of view belongs to the days of George Washington, who was made C in C of all the forces and just did it,' reported Dill, aghast. 'Today the President is C in C of all the forces but it is not so easy just to do it!'[3]

Little wonder then that chaos is the predominant impression of Dykes's first few weeks in Washington, 'with its maddening traffic system and its hopeless transportation facilities, with its sky-rocketing rents and prices, its endless stretches of wretched slums and dismal boarding houses, its confused and confusing atmosphere of an old Southern town, combined with a roaring Northern metropolis, hell-bent on 20th century business'.[4] His diary chronicles the immensely difficult and often acrimonious process of giving effect to the decisions of the Conference, breathing life into the combined organisation after the Arcadians had gone home.

In retrospect the Combined Chiefs of Staff organisation appears as the indispensable midwife of victory.[5] Dykes's diary makes quite clear that its novelty and its fragility are easily underestimated. In the early months of 1942 it might well have been nullified altogether. Inured to backstairs brokerage, Washington insiders like Jean Monnet – who makes frequent appearances in the diary – had no faith in the new committees, but looked instead to personal relationships, above all to Dill and Marshall, to make things go.[6] Bedell Smith consistently advocated some kind of inner council, a triumvirate of Dill, Marshall and Admiral King, with the added flourish of the Combined Chiefs of Staff meeting once a month 'for purely formal purposes with all allied nations' representatives present'[7] – a gesture perhaps towards the aspirations of the Commonwealth and China, but what of the Soviet Union?

The idea was fleetingly embraced by Dill himself in March 1942. The diary reminds us of the very natural preoccupation in Washington with the dismal series of events that unfolded as the Japanese romped through the Far Eastern empires in the opening weeks of the Pacific war. By early March, however, Dill began agitating for some reorientation. First he sounded out Brooke. 'Are you as bothered about the Middle East as I am?'

> My feeling is that the Middle East will be decisive of this year's campaign. If we and Russia hold, Germany is done. If we break we may well see Germany and Japan joined and America driven back to the Western Hemisphere with Great Britain as an outpost. What I would like to be able to do is to go to – say – Marshall and King with [the] shortest of short papers and say: 'Unless the Middle East is reinforced strongly and fast we shall be defeated there and our combined efforts will not enable us to win the war in years. You alone can send the reinforcements the Middle East needs and you must do it with land as well as air forces. The shipping problem we must solve together somehow.[8]

Next he put the proposition to Marshall, who sought advice from Eisenhower, then Assistant Chief of Staff at the head of the key Operations and Plans Division of the War Department. Eisenhower was generally receptive, and particularly enthusiastic about 'the suggested meeting of the three individuals, the only three, who can really make effective progress towards integrating our war effort'.

Echoing Bedell Smith, he went even further: 'I believe that if this suggested meeting could be used as a precedent for starting a weekly informal conference among the three individuals named, *with no other person present*, it would constitute a great stride toward bringing about the agreements we need.'[9]

In the event the proposal was never instituted; or never as completely or consistently as some might have wished. The Combined Chiefs of Staff committee was to a great extent built around the friendship of Dill and Marshall. But the informal special relationship was used always to promote, rather than subvert, the formal one.[10] As the need arose Dill, Marshall and King, and sometimes the head of the British Admiralty Delegation too, might continue their discussions after the weekly meeting of the full committee had broken up and its intimidating apparatus of secretaries and staff officers and dispersed. These discussions were often productive. But they were unplanned and irregular, and any decisions were strictly channelled through the combined organisation.[11]

The very existence of such ideas was, however, symptomatic of the frustration latent, perhaps inherent, in the infant organisation. They were held after all by those most deeply committed to the system. Others again had serious reservations about the principle of 'combination', or its outcome. When the Prime Minister's party returned from Washington in January 1942, Brooke, who had stayed in London, told them bluntly that they had 'sold our birthright for a plate of porridge'.[12] He never recanted the view that the Combined Chiefs of Staff should have been based in London, not Washington, possibly migrating later when the Americans had learned something of how to wage war. With time and reassurance from Dill some of his early resentment faded, but a strong undercurrent of exasperation with the whole organisation remained. More seriously, there were the malcontents in the US Navy Department. Dykes had the unenviable task of dealing with the captious Admiral Richmond Kelly Turner, later to find fame in the Pacific, who took exception to 'large unwieldy bodies . . . in which British officials would be given half the total authority for matters now solely under US control'. Turner also gave voice to the not uncommon American suspicion that 'since the British authorities do not understand the fundamental policies and strategic necessities of the US, it would be expected that US interests would be subordinated to the interests of the British Commonwealth.'[13] Turner's successor, Admiral 'Savvy'

Cooke, was little better. Dykes's diary offers a trenchant commentary:

> A spot of trouble over today's CCS meeting – the combined planners' papers seem to have been bitched up by that bloody little man Cooke who doesn't attend CPS [Combined Planning Staff] meetings and then throws his representative overboard.[14]

Such behaviour was often ascribed to the attitude of their redoubtable chief. 'What King does not understand,' wrote Admiral Cunningham, 'is that his subordinates all take their tune from him, and it is the absence of cooperation and wish to cooperate on his part which spreads itself throughout the whole American Navy.'[15]

This state of affairs was not without its Anglo-American compensations. As Bedell Smith noted in February 1943, when consulted by Ismay about a Royal Naval replacement for Dykes, 'the fact is that the Army has been more sympathetic and cooperative to the CCS set-up than has the Navy, as you well know, and your soldiers speak our language and can play closer to the Operations Division of the War Department.'[16] It was of inestimable significance for the establishment of a combined organisation that in the early months of 1942 Marshall and Dill, Bedell Smith and Dykes, and many of their Army colleagues were able to work more closely together than with any US Navy officer. Organising for war creates strange bed-fellows.

Diary
12 December 1941 – 5 April 1942

Friday 12 December 1941

I had been told on 9 December to stand by to leave the following night for Washington with Sir John Dill, Macready [Assistant CIGS], the Chief of the Naval Staff [Pound], the Chief of the Air Staff [Portal], Dickson [RAF Director of Plans], Lambe [RN Director of Plans], Hollis and Jacob [Cabinet Office], who were going with Beaverbrook [Minister of Supply] and the PM. That same evening Kennedy [Director of Military Operations] told me that the [incoming] CIGS [Brooke] had decided to have a new Director of Plans! No reason given at all which I feel is a bit hard. Went down that night to Camberley [his home]. A great comfort to see W.

By the next morning the trip was off, Roosevelt having asked for a postponement. Guy Stewart is to take over from me as Director of Plans. By 11.12 a.m. the trip was *on* again, so got packed up and tidied out my cupboards etc., while feverishly collecting briefs. To top [it] all, I was smitten with acute conjunctivitis at about 10.00 which practically blinded me. All my chaps [War Office planning staff] were very good about my going. I think they were a bit shaken. Saw C. J. S. King who said there should be no trouble in getting me a run as a Chief of Royal Engineers [i.e. an active command]. Jock Whitefoord wanted to run me for Director of Military Intelligence, Home Forces, but I told him not to press it. By the next morning my eyes were improving, and during a long Joint Planners' meeting they suddenly cleared completely.

Went off to Tite Street [Chelsea – his digs] in the evening after saying goodbye all round in the War Office and packed up my kit, Mrs Howe and Mrs Hueffer assisting with drinks and presents of chocolate for the journey! Left Euston by the 9.30 p.m. special train, arriving on the Clyde at 9.30 a.m. on 13 December.

Saturday 13 December 1941

Thence we embarked in a motor launch which ran us out to HMS *Duke of York*. Mary Churchill, the PM's youngest daughter, travelled up on the train and came aboard to see him off – a nice girl – bombardier in the ATS.[17] Met

Harcourt (the ship's Captain) who was at the Admiralty early in the war; and Macintosh (Commander). The lay-out of the ship is very similar to the poor old *Prince of Wales* [sunk by the Japanese on 9 December],[18] but more staff accommodation aft.

The arrangements are very good. A minute midshipman, Smith, was detailed to look after me which he did excellently. We got under way about 12.30 and finished up the evening with the usual cinema show.

Sunday 14 December 1941

Speed down to about eight knots. The ship rolling violently. Staggered up to see Dill for about one hour before lunch but could not face more than a cup of tea all day.

Monday 15 December 1941

Worked with Lambe and Dickson on a revised strategy paper (for discussion with the US COS) all day, and on notes about the defence of Malaya for Dill all evening. Things are going very badly there. The 11th Indian Division in Kedah [Province] has been pushed back.

Stomach feeling somewhat better, though the ship is rolling very hard at times (25 degrees each way).

Tuesday 16 December 1941

Finished off our strategy paper at last and got it up to the Chiefs of Staff. The weather is improving. Speed up to 17 knots by the evening. The latest idea is that we should go as far as Bermuda only and fly on thence in Clippers. The party is about 47 strong though, with a *mass* of strong boxes and documents.

Beaverbrook is an interesting study on these trips. He has the largest entourage of all – two private secretaries, a valet, a messenger, a doctor (Sir Charles Wilson [later Lord Moran, actually Churchill's doctor]) and a horde of advisers. Thomas is his 'private' Private Secretary – quite a nice fellow; and Poynton, ex-Colonial Office, his official one. With the PM are the toad-like Commander Thompson [naval aide], Inspector ditto [detective],[19] Martin and Brown (Private Secretaries), Averell Harriman [Roosevelt's personal emissary and Lend Lease expeditor].

Charles Lambe has Currie of the [Naval] Plans Division with him, and with Dickson there are Baker (Group Captain) and Deane. Jones and Cooper head the office staff. Old Jones was in great style the first night out – very dressy in a dinner jacket – but as all the rest of us refuse to dress up at night (except Dill and Portal) we haven't seen him in it again. The only exception is Macdonald-Buchanan, Dill's ADC, who appears resplendent in dinner jacket and white waistcoat each evening.[20]

Friday 19 December 1941

For the past few days we have been busy getting stuff ready for the conversations with the US staffs. Charles Lambe is a tower of strength. He did all the donkey work of producing a review of strategy bringing up to date the RIVIERA review [the 'Atlantic Conference' meeting of Churchill and Roosevelt in August 1941] in the light of new conditions. The PM also wrote a long dissertation [on strategy] – though good stuff. Out of it all Jo and Ian [Hollis and Jacob] have distilled a short COS paper setting out the five main planks in our policy which we intend to put forward. We discussed it with the COS this morning at a meeting on the Admiral's bridge. The ship was rolling violently, but it is fresh up there. It had been appallingly rough during the night.

I delved into the UK defence scales [of available men and equipment] and ground out a very short note while Dickson did something on the [possible] scale of attack on the West Coast of America.

Jo tells me he fears that Pound will not seize the reins and really take charge of the party in Washington. If *he* doesn't no-one else will, and we shall never get really going with the Yanks.

News in tonight that the Japs have got a firm footing on Hong Kong Island!! The news from Malaya is slightly better – but Duff Cooper [Minister sent to Singapore to report on the defences] evidently does not think much of Percival as a commander. 11 Indian Division seems to be sorting itself out a bit in the Penang area.

Saturday 20 December 1941

The sea was really smooth for the first time during most of the day. Had a long discussion with Weeks (Ministry of Supply) on the Victory Programme [of munitions production] and explained its origin etc. Worked on a few notes for the CIGS in afternoon.

The news from Hong Kong is very bad: the whole island seems to have been overrun by the Japs. I can't understand it at all seeing how many automatic weapons they had there.

Charles Lambe is a most attractive person and extremely able. I am very sorry indeed that I shall not be working with him on the Joint Planning Staff. It would have been such good value.

Monday 22 December 1941

Yesterday was rough again and no access to the fresh air was possible. We had finished off all our stuff so had a stand easy for the day. During last night we shed two of the three US destroyers which had come out to cover us on the last lap. By lunch-time signs of approaching land were visible in shipping and gulls and soon after we made out land fall. The water had got very shallow indeed but we stuffed on at full speed. The result was a *stern* wave 10 feet above the quarter deck – which incidentally flooded the PM's after-cabin and all those on the middle and lower decks through the wash basin wastes!

We picked up a pilot and two US Navy officers and Maude (Security Officer of the British Missions) about 1.30 p.m. and they gave us the latest proposed arrangements. We were four hours behind time owing to the weather, and every conceivable permutation and combination of destroyer and car; destroyer and aeroplane; train etc. was being mooted! Finally at 4.30 p.m. we anchored in Hampton Roads at the southern end of Chesapeake Bay. The PM and the COS went off and got away to Washington by air. The rest of us disembarked in launches at Old Point Comfort, a one hoss little place on about the scale of Lee-on-Solent. There, we entrained in a special train about 7.30 p.m. and set off for Washington. Everything was so secret, none of the railway people had had much warning. However they laid on the railroad vice-president's private saloon car and put on board 87-odd lunch baskets for the party, which included a party of marines and all the cipher staff. Very good food – two eggs, chicken, fruit and rolls and excellent coffee. It was very welcome.

Tuesday 23 December 1941

We reached Washington at 1.30 a.m. and were whisked off in cars under police escort across all the traffic lights to the Wardman Park Hotel – an enormous place, stifling hot inside. My bag arrived at 3.00 a.m., when I had turned in. But others did not get theirs till breakfast time. Bramwell Davies of the [Joint Staff] Mission was very helpful. After breakfast we went down to the Embassy Annex: met Frank Vogel [JSM planner] there who told me poor old Bundy [US planner/secretary at the Atlantic Conference] had been lost in an aircraft that had left for Hawaii just after the Pearl Harbor show. His loss will be a serious one.

At 11.00 a.m. the COS had a meeting with the Mission and us to draw up the final draft of the strategy paper (one and a half hours of nit picking).[21] Dickson, Lambe and I brought Vogel, Strafford and Belper [JSM planners] back to our pub for lunch – a colossal amount of very good food I must say. In the afternoon I went down with Vogel to meet Gerow (Director of War Plans). He is a very good chap and most cooperative. We had a good long talk all round the war and joint planning which lasted till about 5.30. With him was Colonel Handy his GSO1 [staff officer] and General Eisenhower, a Deputy Director. The latter seemed pretty alert, but has only just been pulled in from a formation HQ.[22] Handy is elderly and rather colourless.[23] I think the time was very well spent.

At 7.30 p.m. the COS and all staffs went to an enormous dinner given by Knox [Secretary of the Navy] and Stimson [Secretary of War]. (Rafts of food and good drink!) I sat next to McCloy [Assistant Secretary of War] – young, forceful and very alert. Bundy, I remember, had spoken very highly of him to me. We had a very good talk together. He is full of the offensive spirit and complains of the stonewalling staffs – whom I had to defend a little! My other neighbour was Lieutenant General McNair (a staff officer of General Marshall's). We had a great chat about unity of command which is like a King Charles's head with the Yanks! The whole dinner was quite in the Hollywood style but certainly very well done. I tasted for the first time the American oyster (cooked) – a great fat thing as big as a poached egg!

After dinner we all came back to the Embassy to clear up the masses of telegrams etc. which had come in. Got to bed about 1.30 a.m.

Wednesday 24 December 1941

Walked up to the Embassy at 9.00 – lovely fresh bright morning. Slight flap to get the CIGS [Dill] off to a meeting at 10.30. Macdonald-Buchanan is a very helpless sort of person and couldn't get him the papers he wanted. I got onto it and raised a copy of the minutes of a Staff Conference of the previous night (President and PM present). The COS went to a general all-round discussion with the US COS. We were warned for [an Anglo-American] Joint Planners' meeting at 3.00. When we arrived for this we found Turner (US Navy Director of Plans)[24] and Gerow and about 20 other officers of all sorts. Turner produced a long waffling list of the 'Tasks' set by the COS. He was in the chair (very much so) and his list was what he said the COS wanted: he had been at their meeting. Coleridge, our [JSM] secretary, didn't agree at all with his lay-out, but we started work on it. The idea was to appoint sub-committees to do everything. By a *reductio ad absurdum*, we torpedoed that idea and only set up a shipping sub-committee. After a bit we managed to get the room clear of everyone except the three of us, Turner, Gerow and George (Army Air Corps). We then got down to GYMNAST [the invasion of North West Africa] on a joint basis and by 7.30 p.m. Turner got quite mellow. The meeting lasted till 8.30 p.m. After dinner we three further discussed GYMNAST and the form of a paper on it, knocking off at 12.30 a.m.

I stayed up till 3.00 a.m. talking to Ian [Jacob] and Jo [Hollis] about a possible planing and co-ordination set-up. They feel one of them will have to stay here for the nucleus. Coleridge does not carry enough guns.[25]

Thursday 25 December 1941

Got to the office at 9.00; dictated off a draft of the GYMNAST paper. We all went down at 10.45 and had a preliminary informal discussion on it with Gerow. This went very well and all difficulties were settled – though the US insisted on doubling the number of forces all the way! I feel they are unduly optimistic about providing them and about timings.

I went to lunch with Bill Donovan: Robinett and Siberg, two officers from their GHQ, who have been pulled in to do secretary opposite Jo and Ian, were there too. Pleasant but not very impressive.

The Joint Planners met again at 3.45. We went at it hammer and tongs, with the size of the committee and the bedlam increasing all the time! Turner became increasingly difficult. Finally about 7.00 he tabled a draft purporting to give our views on the absolute priorities of all the various projects on the *tapis* [under consideration]. The relief of Iceland and Northern Ireland came at the bottom. He simply reiterated that it was *impossible* to relieve Iceland till May, and we could get no real reason why. We compromised finally on a very emasculated version which simply gave the implications of doing GYMNAST. (A disgraceful attempt, this, by Turner to bounce us into supporting him against the President's and PM's agreed views.)

We got away at 8.10 p.m. and went to the Embassy for dinner. Lady Halifax [wife of the Ambassador] looks very ill and frail but was very charming and simple. I sat next to Angus McDonnell, Halifax's 'contact man' – a railway engineer who has lived here and in Canada a lot – good company.[26] He gave me one good thought – we are the only nation in the war now who went to war with Germany to uphold liberty *of our own free will without being kicked into it* by a German attack. After dinner we were all taken down in a bus to see the Disney film, 'Dumbo', the baby elephant in the circus with the abnormally large ears – very good. A pleasant evening – in bed by 12.30 a.m. for a change!

Friday 26 December 1941

At 9.30 we had a Planners' conference among ourselves to sort out our ideas a bit and at 11.00 we went up to the COS to report progress. We explained Turner's dominating position and our difficulty when he attended the joint COS meetings and we did not.

At 11.50 we got away and went down to the Senate to listen to Winston address both houses [of Congress] in informal session. It was a very interesting show. The three of us were much photographed as we walked up the road together with Harriman. The Senate Chamber itself is very much in the Crystal Palace style of decoration and architecture – not a very dignified appearance, but certainly with a style of its own. I almost expected to see aspidistras about the place – the bentwood chairs were there. Winston made a magnificent speech which was received very well. Danny, my enormous chauffeur, was most enthusiastic over it as we drove away. An interesting sight was the soldiers complete with tommy guns looking rough on the roof of the Senate! Altogether a very moving experience.

After lunch we had further discussions among ourselves on the GYMNAST project.

About 6 p.m. Ian [Jacob] rang up to ask us to draft a telegram requesting information on the broad implications of carrying out GYMNAST, the relief of Iceland, the relief of Northern Ireland troops *and* Middle East convoys all together!! We hatched out a draft which I took down to the White House where the PM was sitting with the COS. Beaverbrook had apparently said that we *could* produce a lot more troop shipping if we really tried. The PM OKed the draft 'with acclamation'. The White House is a fine place inside – with the same house-and-office atmosphere as No. 10 [Downing Street]. From there I went off to dine with Bill Donovan who brought out a number of his people. Bill Whiting has just arrived there by air from London. Also met Bob Sherwood, the playwright, an interesting chap. I fear Bill Donovan has lost the end in the means, and doubt whether he is yet producing much of practical value. He showed me with great pride charts of Dakar [Senegal] which were exactly the same as ours, but which he was evidently very proud to be able to turn out at short notice.

Came back from there at 11.00 p.m. and cleared up in the office, calling in with Charles Lambe for a drink with Belben [JSM] on the way home.

Saturday 27 December 1941

Called up to the COS in the morning to go through our paper on GYMNAST. The COS very peeved at the size of the forces shown therein. We explained that the US Joint Planners insisted on raising all our figures.

Joint US/British COS meeting at 3.00 which we attended. Pound reared up to them because papers which had presumably been passed had been reissued with a lot of amendments. Their secretarial arrangements are just non-existent; they don't understand the drill at all. Marshall then broached the idea of a Supreme Commander in the Far East: he made his points very well – nothing could be worse than the present system! It is a fine bold conception – but who is the *man*? At 4.30 p.m. the US and British Joint Planners retired and got down to a draft prepared by the second eleven on reinforcements to the Far East; also to a revise of GYMNAST to lower the [force] requirement figures in accordance with COS instructions. Turner was very much more amenable and did some pretty good drafting. As a result we got through by 9.00 p.m.

Very exhausted, I rendezvoused an hour later with Reggie Kerr who is Deputy Quartermaster General, North America. We fell in almost at once with Douglas, a Treasury man out here on inspection duty, who took us off to the Escargot where we had an excellent dinner at his expense, returning home at midnight. I went up to the Embassy and dashed off a letter to W. to catch the air mail next morning. Returning about 1.00 a.m. with Ian and Jo, they told me that the Supreme Command idea was going hard and *Wavell* was the American choice!

Sunday 28 December 1941

Joint Planners' meeting at 10.30 a.m. at which I reared up about the Yank secretariat issuing papers as a final draft, before we had finally given the OK. Their secretaries are Scobey, an aged Lieutenant Colonel, and McDowell, a moon-faced Commander – both *completely* dumb and appallingly slow. In the course of the morning we hammered out a draft agenda for further Joint Planning work.

In the afternoon we were called in to the COS who told us that unified [tri-service, Anglo-American] command in the Far East was to go through. The basis of the directive was a draft prepared by Marshall's staff. We got down to this draft and, with an interval for dinner, got our ideas on it sorted out by 12.50 a.m.

Monday 29 December 1941

Went through the draft directive for Wavell with the CIGS [Dill] as soon as he came in. Danny [the chauffeur] tells me that Dill's secret service guard has a hell of a time following him on foot to the office in the mornings. No American is apparently capable of *walking* a mile.

Joint Planners' meeting to go through the directive at 10.45. We went at it all day, with an interval for lunch in the building, till 6.30. Turner very amenable. Eisenhower, the author of Marshall's draft, was there. He proved himself first-class. The atmosphere was excellent – everyone flat out to cooperate. The work was much hampered by the uselessness of their secretariat. I found myself doing the job. The final paper does not look too bad at all, though somewhat long and definitive. They very much want Wavell to be under the British COS, but we see the political danger of having all responsibility (and blame) centred in London.

The COS have decided this afternoon that orders will issue from *Washington* to Wavell. This would be far better for Australia. Curtin [Australian Prime Minister] has played the complete shit there and says we have let them down. (New Zealand as usual plays up fine.) The PM had left for Ottawa yesterday so all this stuff has to be cabled up to him as well as home.

Dined with Charles Lambe and discussed the merits of communism at great length! He is a great idealist – but *such* an attractive personality.

Rather a historic day to look back on, if all this goes through.

Tuesday 30 December 1941

Spent most of the morning, after walking up to the office, at the COS meeting at which they went through the Joint Planners' draft directive to Wavell. No amendments of any importance were put forward. At 3.00 p.m. there was a joint US/British COS meeting in the Federal Reserve Building to take the draft. Again quite successful. Trifling amendments only. They also agreed on the 'controlling agency' for Wavell: the COS in both capitals advising the President and the PM – the orders to go out from Washington. This presupposes a strong *British* secretariat here. The President wanted a new 'Joint body' in Washington on which, in addition to British and US representatives, there would also be Dutch, Australian and New Zealanders. Our COS pointed out that these latter *must* be dealt with in London. The US COS agreed and it was decided to return to the charge with the President. The PM signalled his OK [from Ottawa] on the draft directive from Washington in the evening.

Admiral Turner told me during the COS meeting that they were probably sending some troops to Northern Ireland pretty soon. These joint COS meetings are a staggering party. On our side there are our men, our Heads of Mission [Army, Navy and RAF representatives from the JSM] and us three [planners], plus the Secretariat. On their side are their two COS, [Admiral] Stark and [General] Marshall, plus Turner and Gerow [planners]. In addition there are all sorts of hangers-on who seem little interested, as well as Admiral King [soon to replace Stark]. The latter has a magnificent face, and I should say is pretty good. The hangers-on include people like the Chief Marine, heads of various Navy Department bureaux, Raymond Lee [long-standing US Military Attaché in London] who is posing as Secretary-General, and several so-called secretaries who do absolutely nothing at all. They have apparently realised that their efforts at keeping minutes in parallel with ours make them look *too* amateurish as they now accept ours as agreed after vetting the drafts. This is a big advance.

Charles Lambe, Jacob and I took dinner off Bill Donovan. Good talk, as usual, with him. The only other guest there was a 'financial' friend of his − a nice chap who apparently runs a model farm as a hobby but talked a lot of balls (e.g. cannibalism is rampant in Moscow; all cattle dealers will tell you the dead weight of a steer to within not less than three pounds).

Back to the office after dinner till 11.30 p.m. Scribbled off one or two letters to catch the air mail.

Wednesday 31 December 1941

No meetings all day for a change except for the COS who took the Joint Planners' papers on: (1) GYMNAST; (2) South-West Pacific reinforcements; and (3) terms of reference for future work. All went through OK in addition to a telegram to commanders in the Far East (to be sent by both sides), a draft of which we gave the COS to take with them. A large part of the morning was taken up by the arrival of a Colonel Ross from the US Army's movements side. He described their movement layout and said they were moving up the first contingent [of troops] from Louisiana to New York *en route* for Northern Ireland. War Plans apparently knew nothing of this at all, the move having been ordered by Stimson, the Secretary of War!! I never heard a chap talk so fast and continuously as Ross − but he seems all-out to help which is the great thing. The US system is totally different from ours. The whole job is decentralised – the formation commander is just told to get on with it!!

We heard that Napier, Bourne, Pratt and company [Executive Planning Staff from the War Office] are due to arrive tomorrow midday. Shall be very glad to see them.

In the afternoon we got all the signals from New Zealand, Australia, the COS and home and Wavell on the [new] ABDA [Australian–British–Dutch–American] area directive. (Stimson objected to ABD*U* – U is not used as an abbreviation of USA!!) Charles [Lambe] and I drafted a note for the COS on them. The COS in London press for Burma to be excluded. But the US are very keen to have it in. (Wavell also says leave it out.) We advised to include it. The US are apparently very afraid that, if not included, Chiang Kai-Shek will chuck his hand in. They say Wavell and CKS did not get on well together at all when they met at Chungking recently; the latter being very cross because we had grabbed a lot of stuff for Burma which was *en route* to China. Australia and New Zealand both want the ABDA area extended to include them. The difficulty is to get the US to come so far west. But there is hope. King told Pound that if we would cough up two capital ships they would be ready to take the offensive against Japan. The question is whether to maintain *two* inferior fleets or to combine forces and try to bring the Japs to battle. A victory at sea would solve all our difficulties.

For the first time here, I did *not* have to work after dinner. I shall see the New Year in *in bed*!

Dill told me I should certainly have to stay on a bit. I told him I was diffident about doing 'Director of Plans' here if I had not got the CIGS's [Brooke] confidence in London. He assured me I had nothing to worry about on that, but I could get no more out of him. I should very much like to know the real truth about it all [i.e. his unexplained relief as Director of Plans]. I have an uncomfortable suspicion about John Kennedy [Director of Military Operations] having made me a scapegoat.

Thursday 1 January 1942

Dill [as outgoing CIGS] got a GCB[27] in the New Year's Honours. Jacob got a CBE[28] at which I am delighted. He also heard his son had passed into the Navy and got a scholarship too. Ian very bucked about it all, bless him. Portal and the PM returned from Canada in the morning. The PM had apparently had a great personal triumph there.

At 11.00 Lambe and I went down to see Sir Arthur Salter and Sir Ashley Sparkes [Shipping Mission] about shipping for GYMNAST, Iceland, Ireland etc. The latter thinks that we would rake up a bit more personnel shipping for transatlantic moves by converting some cargo ships. Rather doubtful owing to its effect on the import programme. The trouble is that Beaverbrook is horning in and saying that there is tons of shipping to be had for the purpose!

Went down to see Gerow in the afternoon about the Victory Programme, on which Dickson is very keen to put up a paper to the COS. Gerow's idea is to get the production to equip about 215 divisions: he freely admits that he does not know where all these are going to be used. Macready tells me that on their present programmes there ought to be enough for all we want.

At 8.00 p.m. we went to an official dinner given by the COS to the American staff etc. I sat next to Gerow and [Rex] Benson, our Military Attaché. Gerow is very bitten with the idea of a Secretariat like ours; and also, I think, with a Joint Planning Committee of permanent members on our model. A very good dinner.

Got back to the hotel about 11.00 p.m. and found the Executive Planning Staff party had arrived safely – Bourne, Napier, Pratt, Picknett (Ministry of War Transport), Besant (RN) and Tyzack (RAF). They had flown across in a Liberator to Gander [Newfoundland] – thence via Montreal to New York; thence by train. Napier had held his water from England to America!! Most of the journey was in oxygen [masks] at 20,000 feet. They had had engine trouble just after taking off the first time and had to fly around for three hours to reduce petrol load before landing. Poor Picknett (making his first flight) had thought they were on their way, but had taken very calmly the idea of touching down in mid-Atlantic!

Friday 2 January 1942

Walked up to the office with all the new arrivals – bright but mild morning. Had a long discussion with them on GYMNAST and the shipping position generally. They then went on down to meet General Somervell [Army Service Forces commander] who is apparently being badgered by Beaverbrook. After lunch we tried to knock out some sort of a draft on the Victory Programme, in the intervals of dealing with all the Executive Planning Staff troubles [associated with their arrival].

Dill warned me that he had now asked for me to stay on to run the Secretariat here – which will be a big show with all the ABDA to run. GOK [God Only Knows] how long I shall be stuck here now! – but in many ways I would sooner work under the Cabinet Office [as Secretary] than the War Office [as Planner]. Went to dinner with [Raymond] Lee; Hollis, Jacob and Sibert, who has been acting as a [US] secretary, were the others. Lee and Sibert were anxious to hear all about the Secretariat. They want to start one up. Lee has a very nice house – evidently oodles of money: he appeared resplendent in a blue velvet smoking jacket. I found it very difficult to get them to understand that a Secretariat was *not* part of the General Staff or Naval Staff and owes its allegiance only to its committees.

Earlier in the evening Gerow rang me up in great trouble. The President wanted to insert in the ABDA Directive, which had been previously signed, sealed and delivered, a paragraph to say that he must establish HQ in Java [then a Dutch colony]. They wanted to tell the Dutch this. Jacob would not at first raise it with the COS who were meeting the PM in the White House. But at Gerow's most earnest request I got him to do so and the PM sent off a separate telegram.

Saturday 3 January 1942

More discussion with the Executive Planners over GYMNAST. Napier pointed out the wastefulness of sending the US Marine Division which is not mobile – but we emphasised the political angle of it all.

Lambe, Dickson and I went down in the lunch hour and bought silk stockings!

In the afternoon we had a long Joint Planners' meeting on: (a) the defence of the Pacific Islands in the air; (b) the Victory Programme. Turner very insistent that Australia and New Zealand must do the protection of New Caledonia and Fiji. I stressed the smallness of their forces – but they [the US] are very sticky about sending anything outside their area! It was left that we were to press the Australians more. Discussion on the Victory Programme went on for a long time. We did not get very far, but *did* succeed in getting from them a copy of *their* Victory Programme – which has never yet been passed over to us. The totals are pretty staggering – e.g. arms for 8,000,000 men!

Dined with Ian and Jo. Lambe and the Coleridges were the other guests. Mrs C. is a nice person, due to calve in about a fortnight. If I do take on the Secretariat, I shall like working with Richard Coleridge. Jo and Ian agreed to send Drysdale [from the Cabinet Office] as chief clerk which will be a great help.

My nice new pair of socks have come back from the hotel laundry so shrunk I can't get them on at all – damn them! Weather turning much colder. The Japs reached Manila [in the Philippines] today.

Sunday 4 January 1942

Hard at it all morning with the Executive Planners and Napier who had produced a general shipping appreciation during the night. It appears that we *can* do all the projected moves in the East *and* do a lot to help the US get to Iceland and Ireland. Putting on GYMNAST would only cut out 25,000 from the War Shipping Convoys and all movement from America in *US* ships. We knocked out an *aide-mémoire* on it all and fixed up a draft cable home about GYMNAST. These were taken by our COS at 4.00 p.m. They went out to a White House meeting at 5.30. I gather this was a fearful show. The US team was all on, dozens of them, with old Stimson (Secretary of War) trying to explain the plan!! The President and PM profoundly gloomy about it apparently. It looks as if the President will get these meetings cut down to essentials on their side.

All the evening Lambe, Dickson and I discussed the Victory Programme –

whether any paper was needed or not. I feel it has done its stuff so far as the Army and Air are concerned. But apparently the Navy Department (i.e. Admiral Turner) did not include any of the British requirements in their Victory Programme, as Bundy did for the Army and Air. Consequently the programme for small craft is hopelessly small. After dinner I went back with Dickson and dictated a note on the working of our Secretariat for Sibert.

Monday 5 January 1942

Finished off my draft on the Secretariat. Bourne and Napier were down to it with the US staffs – getting quite good value. The PM has gone off to Miami for a brief holiday. I had lunch with Sibert, Lee and Hammond at the Army and Navy Club. Lee wants us to put over to them what our set-up will be for the ABDA Secretariat.

The Dutch have asked to be represented permanently on the US/British COS Committee in Washington, but the PM and our COS are insisting on this being done in London only. Discussed secretarial staff in the afternoon with Jo and Coleridge. Also there: Sir William Douglas (Treasury), Sir Henry Self (who is to be Permanent Under-Secretary to Dill when he becomes the Minister of Defence's [i.e. Churchill's] representative), Wemyss [Head of the British Army Staff in the JSM] and Harris [Head of the RAF Delegation in the JSM; later 'Bomber' Harris]. Douglas quite agrees there must be a considerable increase of secretarial staff.

After dinner we all went down to a music hall show at the Gaiety. Dud and lifeless except for two comedians who were good, and a fat girl who did contortionist dances. Otherwise a lifeless chorus and striptease acts by full-breasted girls who couldn't dance at all.

Tuesday 6 January 1942

Worked on Secretariat proposals in the morning and at 12.30 went down to see Sibert about them after talking things over with Ian [Jacob]. Had lunch in the Federal Reserve Building with Sibert, Hammond (his winger) and old Scoby. The FRB is the most palatial place I have ever seen – a real temple of Mammon! Everything inside is of marble, the outer doors of solid bronze, all the fittings of the most beautiful chromium. God knows what it must have cost to build. Luncheon in the 'officers' room' is most beautifully done and is 'on the house' for the Service staffs who are temporarily housed there as Secretariat for the Conference. We had a most satisfactory discussion about proposed Secretariat arrangements for ABDA. The War Department (or at least Lee and Sibert) are absolutely sold on our secretarial ideas, and their anxiety is to get an organisation of their own, on similar lines, under way before the 'Arcadians' [the conferees] leave. The difficulty is going to be to get it across to the Navy Department, i.e. Admiral Turner.

In the evening I went down to see Bill Donovan, primarily to talk to him about a damn silly report from his man in Cairo which he had sent to the President. This said that 'the situation was deteriorating rapidly: Huns were moving in tons of aircraft: London would do nothing: situation in Alexandria pathetic; morale dropping owing to exhaustion'. I think he was peeved that the President had showed it to the PM who had of course passed it to the COS, who had taken considerable umbrage. Bill counter-attacked at once by saying he had only done it to help keep the President's eye on the *German* ball [rather than the Japanese one].

We talked of this and that and I told him of our difficulties with Turner: his obstinate refusal to send any US stuff to New Guinea or any British area; his failure to include our naval requirements in the US Victory requirements (in contradistinction to the Army's action through Bundy's good offices). He said he would speak to Knox [Navy Secretary] and work for Turner's removal. I think it is the only way to get any good co-operation on the naval side. [Jean] Monnet [the European visionary, then an influential member of the British Supply Council in Washington] is emphatically of this opinion and says we should openly demand this from Hopkins.

I listened to the President's address to both houses of Congress before lunch – a very fine fighting speech in which he outlined the figures aimed at in 1942 production. Beaverbrook has done a good job in setting them a terrific target – e.g. 45,000 combat aircraft in 1942 and double that in 1943! I think the figures are impossible of fulfilment and there will be some priority clashes. Some machinery will have to be set up to sort them out on a strategic basis.

Walked back from the office before dinner. Temperature down to about six degrees, but a lovely sunny day all through. The air is so dry that you get sparks off everything you touch. After dinner, which I had with Jo and Charles Lambe, one of the American Naval Department officers, Kremer, came up with some intercepts showing that U Saw, the Burmese premier, is apparently going to do a Quisling act and go over to the Japs. I think he was a little shocked at our lightheartedness in the matter! As Jo said, we take things like that but do something quick (telegrams were roared off immediately) whereas they take it terribly seriously and talk a hell of a lot, but do precious little!

Wednesday 7 January 1942

Worked on Joint Intelligence Committee stuff with the others all morning. Discussed a Victory Programme paper with Macready and got out a draft – but it has been overtaken by a paper the COS are putting in to the US COS setting out what our set-up is going to be here in future. We are having trouble with Australia who, unlike NZ over Fiji, say they can send nothing at all to defend New Caledonia. The Yanks are very sticky about sending anything at all to our territories. They are quite shamelessly pressing the small Dominions who are in the forefront to strip themselves of all home defence troops, while they themselves with a population hundreds of times bigger sit cowering on their west coast!

Jo is having trouble over Dill's directive. The PM agrees he should deal only with the military side, merely 'keeping touch' with the Civil Missions; but Self wants to get in as the local Bridges [Cabinet Secretary] and is trying to pull him [Dill] in as a great panjandrum over the whole lot – thereby making a good job for himself.

Went down after lunch and did some shopping – mostly foodstuffs. It looks quite strange to see all that stuff in the shops again. In the afternoon we did more Joint Planners' stuff on GYMNAST; on the Pacific air route; and on Atlantic strategy. It is very difficult to produce any useful papers owing to the chariness of the US Joint Planners in producing any concrete recommendations at all. Their Chiefs don't use a staff at all. Admiral King told Pound today, for example, that he would not mind the Planners examining a certain question 'providing they made no recommendations'!

Macready sat with us at dinner and told us some most amusing stories of his time on the Polish Police Mission after the last war. Wilkinson telegraphed today about secretarial staff here. Charman is to come as chief clerk, the others being Maynard, Miss Shephard and Joan Mainprice [from the War Office]! It will be nice to have some faces 'I knew and loved when all was young'.

Thursday 8 January 1942

The Planners worked all morning. A Joint Planning meeting in the afternoon which lasted from 3.30 to 7.55 p.m. – Pacific bases defence. (The US agreed to reinforce New Caledonia!) Great diversity of opinion between the US Army and Navy developed over Atlantic operations projects. We had to break up before they had resolved it. Coleridge, Dickson and I dashed off at 8.00 to see an invitation show of [the film] 'The Target for Tonight'. We had a hurried snack of spaghetti in real Italian style in a little café near the theatre. It was a very good picture. After it the Davieses [JSM] came back with us all for a drink.

Friday 9 January 1942

Started taking over the Secretariat. Very gloomy telegram in from Wavell about conditions in Malaya. 9 and 11 Indian Divisions are melting away. Great bobbery going on over Dill's functions. Henry Self wants to set himself up as Permanent Under-Secretary and to get Dill to co-ordinate all the Civil Missions. Jo was certain this was not the PM's idea. Jo and I went down to see Self after lunch. He was quite frank about it – Macready had told him that a certain diagram which had been roughed out showing responsibilities had been approved by the PM – but it had not. Jo drafted a minute to the PM for Dill suggesting the two alternatives, i.e. complete co-ordinator; or in charge of the

Military Mission [JSM] only. Dill quite shirty about the latter idea! However I told him Jo was only keen that he should not be put in a false position. After dinner I went up to his room and helped him draft his own suggested directive. He was quite pleasant then.

Saturday 10 January 1942

To a COS meeting in the morning. Chief items were the US proposal for Drum to be in charge of the Burma route from Rangoon to Chungking and to command all US and Chinese forces in Burma independent of Wavell, though co-operating. The COS would not have that and produced amendments. The other point was trying to fix up for Wavell to assume command as soon as possible, before the directive was finally OKed by the Dutch and Australians, who are both being tiresome about consultation machinery.

US/British COS meeting at 3.00. Complete confusion over the agenda. The really important paper, 'Post-ARCADIA Collaboration' [i.e. the form of Anglo-American collaboration after the conference], had never been circulated to the US Navy by their secretariat![29] Old Stark produced one item after another out of a hat – in none of which were our men prepared. Little good work done. Tried to get their secretarial organisation sorted after the meeting, but it is really a hopeless task. Robinett, one of the Army secretaries, I mistrust. Macrae, USN, and Sexton, US Army, are plain stupid.

Went back after dinner and tore off a note on SUPER-GYMNAST [revised codename for the same North African operation] for circulation.

Heard that all the Supply missions had reacted *most* strongly to the idea that Dill should have any jurisdiction over them! They had presented him with a draft suggesting he should be only in charge of the Military Mission. This apparently he had accepted, after seeing Beaverbrook.

Sunday 11 January 1942

COS meeting at 10.15 in silence while they read a PM's appreciation indited [composed] from his retreat in Miami. Ian and I went through it paragraph by paragraph scoring as in boxing rounds (WSC v. Hard Facts). He won heavily on points but was nearly KO about the 12th round. They then went off to the White House to meet him on his return. At 3.00 p.m. a US/British COS meeting. They were not ready to discuss post-ARCADIA collaboration. A Joint Planners' paper on US reliefs to Ireland and Iceland was taken and OKed; also one on Pacific Islands' defences. The latter was approved subject to Marshall's approval. Most of the time was taken in discussing the possibility of speeding up US reinforcements of the Pacific Islands and ABDA. They can't raise the ships and are badly rattled by the Malaya news and a tip and run raid on Samoa. I don't think Dill was wise to show them a gloomy Wavell telegram on the subject!

Came back and did the minutes. Then went out with Ian to dine with Monnet. Macready there too. Monnet is a very shrewd fellow. He stresses the importance of the Dill–Marshall liaison. I think he is right that the Yanks won't work to organisations – they deal only in personalities. Late to bed as usual.

Monday 12 January 1942

Beaumont-Nesbitt [JSM] spoke to me about his proposal for a Director of Intelligence to co-ordinate Intelligence here. I think it sound and he would do it quite well. The COS were down with the PM all morning, and a 2.00 p.m. meeting had to be postponed till 4.00 p.m. Marshall then produced a shipping plan for US Far East reinforcements quite different from what had been fixed up at a rush meeting of Napier and company with their movements people the evening before. Ireland and Iceland convoys are to be cut down and probably Russian supplies too – though *not* Middle East aircraft supplies. Had a long talk with Gerow after the meeting. They are evidently nervous of our Post-ARCADIA Collaboration paper and quote the American–British Conversations [on secret collaboration, Washington, January–March 1941] at us.[30] I explained the paper was only intended to supplement on the *joint* bodies required, and think he was satisfied. I finished off the minutes and did a telegram home on the Burma–China proposals after dinner. Nothing definite yet about Dill's directive.

Tuesday 13 January 1942

COS meeting at 10.30. Macready expounded his scheme for [munitions] allocation from US and UK pools by military committees in Washington and London. He was sent off to expound it to the PM, but apparently failed to get it across at all in the morning.

At 4.00 there was a US/British COS meeting, the main item being post-ARCADIA collaboration. The US COS objected strongly to any British military representative being allowed access to the political heads above *them*.[31] It looked as if that was going to torpedo the whole set-up, but at a private huddle with no-one else present they apparently managed to come to some agreement satisfactory to all. At a later meeting with the PM at the White House, Dill got some sort of a directive OKed by the PM, and also agreement to Self as his head man for dealing with the Civil Missions.

Macready had a further session on allocation up till 2.00 a.m. It finished up with Beaverbrook and the President objecting, but with the PM and Hopkins on his side. The PM took some time to hoist in that allocation was a matter of close detail that could only be done by the staffs. Also that pooling everything would be much better for us than sticking rigidly to lease-lend procedure. The US COS only accepted the general principles in the post-ARCADIA collaboration paper. All detail of the methods was 'stricken out' as Admiral King says. They explained that their own organisation was as yet too indeterminate. We did however get them to agree to a short minute to the President and PM proposing allocation on strategic considerations, guided by COS directives. The other paper taken was the Joint Planners' paper on Atlantic projects which went through with little amendment.

Ian had a fearful day fixing up arrangements for the departure of the Arcadians. Riley of the White House security police insists on a fearfully complicated show with a plain clothes man on every car. They are going by train to Norfolk [Virginia]: thence by flying-boats to Bermuda to embark in the *Duke of York*.

Light relief was provided by a copy of the US version of the minutes of a White House meeting produced by Sexton, their secretary. It read just like a child's comic story.

Wednesday 14 January 1942

Dashed down during morning to finish up shopping for my hamper home. Lunch for the COS and secretaries of both sides at the Federal Reserve Building – very good too. Sat next to MacCrae, the naval secretary who is just going off to be naval aide to the President – a very nice fellow.

A US/British COS meeting followed lunch. A US paper, based on a Joint Planners' paper, was tabled at the last moment to show what could be done about SUPER-GYMNAST. They say they can't raise *any* more shipping, so have to wait until the ships which are being sent off to take reinforcements to the Far East return to the USA before they can get anything away, other than the Marines in combat loaded ships. They have at last agreed if necessary to take up South American liners, but in default of any Ministry of Shipping have no view of the whole shipping picture. They don't understand at all that to get ships for operations you have to cut into trade and imports. The paper was accepted as a basis from which to answer the President on the time factor for the operation. The US COS also tabled at the last moment a draft paper on post-ARCADIA collaboration which though in very general terms was not too bad. Our men accepted it subject to certain amendments.

After a hurried dinner, Jo, Ian, Dickson and Napier got away to the station on departure. I saw Jo and dear old Jones off from the office and came back feeling very forlorn indeed.

I am afraid Dykes has a number of fractious babies to nurse [Hollis reported]. Apart from ABDA, GYMNAST, and several joint surveys, our main task has been to try to establish firm US–British machinery for dealing with:

a. Strategy.
b. Planning.
c. Intelligence.
d. The allocation of finished war material.
e. Movements, including the allocation of shipping.

f. Secretariat.

a. A fairly sturdy growth.
b. Very promising.
c. Almost hopeless at present.
d. Promising?
e. Doubtful.
f. A sickly plant.

It is no good saying to our friends we have the machinery for this and that and the other, you must have a similar. It gets us nowhere. They must be allowed to develop their own machinery in their own time.[32]

Thank God Charles Lambe and Geoff Bourne are remaining here for a bit. Frank Vogel left last night to catch the first US convoy to Northern Ireland. I have got hold of Vincent, chief [shorthand] writer, to stay on as a clerk here. Dill has taken on a Paymaster Commander Montgomery [Royal Naval Volunteer Reserve] as his personal assistant.

Thursday 15 January 1942

Very busy day. Moved down to a proper office on the first floor [of the Embassy annex] and installed Vincent and Miss MacAuley. Met with the Joint Planners in the morning and sorted out all the left-over jobs to be done. At lunch a telegram came in from Wavell saying he was proposing to assume [ABDA] command as from 15 January. Whacked it down to the US COS. Went down with Coleridge to see Leslie Chance, secretary of the British Supply Council, in the afternoon to get the form on the Self/Dill set-up. He foresees trouble, as Self overcalled his hand at the start. Found [Admiral] Little [Head of the British Admiralty Delegation at the JSM] in a flap on our return over Wavell's signal, but calmed him down.

Called in for half an hour at a small CTP [cocktail party] of Coleridge's before dinner; then had dinner with old Dill who is pathetically lonely, as Macdonald-Buchanan is ill with chicken pox! Back to the office till 12.10 a.m., sweating out a note on all the conference papers and what has happened to them.

Friday 16 January 1942

Very soon after I arrived in the office, Eisenhower dashed in with a draft US COS telegram prepared by the War Department about Wavell's assumption of command. Simultaneously Little was called up by King to come down and see him. We waited there a long time talking, while two short pages of type were knocked off. The President on the previous evening had apparently sent off a cable to Wavell without reference to anyone but King, authorising assumption of command. The War Department were anxious to include the Philippines which Wavell wished to leave out for the present. Dill furious when we got back from King because we had not roared up King for not having ensured Dill was consulted as the representative of the Minister of Defence! Berry for Little and me!! Dill spent all afternoon drafting a cable for the PM explaining, and a letter to Hopkins giving a strong hint.

After that flurry, there was a meeting of Dill, the Heads of Missions [i.e. the Service delegations at the JSM], and Self at which the latter developed his ideas. Nothing really decided at all. He wants all to move down to town [central Washington], but the JSM and Dill want to stay here [in the Embassy annex]. I fear Self will swallow us up if we are not careful. He has a large well-organised staff. JSM meeting in the afternoon to review the position.

Got back late to dinner. Shifted over to a cheaper room at $3.50 instead of $7.00 a day.

Saturday 17 January 1942

Monnet came in to see me during the morning. He is very anxious to get a right approach to the [munitions] allocation problems. The organisation is to be a 'sub-committee' of the Combined Chiefs of Staff under the chairmanship of Harry Hopkins, *reporting to* the Combined Chiefs of Staff. GOK what that means. What Monnet is anxious to ensure is that equipment is allocated by *theatres* and not on a purely nationalistic basis – i.e. that the US should not be allowed to say 'we have X men who must be equipped – what is left over can go to the British and elsewhere'. He feels that the Combined Planning Committee will never achieve agreement on these lines – nor will the CCS on their own. His proposal therefore is that the secretariat of the allocation sub-committee should interpret estimated production in 1942 into terms of squadrons and formations that can be equipped and maintained on various dates; that the sub-committee should then present this to the CCS and say, 'where do you want these forces applied?'. In this way, by a *reductio ad absurdum*, the equipping of huge US forces in the USA at the expense of the fighting fronts will be ruled out.

General Burns is apparently selected as the secretary of the sub-committee and Monnet has a very high opinion of his honesty and objective outlook. He asked me then to lunch with Burns, whom I had met at Placentia [Bay, off Newfoundland, the venue for the Atlantic Conference] and in London before the Moscow conversations [of August 1941]. I must say I am *very* favourably impressed by him. We had a good talk on a possible organisation. It is clear there will have to be sub-committees for air, army and navy material. How much of the interpretation of production into terms of formations will be done by the sub-committees and how much by the secretariat will want working out. But Burns was quite clear, the secretariat must be *international* and *impartial*, serving the committee and *not* any one nation. The conception is good, and I believe Monnet's approach is sound.

I foresee difficulty working the CCS Secretariat with McDowell – his ideas are obviously to be the secretary of Admiral King. I hope something can be worked out with him.

At 4.30 Geoff Bourne, Charles Lambe and I left for a weekend rest in a country house in Virginia about five miles west of Middleburg, belonging to a Mrs Morrison: Welbourne, near Purcellville. We went out through the area of Bull Run and Manassas [Civil War battle sites] – through rough woodland and brown pasture land, and arrived at 6.30. A charming country house approached off a country lane – built about 1830 – furnished with nice old stuff and lots of books. Morrison is a tall thin elderly man who would pass for an Englishman anywhere – of the thin lean country-gentleman type. Mrs M. is a large body, very pleasant indeed. Both talk with the pleasant southern accent with very little twang in it. After an excellent dinner we turned in fairly early.

Sunday 18 January 1942

I didn't wake till 10.00, when I had a spot of breakfast in bed. Turned out very leisurely and had a poke round the place with Geoff and Charles. The house is in the Colonial style with a high-pillared verandah up to above the first floor. On the east side lies a garden, quite in the English style – flowers and vegetables etc. mixed. The farm lies out at the back, on the south. From the top of the hill at the back you get a wonderful view of the country, all quite brown now.

At lunch there was a Mrs West, widow of a Marine general – an amusing person. Her husband had been in the Boxer [Rebellion] show, and got away with some of the Imperial seals from Peking. These he had shortly afterwards sold to raise the wind, and they now are in the Metropolitan Museum in New York. He had been a great friend of Smedley Butler who was in Shanghai in 1927. Butler died about two weeks before him and his remark on hearing the news was: 'Damn it – Smedley *would* get there first!' After a very good lunch the three of us set off for a walk and covered about five or six miles across country.

Mrs M. is very keen on gardens and music. We had a lot of pleasant talk after dinner and turned in at peace with the world at 10.00 p.m. One of the best week-ends I have ever spent in my life. Such an enormous relief to get out of that prison of a hotel into a home, and to be off the pavements and away from motor-cars for a bit.

Monday 19 January 1942

Our car failed to turn up at 8.30 and we did not get away till 9.30 arriving back about 10.50. The weather had turned to a 'fine soft day' of mist and rain.

McDowell came up in the afternoon and Coleridge and I had quite a satisfactory talk with him in which we got him to agree to all our proposals for the running of the Combined Chiefs of Staff Secretariat. A long bleat from the [British] COS came in to the CCS asking for naval reinforcements for ABDA. News also in that Maynard, Charman, Joan Mainprice and Miss Shephard [secretarial staff from the War Office] are leaving for here by fast convoy on the 20th. Self and party of about six arrived and installed themselves in the office.

I dined with Reggie Kerr [JSM], who told me all about his Quartermaster organisation which has grown enormously since he arrived a few months ago.

Tuesday 20 January 1942

Called in to see Hoyer Millar and Ronnie Campbell [Counsellor and Minister respectively] in the Embassy in the morning. Had lunch with Morris Wilson of the British Supply Council and Monnet who talked much of the new allocation committee and Self's position. They can see no job for Self on Dill's present directive which is merely to 'keep touch' with the civil missions – nor can I. They read it that Self wants to get himself promoted at any rate, so that if the job folds up he can at least secure a good job at home. After lunch Burns came over and we had more talk on the approach to the allocation problem, Monnet further developing his thesis. The principle is undoubtedly sound, but the machinery to apply it is not easy to work out. Salter then was brought in and shot us a line about the shipping angle. Our trouble is that the agreements on shipping allocation and raw materials have not yet been promulgated: Hopkins is sick; so nothing at all is happening!

When I got back I found a telegram from the PM to Dill to say he had decided to regularise his position by making him Head of our Joint Staff Mission, taking the place of Wemyss [Head of the Army Staff] who would be moved on! This puts the poor old man in exactly the position he always said he would refuse to occupy! GOK what he will say when he gets back tomorrow [from Canada]! What happens to Self now?! Dined with Campion and Davies [JSM] at the Army and Navy Club, and had much discussion with them on the allocation committee set-up. Campion agreed with Monnet's idea and thinks it could be translated into action – though Macready apparently thought it impracticable.

Wednesday 21 January 1942

Had lunch with the Coleridges. They have a nice little house in a wooded suburban area. She is a nice person, due for her second child any day now.

Dill returned in the evening from Canada and I had a talk to him about his new directive. He was naturally very annoyed about the whole thing and I think he has been treated *most* shabbily. He gave the news to Self who was completely taken aback. He [Self] sees his position collapsing completely. As head of the Military Mission only, Dill would not have the status to coordinate the civil missions in any way.

Thursday 22 January 1942

Monnet called me up in the morning and asked me to come down as he was engaged with Burns in drafting the terms of reference etc. for the allocation committee. Aurand [US Army] was with them when I arrived but had to leave very soon after. I had to inject a few ideas to get the set-up on to a basis of equality between the US and British instead of our being suppliants as heretofore. We worked on the draft till 2.30 and then went to lunch with Burns at the Army and Navy Club. Coleridge called for me at 4.00, when we were still drafting, as McDowell was in a jam with Turner over CCS stuff. Turner is running the US Secretariat which I object to most strongly, as he has no *locus standi* at all. We spent a patient hour with McDowell trying to straighten things out. Getting back from the Navy Department we had a long wait to get a car. Washington is the most difficult place imaginable to get about in. There is no room to park a car anywhere and there are no buses. We should have been quicker walking the two miles home.

On return about 6.00, Monnet was calling up about the allocation committee stuff. I had a chance for a word with Campion about what had been produced. Monnet asked me to dine with him to talk about it more. Dining there were a Mr and Mrs [Felix] Frankfurter. He is a Judge of the Supreme Court – a cocky little man, rather vain, I should judge, but quite pleasant. His wife is a handsome old lady – very nice, I thought. Monnet and I retired to discuss the latest US draft. I fixed with Campion to meet him in his quarters at 11.30 and we sat up till 1.30 a.m. going through the latest revised draft which he had produced. He has rather a zid [prejudice] against the Civil Supply side and wants to keep Stacey May and company right out of it. Monnet insists that only from them can any useful statistical data be obtained. Campion says if you get the civilians in, the War Department won't play and will sabotage the whole show. To bed at 2.00 a.m.

Friday 23 January 1942

Had breakfast today in the hotel drug store: for 15 cents I got the same as I had paid 70 for in my room. Lovely bright sunny day. Much talk with Dill and Self on the alloctions committee directive in the morning. Self is fairly happy, but I can see many points of difference between him and Campion. Burns came along at 11.00 a.m. to see Dill about it all and get our representative's names. Dill put Self in as the counterweight to Burns. I hope this will not wreck the whole show.

McDowell having rung up at 9.30 to say the CCS meeting proposed for 3.00 a.m. was *off*, called up about 10.00 to say it was *on*. Had a fearful chase to get the agenda out, and to brief Dill. McDowell whacked in about three papers at the last moment – and then some relevant signals came in too. All rather a rush. But the meeting went off much better than I had dared to hope – the most orderly performance we have ever had, owing to there being an agenda etc. Dill told me in the evening he had replied to the PM to say that he didn't want to stay under the new terms, but at least insisted on being outside the Army Staff as the representative of the COS committee [as a whole]. This would leave Wemyss *in situ* [as Head of the Army Staff].

Went with Dill to dinner with T.V. Soong, the Chinese minister. Casey [Australian minister] was there too. Also two Chinese generals, and the air attaché – all very nice people. Soong seems a pretty tough nut. Chinese food and chopsticks – quite good. He has a nice place there. One of his secretaries had been at Winchester and Christ's [College, Cambridge]. The conversation was fairly general – Soong did not try to extract any promises of further aid to Chinese out of Dill!

Saturday 24 January 1942

Coleridge got the minutes of yesterday's meeting through McDowell, by a personal visit, without alteration. Had a busy time getting signals off and agreement with the US on them, but we got away the first two CCS signals to ABDA command, which is rather a triumph. Went down to see Eisenhower about them in the afternoon.

At 6.30 p.m. Geoff [Bourne] and Charles [Lambe] dragged me away with Foster (Public Relations here) in the latter's car to see intercollegiate basketball and boxing in the Maryland University stadium. An interesting performance: it was held in a magnificent gymnasium seating some thousands; all equipment and fittings beautifully done. The cheer-leaders in white sweaters and trousers were very active. The basketball was very fast and skilfully played. George Washington University beat Maryland comfortably. The boxing was poor – little skill and not much guts, we thought. A typical American crowd – all very friendly: two *extremely* shrill-voiced girls just behind us. Not having had any dinner we had Coca-Cola and peanut candy in the intervals. On the road out we passed two or three 'trailer camps' – parks of luxurious looking caravans. All along the roads there are groups of 'cabins' which act as 'dak bungalows' [houses for travellers in India] for the motor-traveller in this country. On return we fed at O'Donnell's seafood restaurant on oysters in large quantities – both fresh and cooked oysters are one of the few things that are fairly cheap here. A very good evening indeed. Lovely bright, mild day.

Sunday 25 January 1942

Clocked in an hour late to mark Sunday. Had a busy morning till about 2.00 p.m. getting stuff squared up for a COS meeting tomorrow afternoon and a Dominions Committee meeting in the morning.

Before tea I walked down to K Street and caught a bus out to Falls Church [Maryland] to see the Davieses [JSM] who have a house out there. It is a growing 'suburb' – all very messy and untidy, like Hayling Island in the bungalow area. The Davieses' house is quite nice though, standing in a bit of land of its own which unfortunately for them has no fence in accordance with the normal American practice. Old John is a very gifted fellow – very handy with his pen and paintbrush – does a lot of photography and cine work too. After supper their neighbours the McLoughlins came in. He was a Middle West farmer who is now employed by the Department of Agriculture, mainly going round instructing in scientific farming and supervising government loans to farmers. Had an interesting talk with him about their problems. A pleasant evening's change from the dreariness of the Wardman Park Hotel.

Monday 26 January 1942

Dominions Committee meeting in the morning to discuss Burns's draft of the allocations committee directive – also the question of Dominion Missions [in Washington]. Dill had put up a draft telegram which was distinctly ill-considered. Meanwhile ABDA stuff is pouring in, nearly breaking our small staff. I hope we raise some reinforcements soon. Dill started roaring for a revised draft of his Dominion Missions telegram almost at once. I had dashed off a first draft which he was rather sniffy about. Self then tried his hand at a second draft (which turned out very little better). Self and I then went down to see Burns about the allocation committee draft which Self had drawn up after the Dominions meeting. This was accepted by Burns. Ploughed away at CCS and other odd stuff till nearly 8.00 p.m. and then went back. Dined at Mays. They give you a very good dinner there for 75 cents.

Tuesday 27 January 1942

Dill had a meeting with the Heads of Mission at 12.00 to go through the agenda for the CCS meeting in the afternoon – a very tedious affair in which he solemnly read aloud (twice over) several long telegrams to and from Australia to the PM etc. I thought we should never get through – nor did we till nearly 2.00 p.m.! Considerable bother being caused by Casey [Australian minister] going to see the US COS, President etc. and pressing for help to Australia. He is only doing his job, but it does complicate things. Curtin [Australian Prime Minister] had sent a bloody awful telegram to the PM a short time ago saying that Australia was being let down etc., etc. Casey gave a copy to the President who said 'CCS to consider'!

The CCS meeting in the afternoon was not too bad. We had hoped to get through agreement for the Anzac Area, but owing to the Australians as usual wanting to have it both ways, it couldn't be fixed without further reference to Australia. Curtin's telegram to the PM was then discussed. Our side had some difficulty in persuading the US that it was *not* for the CCS to answer! I told Dill he must report personally on it to the PM as there were sure to be sparks about it ever having got to the CCS. He agreed to do so. As usual they tabled one paper that had never reached us, though they had circulated it on their side, from the War Department, *days* before! I *wish* they would get their Secretariat set up. Got through with the minutes etc. by 8.40 p.m. The McCloys [Assistant Secretary of War] asked me to dine and go to a horse show tomorrow, but I had to refuse, as Coleridge is not too fit and must have a day's rest. Davison arrived from the UK [to join the Secretariat]. Dull and cold.

Wednesday 28 January 1942

Winston's speech in Parliament reads very well. He counter-attacked heavily [against a motion of no confidence, defeated by 464 votes to one]. Very hard at it all morning. Warned at 12 noon that the President would hold a staff conference at 2.00 p.m. 'Pa' Watson [President's aide] said the agenda might be anything from bears to ducks. Went down with the FM [Dill] after a very hurried lunch. It was a general *tour d'horizon*. The principal item was Dominion and Dutch representation. The PM has conceded the principle that they should be represented more strongly in Washington. The President suggests to divide all matters into (a) political and (b) military. (a) to be dealt with in London and (b) in Washington by the CCS. The Dominions and Dutch to be brought in on a 'consultative' basis here. The US to deal with the Dutch, and us with the Dominions. GOK how it will ever work. The CCS are to consider and draft a reply to the PM from the President on the subject.

A very hard day indeed. Dill does not make things any easier by keeping one on the jump about every little thing, which he keeps getting mixed up. He cannot realise that he has not got the whole War Office to work for him [as he had when CIGS].

Thursday 29 January 1942

Managed to persuade Dill to send a cable home asking for guidance on Dominion representation here before whirling in with a CCS paper. Drafted something which satisfied him and got it off in the evening.

Went along to the Bensons' [Military Attaché] at 7.15 and had a buffet supper with them, Wemyss, Dill and the Beaumont-Nesbitts before going on to the Horse Show at Fort Myer at 8.00. Very high class jumping there – all done *very* fast. Some *beautiful* horses – the general standard very high indeed. Four hours of it was too long though – on very hard seats in a very cold atmosphere. I had to lend my British Warm [overcoat] to Mrs Beaumont-Nesbitt to prevent her being frozen. We all three shared Paddy's coat as a rug!

Friday 30 January 1942

Rather a less busy day than usual. Wavell reported that we should retire to Singapore Island during the night. It looks as if Rommel has retaken Benghazi. Had a long chat with Leslie Chance after dinner about British Supply Council personalities, Dominion representation etc. He is a Canadian though hardly detectable as such – and a *very good* chap indeed.

The President's birthday. Balls going on everywhere with film stars making triumphal progress round!

Saturday 31 January 1942

Noel Hall [Minister of Economic Warfare at the Embassy] got hold of me early to try and get action taken by the State Department to prevent French Indochina letting Japan have ships. Tore off a note and got the FM to send Little down to see King. Went to the Munitions Assignment Board's first meeting at 10.30 with the Heads of Missions and Self. Burns tabled his drafts. Hopkins looked *very* ill indeed, but all went quite well. A Major Kielkopf produced what purported to be a note of the proceedings – a bloody awful abortion as usual! I did my own draft and sent it down to Burns with, I hope, a tactful hint that it was in a more suitable form.

Paddy Beaumont-Nesbitt came and had a long chat in the evening. He wants to secure himself a job out here as chairman of a Joint Intelligence Committee and general contact man with the press. I think he certainly has a useful function to perform. Dined with them. Val Wilson there too. He reports very well on the material of the US Army, but very unfavourably on the leadership· and discipline. I wonder if they will ever learn. The democratic spirit of the country results in the officer caring nothing for his men – on the principle that they are as good as he is and therefore just as capable of looking after themselves as anyone else!

Sunday 1 February 1942

Lay in till 10.30 and had breakfast in my room. Went up to the office about 12.00 and found Dill determined to submit a paper to the CCS outlining as from *us* proposals for Dominion representation [in Washington]. He had apparently told Stark he would. I argued hard, but could not persuade him. He agreed however to send a signal to the COS asking them to expedite a reply to our cable setting out the President's ideas. I was so disturbed that I sent Jo Hollis an SOS asking for definite instructions to hold hard. The old man [Dill] is very obstinate at times – it was clearly up to the US side to put something up if the President was in a hurry.

Called up Bill Donovan and he asked me to lunch with him. Poor old Bill can't make up his mind to give up any idea of commanding troops. His idea now is to train a corps of special scouts rather on the Commando model, units of which would be lent as Army troops to formations for special jobs – and also set an example. He showed me one or two papers. Their Intelligence people are not passing their papers across to our side as they should – Heaven knows why they are so cagey.

Worked till about 7.00 p.m. then dined and wrote letters. Fine and bright. News in of the first US naval offensive of the war – a bombardment attack on Jap bases in the Marshalls [Pacific islands]. Results not very great – only a few small auxiliaries sunk, but a great blurb in the papers. Still it is a start.

Monday 2 February 1942

Tore off a draft, with one alternative, for the CCS on Dominion representation. Heads of Missions discussed it at 12.00, and after a bit decided, thank God, that it would be unwise for us to commit ourselves without guidance from London.

Lunched with Campion and Davies and discussed Munitions Board procedure etc. Campion is unhappy about it – he thinks now that Burns *will* succeed in building up his 'Executive' into a kind of super-department, and that therefore we should weigh in heavy with British personnel on the secretariat. I think that is to be avoided if possible. Some disturbance caused during the afternoon by Hopkins receiving a telegram from Beaverbrook telling him of London's decision to sub-allocate (from US allocations to the UK) to New Zealand and Australia – no word to us at all, of course!

Busy day getting ready for the CCS meeting tomorrow. Some snotty rude papers circulated by the US. One points out that as we are not prepared to find a special escort, eight days out of cycle, for a load of US troops for Northern Ireland, we can't be in much of a hurry for them! The other urges pressure to be put on Wavell to accept Chinese troops for Burma in spite of the fact that Marshall has already been told that Wavell has accepted two divisions – all that could possibly be equipped. It appears now that all the fuss made by the US about the amount of forces being sent to Wavell and the Pacific is largely blah. What is being sent is all unco-ordinated – and a good part will be of little operational value at the far end. Moreover they have no precise knowledge of what exactly *is* being sent!

Went to a lecture after dinner by Professor Ayers on the American language – *very good* and most amusing. His theme was that there can be no 'correct' standard. Many American pronunciations and usages are merely 18th century – which have survived – whereas the corresponding English version is often merely 'refined Cockney'. Talking of shibboleths, he said McArthur in the Philippines would doubtless use words like 'lullapaloosa' as passwords and thereby defeat the Japanese completely. Bermuda apparently preserves 18th-century pronunciation perfectly, the upper classes saying gr*a*ss [short 'a'] and the lower gra*a*ss [long 'a'].

Tuesday 3 February 1942

JSM meeting at 11.00 to go through the CCS papers for the afternoon meeting. The PM came up with a signal for Dill saying 'don't put up any suggestions for

Dominion representation yet'. Very glad to get it, as my advice was borne out, which may strengthen my hand with Dill a bit – evidently a result of my SOS to Jo. CCS meeting at 3.00 in the new offices of the US Secretariat. They have taken over most of the Public Health Building – a very fine building opposite the Navy and War Departments [on Constitution Avenue].[33] Each Department is putting up $150,000 for equipment etc.!! ['Beetle'] Smith of General Marshall's secretariat is taking over the US Secretariat, being promoted Brigadier General. They are starting up a Joint Planning section and a Joint Intelligence Committee – all to be housed there.

Two unpleasant papers were put up by them – one cribbing because we couldn't lay on a special escort for a convoy to Northern Ireland without waiting nine days. Our side went into action very well. Dill said 'presume this is meant to be sarcastic'. King's face was a study, as he had drafted it. 'Betty' [Admiral] Stark ordered it to be 'stricken out'.[34] The other wanted a direct order sent to Wavell to accept all Chinese [troops] possible for Burma, Chiang Kai-Shek having said that we refused to co-operate! We produced a draft which they agreed would meet the case. Van Mook, the Governor of the Dutch East Indies, came in. Dill gave him a very good run over the whole world situation. Van M. asked if more ships couldn't be provided so as to attack Jap lines of communication by sea. King was extremely rude to him – and all the US side felt thoroughly ashamed! I think the Dutch will begin to realise that there is precious little to be got out of the US.

Went to dinner at the Embassy. Only McDonnell [public relations], Williams [Assistant Military Attaché] and Bullitt [Roosevelt's Ambassador-at-large in the Middle East] there beside the Halifaxes. Bullitt was very impressed with the morale of our troops in the Western Desert and their achievements with such limited resources. He said the Germans had piled up enormous dumps at Benghazi which unfortunately they have now recaptured as it would be impossible to destroy them. He had a few bullshit yarns about (1) us having shipped 20,000 tons of beer for speculators in Egypt, plus 3,000 tons of toilet paper! (2) they having doubled the throughput of Suez [Canal] by their own unaided effort. He gave a pitiful description of Poles arriving in Persia from Russia. The Russians are playing hell in Persia and ruining the efficiency of the railway, by hanging on to rolling stock etc. None of these chaps realise that we *are* sending out to the Middle East every man and every aircraft that can possibly be got out there. Still, he is certainly on our side! Bullitt is a man in the late 40s I should judge – fresh-faced, not typically American in appearance at all – a great enthusiast.

Wednesday 4 February 1942

A reasonably quiet day. Moved into 1940 Biltmore from the Wardman Park Hotel – quite a good flat on the fifth floor. Had lunch with Ronald Campbell and Noel Hall [Embassy]. Discussed the responsibility of the Service Heads and the Treasury for our unpreparedness for war. Noel Hall feels very strongly that any sort of leadership was completely absent!

Thursday 5 February 1942

Went down to see Gerow and Eisenhower. Got them to suggest to Smith (I think without knowing we wanted it) that the whole of our Staff Mission should move into the Public Health Building which they have just taken over for their Secretariat. Had lunch with them in their office and then went on for a long chat with Smith, who strikes me as very good.

Friday 6 February 1942

Had a long session with Smith again about accommodation for our Mission in the Public Health Building. He is all for it. After thinking it all over, Coleridge and I decided we must go for the top floor which would be self-contained. Worked out a rough 'accommodation' plan with Hayward in the afternoon. It is going to be a tight squeeze, but well worth it. Dined with Morris Wilson [Supply Council] at the Shoreham [Hotel]. I was afraid he was after something, but I think the old man is just plain lonely. We sat talking about 'planning for peace' afterwards – but he has not much original thought in his head.

Saturday 7 February 1942

Dill has got his directive at last. Publicly he is to represent the COS; *privately* the Minister of Defence [Churchill] also. He seems quite happy. Meeting of Heads of Mission with Halifax in the morning, to put him well in the picture – quite useful. Spoke to Hoyer Millar [Embassy] about our possible move to the Public Health Building. He seems quite happy about it. Went down and saw Burns with Evill and Self before lunch. We *must* get the Munitions Assignment Board secretariat fixed up. I shall ask Wemyss to put in Garforth to keep the job warm anyhow. Had another long talk with Smith in the afternoon. There are difficulties with the Navy over getting any kind of joint show going. Turner insists on keeping the US Joint Planners in the Navy Department. I fear we are in for a lot of troubles before the show starts to run smoothly, but Smith is absolutely sound. It looks as if we shall be invited into the Public Health Building all right.

Our Joint Planners knocked out a paper on air reinforcement to the Far East which is all at sixes and sevens now. Burns has made an *ad hoc* allocation of 36 aircraft to the Dutch East Indies! Meanwhile the War Department have changed their orders about diverting 80 planes to Australia, and postponed it quite a bit – but it is all on a hand-to-mouth basis, influenced each day by the latest news from the Far East.

Sunday 8 February 1942

Went up to the office at 10.00 and got through some quick jobs before 12.30 when Ralph Foster [Embassy], Geoff [Bourne] and I went out intending to lunch at the Olney Inn about 20 miles north-west [of Washington]. Found it shut, so Ralph boomed into the Manor Court Country Club (marked 'Highly Restricted'!) and got us in as Honorary Members for lunch. The manager, Mr Crocker, was very welcoming. After a good and cheap lunch, we took a walk round the golf course. Called in on the way home on some stables attached to the place, run by a couple called Cashell. They found us looking round, asked us in for a chat in the harness room, and invited us to have a day's hunting with them next Saturday! – which we had regretfully to refuse. People certainly are most hospitable here.

JSM meeting at 6.00 to consider a telegram from the War Office telling us to put proposals to the CCS for the setting up of unified command in the Anzac Area. Little was very doubtful about the idea as it would remove the area from King's personal responsibility. I advised strongly to put that to London before raising it with US COS. They refused at first, but were finally persuaded to do so.

Went up with Foster, Geoff and Davison to supper with old McDonnell who has a studio flat: cooks all the food himself and lays on a very cheery show. Had a long crack with Foster about planning for the peace. He put some good points about lack of vision at home, e.g. continuing Customs when we want all the imports we can get; waiting for funds to be raised by charity in the US in order to buy blankets in Witney for families in London!

Monday 9 February 1942

JSM meeting at 10.30 to take a Joint Planners' paper on air reinforcements to the Far East. Got it through just before lunch. Strafford [RAF planner] very 'drafty' as usual. He has a small mind, very much a pundit. A signal came in during the morning to say hold hard on the Anzac scheme: I was much relieved as this is the second time I have been right on procedure, all of which is helpful. Went down to see Smith in the afternoon. Finished up the [CCS] agenda. He gave us the official invitation into the Public Health Building.

Jacob rang up from London at 5.30 p.m. They are much worried about the Munitions Assignment Board directive, and could not understand at all a very pompous telegram of Self's on the subject. They had not realised that the CCS had *issued* the directive, the Board being a sub-committee of the CCS! Beaverbrook of course [as Minister of Supply] takes quite a different view. I reassured him as well as I could and promised to elucidate. The issue of a War

Department communiqué about the CCS set-up also had caused some stir at home. I explained that I had been shown it casually to check names etc. and had put in *some* references to the British COS – but as it was a draft speech by Marshall to West Point had not treated it as official and had made that clear to the US. I told Ian [Jacob] to read it again carefully – there was nothing objectionable in it really – and anyhow it was no good beefing about it now! I also roared him up about the lack of timely direction from the COS who never come up with a signal till prodded. I fear William Stirling [handling JSM traffic in the Cabinet Office] is too idle for this job.

Tuesday 10 February 1942

JSM meeting in the morning to go through the CCS agenda. CCS meeting in the afternoon went off very smoothly indeed. We had to put over amendments required by London to 'War Collaboration' in the charter for CCS procedure. London clearly very nervous lest they should be elbowed out altogether! Dill did it very well *indeed* in quite a light-hearted manner, and everything passed smoothly. Coleridge stayed down and did the minutes while I agreed the conclusions with Smith. We got them to swallow complete, as the terms of reference for a Combined Planning Staff appreciation of the Pacific situation, the wording we had telegraphed home some days ago, and on which the Joint Planners are actually working.

On my return to the office I heard that our [secretarial] party from London had arrived – earlier than expected. Called down after dinner and looked up Joan Mainprice and Claud Berkeley who were in the Ambassadors Hotel for the night. They had apparently had a long rough journey, starting with a three-day chase for their ship on the other side, between Liverpool and Belfast. Thick snow when they left London. But all seemed very cheerful now.

Wednesday 11 February 1942

Took Berkeley, and Bob Garforth who is to be at least temporarily in the show, down to introduce them to General Burns, who was very cheerful as usual. Wish we could foresee what sort of a set-up this Munitions Assignment Board is going to be. Very hard to fix up about staff etc. Cabled London to get Berkeley fixed up as a major – as I fear a mere captain would cut little ice in that galaxy of stars!

Thursday 12 February 1942

JSM meeting in the morning with the Dominions and attachés all present. Went off very well – Dill can be very good: now he is less pressed, he is regaining his old form very well. Went out with Geoff after lunch to look for another flat. Ours certainly is a bit dim and he does not want to stay in it. Looked at one furnished one – too large for us. Then saw a new block and in a rash moment signed up an *unfurnished* two-room flat – at $80 per month. Furniture on the never never will probably run about $40 – but I think it will certainly be a good investment as the housing shortage here is bound to increase as the government machine expands. I hope I shall be able to finance it all![35]

Dined with Joan Mainprice [now his PA] at Harveys – which is Monnet's recommendation for sea food. News in that the [German pocket battleships] *Scharnhorst, Gneisenau* and *Prince Eugen* are all out [from Brest] and trying to run the Channel.

Friday 13 February 1942

A Black Friday. The German ships got through all right to German ports although we lost a lot of aircraft in attacks on them. The Japs seem to have got the whole of the western half of Singapore Island.

Saturday 14 February 1942

The President held a Combined Staff Conference at the White House at 11.00 a.m. in his study. He has a passion for stuffed dogs and toys of all sorts – his desk is full of them. Nothing very much came out of it – except he naturally wants more air [forces] for ABDA – and wants to be strong somewhere in that area. There will be a scream now, I am sure, to complete the Pacific appreciation in a tearing hurry. But we shan't get it from home for a day or two.

The US Navy, i.e. Turner, are refusing to put their Joint Staff Planners etc. in the new Public Health Building. He *is* a stubborn old swine – and if they don't come in, the whole conception will fall down: at present he runs them like a circus of his own. Smith tells me Marshall intends to have a show down over it.

Sunday 15 February 1942

News came in from Wavell during the morning that Singapore had surrendered. I never thought I should live to see that. They say they are out of water, petrol and ammunition. I suppose the large numbers of civilians in the city made things very difficult. But we don't seem to have the knack of sticking it out like we did in the last war. Shall we *ever* make a stand anywhere? Wavell sent in a pretty gloomy cable yesterday morning on the great difficulty of holding Java if South Sumatra goes – and already the Japs seem to have landed there. To supper at Angus McDonnell's to meet Surles, Grogan and Dupuis who are the heads of the War Department Press Section – quite a nice lot, though I am bound to say *not* terrifically impressive. Mrs Surles was clearly tickled to death to meet Lord Halifax (who was there for a short time) *and* the Field Marshal [Dill]. Still, we shall need all our good relations with the US Press during the next few days!

Monday 16 February 1942

Went to a meeting of the Munitions Assignment Board in the morning. The agenda mainly dealt with sub-committee organisation and procedure. Hopkins runs a meeting very well in his quiet way. Took Geoff Bourne down to see Donovan in the afternoon. Old Bill had very kindly rung up to condole about Singapore. He is still set on taking control of some sort of Commando show. We argued in favour of building if possible on two Marine Battalions which have been specially set aside, rather than starting a new unit altogether.

Dill hauled me back just after I had left to deal with a telegram from Wavell who is faced with the awful problem of where to send the Australian Corps. He fears that with South Sumatra in enemy hands, Java is now untenable and that troops put into it would only suffer the same fate as Singapore. But it is hard to pull out and leave the Dutch completely out of it all. At the same time the keys are now Burma and Australia and we must try and make sure at least of them. It certainly is a desperate position we are now in. God alone knows how long it is going to take us to get back into the Malay Barrier again.

Tuesday 17 February 1942

JSM meeting in the morning to go through the CCS agenda for the afternoon. Salter came in to discuss his memo on the shipping situation. I spoke to Jo [Hollis] in London at 12.30 to get the form on their consideration of Wavell's telegrams. He was just off to a Pacific Council meeting to discuss it. Also spoke to Ian [Jacob] about the Munitions Assignment Board.

Just before the CCS meeting, there arrived a hell of a telegram from London about the shipping situation, from which it appears that we may be faced with having to choose between the Middle East and the Far East as we cannot possibly meet our minimum requirements for reinforcements unless more personnel shipping can somehow be produced. It certainly is a very gloomy picture. God knows how we are going to get through it. The US COS reacted very well to Salter's memo, but I think I must get Dill to get the paper somehow to the President's eye to screw out the last possible ounce of US shipping. A good CCS meeting. Fixed up the minutes with Smith afterwards very satisfactorily. Coleridge tore them off in great style, as usual.

Wednesday 18 February 1942

Signal in from the COS early giving the Pacific Council's resolutions on

Wavell's telegram. They recommend 'no surrender' in Java, but no more forces to go there. Went down with Smith to see Stark who called a meeting of the CCS at 12.30. Knocked off a draft signal to Wavell before the meeting which was accepted almost *in toto*. The Dutch and New Zealand reps were brought in for the last part of the meeting. The Australian could not be found. Telegraphed our draft to London for concurrence – a hell of a day. We tried to stop the repetition of the Pacific Council's recommendations to Wavell, but heard late in the day that the PM had ordered this. Dill had to explain to the US COS; King was very cross at having action by the US Navy recommended by the Pacific Council! – and Wavell informed of it too! Waited up till 2.30 a.m. hoping for London's OK on the CCS draft signal to Wavell. Nothing in.

Thursday 19 February 1942

Having no reply from London, spoke to Jo at 12.00.

> If we have to do the idiot boy every time, the US COS will tend more and more to take control and you will always be a day behind. I realise the period of gestation in Whitehall is usually much longer than here where the US COS short-circuit the civilian departments entirely. But it is very hard to stall when we do not know at all how the matter is being processed at home.[36]

The Dutch apparently reacted strongly against our cutting out the 'no surrender' paragraph. London had put back certain amendments, but Jo said to hold these – as the PM would now deal direct with the President.

Dined with Dill and Wemyss. After Geoff and I got back, I got a call from Signals to say that the PM's message for the President had come in. Went down and sorted it all out at the Signals office. Took it along to the White House at midnight, hoping to catch the President before he turned in. But nothing doing; so had to leave a message for Hopkins to be dealt with in morning. Jo said they had had a hell of a time with the Dutch, poor devils. They are in their last ditch now.

Friday 20 February 1942

By about 10.45 I got from Smith the reactions of President in form of a message from Hopkins to the PM. He amended the discretionary clause after the sentence to say there was to be no surrender in Java, but was, I gather, peeved at having the Dutch objections put back in his lap. He did not like to refuse Dutch pleas, but it will not do him any harm to have to carry the can for once! I got Jo on the telephone at 11.15 and to my horror found that they intended us to work on the London amended draft! However I got hold of Smith and he got that [passed] by their Chiefs of Staff all right and we pushed the signal off soon after 1.00 p.m. I gather from Jo that the Australians are completely bloody-minded and refuse to allow anything to be diverted even temporarily to Burma – though no British troops can reach them for some time. Had a long conversation with George Price [Cabinet Office] and Ian on the telephone in evening. Asked them to clear up the position of the Pacific [War] Council *vis-à-vis* the Combined Chiefs of Staff.

Foster got hold of me after lunch and pleaded for help to get Paddy Beaumont-Nesbitt into the head of the Service Press Relations outfit. The three attachés are quite incapable of handling the thing properly. The US are only too keen to get our stuff over if we will feed it into them – but at present we have no one capable of doing it. Had a word with Dill on the subject – but he has little opinion of Paddy's capacity! The subject is somewhat urgent as Dewing [Director of Military Intelligence] is to come out – and Paddy is to be sent home and retired. I hope we shall keep him, as there is no doubt he has great influence with the US Press.

News in of Cabinet changes at home. Stafford Cripps comes in as Lord Privy Seal; Oliver Lyttelton as Minister of Production. Beaverbrook is out, but is to come to Washington on munitions. Self naturally somewhat apprehensive, but thinks the Beaver is now a fallen star.

Saturday 21 February 1942

Wavell came up with a signal early to say that Java would probably fall within a few days owing to his lack of air forces. He wanted to know what he should do about evacuating unarmed troops and his HQ. His signal had virtually crossed ours of the previous day. Fixed up a CCS meeting for 3.00 p.m. with Smith. Drafted a short reply to Wavell. Smith came up before lunch with the US ideas and we concocted a revised draft incorporating both ideas. At 3.00 p.m. Stirling and Price talked to me on the phone from London and I got a rough idea of what the COS thought – quite close to our ideas. They said the Pacific War Council would meet very shortly and they would send on their recommendations. The PM was evidently away in the country. The CCS drafted quite a good reply. Most of it was sent straight off to Wavell: the 'evacuation' paragraph was to be referred to London for concurrence – much against US desires, obviously. Called London at 8.00 p.m.: heard they were sending *their* ideas. Waited anxiously till about 10.30 p.m. for news: then got *COS* recommendations only, which dealt with details, e.g. whether the wounded should go before or after the women and children etc. Took that down to Dill at his house: we thought it best to try and get off the CCS original draft.

Called up George Price on the phone, and explained we couldn't go *on* exchanging drafts. The President had already agreed ours – but they had not seen it yet. Got Smith down to the Signal Office about 12.30 a.m. where the PM's telegram to the President giving the Pacific War Council recommendations had by then arrived. We agreed no action required that night, as Dill had authorised the CCS paragraph to go. Smith was firm that the US COS would not want anything else to go. Sent it off to Wavell and a signal to the PM from

Dill explaining why he had had to send it. Smith did a note for Hopkins enclosing the PM's message to the President. Smith very impressed by the efficiency of the WRNS [Women's Royal Naval Service] in the Signal Registry. To bed at 2.00 a.m.

Sunday 22 February 1942

Went down at 10.30 to the White House where Dill was with Hopkins over the PM's wire to the President. Hopkins was in bed as usual – looking very frail, but quite on top of the situation. He agreed nothing further need be sent to Wavell. Discovered that the copy of the PM's signal and Smith's note which had been delivered at the White House at 7.45 a.m. had never reached Hopkins – nor could I discover where they were! Their organisation is *completely* hopeless.

Had lunch with Geoff and Patrick Davison and went for walk after with them for about three miles down Rock Creek – very pretty. Got back about 5.00 p.m. and worked till 8.00. Jo rang up about 7.30. There is evidently great effort to induce Australia to let some Divisions go to Burma – but Curtin [Prime Minister] is refusing. The President has appealed twice and the PM is making a last effort – probably without any hope of success.

Went to McDonnell's in the evening. [Great] numbers of American Press there. Cruikshank spoke to me of the very disparaging criticism of the British Army which is prevalent among the American Army – they say we have no stomach for the fight. He says we *must* get more US War Correspondents with our forces. After I got back Wavell came up with a signal proposing his HQ should not withdraw, but merely dissolve, as it has no longer any command [i.e. troops] left beyond Java. The effect on public opinion in Java would be far better than a withdrawal. To bed about 1.00 a.m.

Monday 23 February 1942

JSM meeting in the morning at which we spent much time drafting a communiqué for issue when Wavell dissolves his HQ. Casey [Australian Minister in Washington] had produced quite a good one with Dill which served as a basis. CCS meeting in the afternoon. Stirling had spoken on the telephone to me in the morning to say that London agreed with Wavell's proposal. Their detailed comments arrived just before the CCS meeting, proposing boundary lines etc. At the meeting the US COS made it clear they were *not* in favour of breaking up the ABDA area completely. The Dutch, Australian and New Zealand representatives were brought in. The meeting was *very* large and unwieldy and I doubt if the Dutch quite understood what it was all about. All the time we were waiting for a call from London to know whether Wavell would go back as C in C India or not. The phone was out of order and two requests for news *when* consent would be received met no response. Finally just after a sandwich supper about 10.00 p.m. the OK arrived. Between 8.00 p.m. and the time I finally turned in, we handled 20 messages in and out – because just after we had sent off the draft communiqué to Wavell and the Viceroy [of India] and cleaned up all round, we got a very late signal from the COS to say the PM had changed his mind and wanted *no* public announcement. This was about 12.30 a.m.! The end of a perfect day! To bed about 2.45.

Tuesday 24 February 1942

Felt very strongly we were putting Wavell in a difficult position by (a) telling him to withdraw, and (b) not allowing him to have a published statement of the circumstances. Represented this to the FM, but he felt it must lie with Wavell. Went in with Smith to see Marshall after lunch. The Australians have asked for details of the 7th–9th Australian Divisions who are in Java to be specially evacuated! What a nerve they have. They have turned down absolutely flat the PM's and President's appeals to let their 7th Division go to Burma – our only possible chance of getting any reinforcements in quickly. Their name *will* be mud when it all comes out. I put my point about Wavell to Marshall who saw it at once. He said he had never liked the idea of breaking up the HQ but realised that behind Java there was probably no other location than Melbourne [Australia]. He would be prepared to tell Wavell to stay on with a small personal staff, if Dill wished it. After a telephone discussion Dill sent off a wire, pointing out the desirability of a public announcement. Marshall is out to do all he can to give Wavell a build-up in the US press.

Cohn of *Harpers* [weekly] came to see me to try and get some local colour for an article on the PM's journey [back to England after the recent conference] in the *Duke of York*. Had to tell him that the voyage had been very uneventful and there was not much story to it.

About 11.00 p.m. Wavell came up with a signal from which it was obvious that he was not clear whether the ABDA *Area* was to fade out or not. Dug Smith out and drafted a cable making it clear that command was merely being transferred to the Dutch with a reduced HQ – due to the diminution of the area. Got it OKed by Dill from his bed about midnight and pushed it off from Naval Signals. To bed at 1.45 a.m.

Wednesday 25 February 1942

London came up with a signal in the morning asking who was to command the Pacific Islands and Northern Australia. They have evidently a fixed idea that the ABDA area is to disappear completely. Drafted a signal to explain what was really intended.

Lunched with Ralph Foster at a 'Raw Bar' on Riverside off oysters and shrimps – very good. Had a long go with Smith after lunch and cleared up a lot of points. JSM meeting at 4.30 p.m. to go through a paper of Wemyss's [Head of British Army Staff] on the procedure for getting a basis for munitions allocations.

Called in at Naval Signals on the way home to deal with a COS signal saying that the PM did *not* want any communiqué about Wavell in a hurry – but no sign that the Dutch East Indies Government had been told to lay off. Rangoon seems to be as good as lost.

Thursday 26 February 1942

Signal in from London to say that the PM did not object to local publication of the communiqué in Java, but *no broadcast*. Asked for the President's views. Smith would not reopen the question at all: wired London accordingly. Wavell closed down for good in the evening, leaving command to the Dutch.

Had dinner at the Bensons' – present Wemyss, Foster, Cruikshank (Press at the Embassy) and Ed Kirby who is running radio publicity for the War Department. Listened to Dill's speech [at an Overseas Press Club dinner in New York] on the radio – *not* as good as he originally wrote, I thought. I slept through [Soviet Ambassador] Litvinoff's![37] Kirby was very interesting on the subject of American radio. They are evidently doing their best to avoid its abuse.

Friday 27 February 1942

A very quiet day. Spoke to Jo, Ian and William Stirling on the telephone at 5.30 p.m. Poor old Richard Coleridge [Dykes's deputy] tells me that the doctors suspect TB in his elder boy.

Dined with the Smiths – a very nice simple couple. Turkey, and strawberry shortcake, cooked by Mrs S. – *very* good indeed. Others there were Dr & Mrs Mann (he runs the Zoo here); and Robinett [US Secretariat]. Smith is a very handy fellow: makes his own split-cane [fishing] rods, and [wooden] stocks for his own guns and rifles. He has two very nice 'bird dogs' – a pointer and a setter.

Saturday 28 February 1942

Another quiet day. First news starting to trickle in from Java after the taking over by the Dutch. The [Japanese] invasion of Java is starting on the north coast. Wansborough Jones has arrived from home for a job in charge of the movement of personnel: he got here by air in 19 hours from Prestwick! Everyone at home is apparently feeling pretty blue about things. There is no doubt we are taking fearful risks in the Middle East by stripping out so many troops.

Fixed up the agenda for the Tuesday CCS meeting with Smith. He had some trouble in getting Stark [US Chief of Naval Staff] to agree to letting the Dutchmen in at the start of the meeting to discuss ABDA, but we prevailed in the end.

Dined with Joan Mainprice at the Napoleon and went to the pictures after – 'The man who stayed for [to] dinner' – a poor show.

Sunday 1 March 1942

Took the whole day off. Lay in till nearly 11.00. Then went out with Ralph Foster and Geoff to Harper's Ferry, after getting lunch in Leesburg [Virginia]. Leesburg and Harper's Ferry are by no means the 'chromium plated' type of American town, but rather flyblown, down-at-heel places – shops very similar to what you would find in the North Midlands small country town in England. Looked at 'John Brown Fort' – the old armoury which he held and which has now been reconstructed in the grounds of the local College – which is for coloured students only. It used to stand on the river bank just by the bridge. We walked up to 'Jefferson's seat' overlooking the Shenandoah and the junction with the Potomac – a very fine view indeed. High wooded hills very steep on the opposite sides. The river is shallow running over rocky ledges – water a lovely light green. It must be very beautiful in spring and autumn. In an old overgrown cemetery near Jefferson's seat we found the grave of John Harper, born at Oxford in 1712 – died 1782. There are several ruined shells of houses round about that look like relics of the Civil War. At Brunswick which we passed there is a very big goods yard. The American trains are very impressive in their enormous size: everything is on a very big scale, and freight trains are about three/four miles long. No wonder Americans laugh at our tiny trains. Came back on the north bank of the Potomac. Maryland is more open than Virginia – much less woodland, but prosperous-looking farms mostly.

Went to Angus McDonnell's Sunday evening party. These parties of McDonnell's are certainly a great way of breaking the ice – a large crowd there as usual and all very cheery under his good influence – and cooking.

Monday 2 March 1942

Fairly quiet day till the evening. I was down with Smith at 5.00 p.m. when he showed me a press flash from Australia proving a leak about Wavell's HQ having dissolved. Almost simultaneously Signals rang up to say a 'most immediate' signal was coming in from London. This proved to be authority to release the Wavell communiqué at 7.30 p.m. But Smith and I both saw that the original communiqué was now completely dead and if issued in that form would cause a fearful stink. So we recast it all in the past tense, and while he got it OKed by the US COS, I put in a call to London. Got George Price [Cabinet Office] about 7.00 p.m. and found that the original text had already gone out to the press and first editions were already printed. So they left their version as it stood, while I just managed to clear our version to the War Department press side before 7.30. A very hectic two hours!

Java has been invaded at two points on the north coast: the naval forces have been dispersed after a sea battle in which the Dutch and ourselves took considerable casualties.

Tuesday 3 March 1942

JSM meeting in the morning to go through the CCS agenda. The chief item is the new set-up in the Anzac–ABDA area. It looks as if Australia and New Zealand favour an American C in C for the whole area: McArthur is proposed by the US Army but [Admiral] King [earmarked as the new US Chief of Naval Staff] would never accept him for the sea.

CCS meeting at 2.30. Dijxhoorn, the Dutch General, gave a résumé of the situation; he seems quite stouthearted. Rather a shemozzle [a mess] followed over the ABDA boundary question. London's views only arrived about 1.30 and Little [Head of the British Admiralty Delegation] had not seen them before the meeting. He arrived 10 minutes late, and apparently didn't read the signal given to him. As a result he was the only person there who wasn't properly in the picture; got thoroughly rattled and fussed; couldn't make up his mind whether to stall or to accept the US proposal which was quite OK really. Finally did the latter with ill grace, and left in a fuming temper. Cleaned up the minutes with Smith and Coleridge after the meeting. Met Maloney who has been brought into Burns's show [allocating munitions] on the Army side – a very intelligent fellow.

Test black out in Washington for the night [an air raid precaution].

The Australians have very grudgingly allowed two Brigade Groups of the 6th [Australian] Division to be temporarily diverted to Ceylon! – evidently in response to the PM's and President's desperate appeals.

Wednesday 4 March 1942

Had high words with old Little who was extremely peeved at having been, as he thought, bounced at yesterday's CCS meeting. I think actually he mistook the tenor of the meeting! I disclaimed all responsibility as far as the Secretariat was concerned; and we parted quite amicably.

Had lunch at the Army and Navy Country Club with Lovett and Deane [US Secretariat], Geoff Bourne and Ralph Foster. A pleasant place but I began to feel a bit [?]diffy as the day wore on. Retired early to bed with a feverish cold.

Monday 9 March 1942

Stayed in bed from Thursday to Sunday, feeding mostly on fruit. Old Lillian [the home help] fixed me up quite well – Joan Mainprice arrived each day with a selection of papers and got me some tea or something. By Sunday

8 March, I was fit enough to stagger across the road for a meal outside. Had a short day in the office from 12.00 to 6.00. Patrick Davison [Secretariat], who has also been sick for a while, returned to work as well. There has been considerable activity over a very despairing telegram from the PM to the President appealing for more help in shipping. The PM is evidently desperately disappointed at the complete ineffectiveness of the US against Japan – as well he may be. The Combined Planning Staff produced a draft reply which the CCS considered on 7 March and submitted to the President. Not *very* helpful. They are going to release the *Queens* [*Mary* and *Elizabeth*] and *Aquitainia* for trooping from the UK – a horrible risk in those waters.

Tuesday 10 March 1942

A quiet day: feeling a bit stronger. We are in our new offices now [in the Public Health Building], but everything is pretty muddly as they are still putting in telephones. Electricians are crawlng all over the place. The officers' mess in the basement is very nicely run.

JSM meeting in the morning, but very little on the agenda. CCS meeting in the afternoon. The Dutch representatives were brought in to give a report on Java's last stages. Marshall was away sick. Stark took the chair for last time: his job is folding up and King is to become supreme head of [the US] Navy. Stark goes to London to replace Ghormley as head of the US Navy there – virtually the 'shelf' for him. He is a nice old boy, but *not* effective.

Wednesday 11 March 1942

All finally fixed up here to get Paddy Beaumont-Nesbitt a job. He can certainly do some useful work here with Public Relations.

I had a long talk with Smith in the afternoon: he strongly advises Dill to have a heart-to-heart talk with Marshall and King about the Middle East. I retailed this to Dill who cracked off a private telegram to the CIGS [Brooke].[38]

Thursday 12 March 1942

Hard day, with a stream of odd people coming in to me. Got off a long private wire to Jo giving him the background of Dill's wire, and pointing out how it looks from here as if we [the British] can't really make up our minds to be strong *somewhere*.

Dined with Leslie Chance [Supply Council] and had a good crack with him about all and sundry. He is a first class chap.

Friday 13 March 1942

Another long day. Dashed off for an hour in the evening to a CTP given by Vereker the NZ Naval Attaché. Had a talk with old [Walter] Nash [New Zealand representative on the Pacific War Council] who was very cordial.

Had a quick meal in a drugstore near the office and worked on till 11.30 p.m. George Price told me on the telephone that my wire to Jo [see 12 March] had been most useful.

Saturday 14 March 1942

Woke early as we were all set to go to West Point [US Military Academy] for the day in General Marshall's private aircraft. Unfortunately there was very low cloud and rain – too bad for flying. This we discovered by ringing up the airfield. Lay in till late and then went down to the office at 11.00. Bill Donovan asked Smith and me to lunch. Smith just before told me he was recommending to Marshall and Stark that Bill should be Chairman of their Joint Intelligence Committee, and thereby be brought into the COS orbit properly. He approached this idea gently at lunch and Bill swallowed it whole. A very satisfactory show – and I am sure it is the right idea.

Dill got a very unsatisfactory and unhelpful wire from the CIGS about the Middle East – but decided to write to Marshall suggesting a private talk with him and King on the subject. Smith feels that if he could only put it over to those two, then the US *could* pull more shipping out of the bag.

Smith told me that Marshall had directed him to find out 'tactfully' whether Geoff and I would be willing to occupy a quarter at Fort Myer *free*![39] A very tempting offer, indeed, though I have a feeling against being under any obligation. Geoff tells me that the Government might try to dock us both $9 a day if we went in, but we could almost certainly get away with paying US rates of single lodging allowance, which would be much less.

Went up to a CTP of Ralph Foster's at 7.00 – large crowd there. Old Surles, head of War Department Public Relations was very mellow. Talked with Mrs Lovett, a nice little body. Had dinner with Ralph afterwards and then went on with him to Ed Kirby, who is in charge of the radio side of War Department publicity. Mrs K. is quite an intelligent person, and I gave her a bit about India and Palestine. Ed slightly pickled as a result of level-pegging with Surles earlier in the evening. Stayed on there till 1.30 a.m. and only got away with difficulty then.

Sunday 15 March 1942

To the office at 10.00. Lunched at Scholls with Geoff, Patrick Davison [Secretariat] and Johnny Grindle [naval planning staff]. Poor old Johnny is having considerable difficulty with Little [Head of the Admiralty Delegation], who insists now on picking over all the naval stuff in the Joint Planning draft stage. Worked then right through to 7.20, as Dill was drafting a reply to the PM on a rather stupid telegram about what our strategic policy should be. The PM keeps harping on offensive action against the Japs in the Pacific, which is fine, but to keep on stating it merely infuriates King and makes him stubborn.

Our principles, suggested by old Handy [Marshall's staff], were security of the UK; security of the USA; support to Russia; and prevention of Japan joining hands with Germany. These if properly applied give you the answer – i.e. take a chance on Anzac and pour all into the Middle East and Russia.[40]

Went to Angus McDonnell's in the evening. Talked about India and its problems – a terrible lot of misapprehension about it all in this country.

The FM put his foot down on our invitation to quarters in Fort Myer [see 14 March] – says we must not be beholden, or let anyone say we're keeping a US officer out of quarter. I see his point but it was Marshall's own idea!

Monday 16 March 1942

Busy day. Dill lunched with Marshall and had some discussion about the Middle East etc., but did not get very far, I gather. Pope [Head of the Canadian JSM] came in to see me. He is a good chap. Dick Dewing who arrived a day or two ago [as Head of the British Army Staff for a brief period] is all for working him in finally as MGGS [Major General, General Staff, i.e. a kind of chief administrator] on the British Army Staff, working up to a Commonwealth Mission as the ultimate end.

Got away from the office at 7.30, and took Joan Mainprice to the 41/42 Society lecture by Mrs [Eleanor] Roosevelt on 'The American Woman'. Very interesting – we got a seat among the elect in the front, the hall being absolutely packed. Mrs R. has great charm and personality, I thought. She spoke for an hour very sympathetically and simply, without any note at all.

Tuesday 17 March 1942

JSM meeting in the morning. Salter [Head of Merchant Shipping Mission] very interesting as usual on shipping: he says, if pushed, it is nearly always possible to ship *equipment* – but units and formations are quite another story.

CCS meeting in the afternoon – quite a good meeting, with Marshall in the chair. McArthur has been got out of the Pacific Islands and is announced as supreme commander in Australia. Arnold very difficult about air [forces] for the Middle East. Offers US squadrons (a few) if *we* ship *and* equip them! Not helpful at all. Smith tells me Arnold is convinced we have any quantity of aircraft, and till disabused will always be non-cooperative. Some discussion on new Anzac area set-up. King very positive that he would brook no interference by a Pacific War Council in London! Geoff Bourne had produced a very good paper on strategic priorities for allocations [of munitions]. Turner and Handy say it is an impossible task. Smith very peeved at this, having seen Geoff's paper! We are taking his advice as to how to put it over, as it leads to the inevitable conclusion that far less equipment should go to US Army expansion!

King clearly very peeved at a telegram from the PM to Hopkins which we had never seen. The PM won't realise that that sort of thing does not help at all,

PLATE 1.　On commissioning into the Royal Engineers, 1917.

PLATE 3. In Shanghai, 1927.

PLATE 2. The wedding of Dykes and Ada Winifred Smyth at Shortlands Parish Church, Kent, on 8 June 1922.

PLATE 4.   Winifred with Richard and Evelyn, 1931.

PLATE 5.   With Winifred outside her family home,
Castle Widenham, Castletownroche, County Cork, 1937.

PLATE 6.   With Richard at Castle
Widenham, 1937.

PLATE 7.   Consulting map boards on a Staff College exercise, 1939
(Dykes second from right, with hand raised).

PLATE 8. The Committee of Imperial Defence Secretariat assembled on what Dykes called the 'Jubilee of Sir Maurice Hankey' in April 1937. A keen photographer, Dykes both took the photograph and managed to appear in it himself, popping up at the rear towards the left. The front row, left to right: Admiral Barry Domville, Sir John Chancellor, Hankey, Lawrence Burgis, 'Pug' Ismay. 'Jo' Hollis, a particular friend of Dykes, stands in the second row on the left; Gordon Macready, later Head of the British Army Staff in Washington, third from the left in the back row.

PLATE 9. The opening session of the Imperial Conference, 14 May 1937. Chamberlain is second from the right. Dykes sits by the curtain

PLATE 10. The Combined Chiefs of Staff in session in Washington, 23 October 1942. Dykes is fourth from the left, with Field Marshal Dill on his right. For the US Joint Chiefs of Staff, Admiral King is second from the right, Admiral Leahy third from the right, General Marshall fifth from the right. (Official US Navy Photograph; Marshall Research Foundation.)

PLATE 11.   Winifred receiving Dykes's posthumous US
Distinguished Service Medal.

PLATE 12.   A portrait of 'Beetle' Smith, Dykes's devoted friend and
US opposite number in 1942. (Marshall Research Foundation.)

and that all his telegrams are passed on to US COS but that we *don't* see them always.

Wednesday 18 March 1942

Had a long talk with Eisenhower in the afternoon and discussed:

(1) Command in Burma. Chiang Kai-Shek *won't* have any Chinese under British command: wants ['Vinegar Joe'] Stilwell, the US commander, to be the boss – how to fix up this stupid quarrel?
(2) The importance of the Middle East. He wants us to say what we need. I really think they would make a special effort [if] it is well put over to them.
(3) The possibility of invading France this year. Went through the [?]'first phase' plan with him.
(4) The need for better liaison between us and the Americans, by *daily* personal contact *other than* in committees.

A long telegram in from the PM to the President giving his ideas about the new set-up in the Anzac and Pacific area – *not* a good telegram, I thought. Dill sat down and fiddled till 8.00 trying to draft a quick reply, which was quite unnecessary till we had got US reactions.

Dined with the Monnets. Monnet discussed the making of peace. He maintains it will be essential to dictate final boundaries etc. *immediately* after an armistice – they will then be accepted quite naturally. A year's gap for negotiating a peace would be fatal. He always has an interesting viewpoint.

Thursday 19 March 1942

Meeting of Heads of Mission with the Ambassador in the morning. The Combined Planners met the Combined Munitions Assignment Board to discuss directions. Bourne put his ideas over quite well, I gather. Got the FM to telegraph the COS asking for a clear picture of our deficiencies in the Middle East. Hope it will bring us something useful to go on.

Friday 20 March 1942

Combined Planners hard at it all day hammering out a paper on strategic guidance for munitions assignment. Geoff seems [to be] keeping up his end well with old Turner, who is being very difficult as usual. Dined with Joan Mainprice at the Escargot.

Saturday 21 March 1942

Quiet day. Dill showed me a telegram from Bridges [Cabinet Secretary] asking if there was really a job for Self [in Washington]. I drafted a reply asking for some delay till Lyttelton had got going in London [as Minister of Production] and Beaverbrook had arrived here.

Sunday 22 March 1942

Did not go to the office. Smith picked me up about 12.30 and I had lunch with them. Waffles and bacon! Great fun over making them on a new waffle iron! Went down with them after lunch to Manassas where we spent the rest of the day with the Desslers. He is managing director of Louis Marx, one of the biggest toy manufacturers in the world. The party there consisted of Marx, his brother David, Dessler, their wives, a Mr and Mrs Markham, Louis's two children – *very* nice children (about 12 and 14), Mrs Dessler's mother. All the men were New York Jews, fabulously wealthy and very vulgar but *very genuine* people which excused all. Drink and food and cigars in profusion. Had short walk in the afternoon to the site of the 1st Manassas battle. David Marx almost 'out' after one mile! All very thrilled at seeing Smith's 'bird dogs' make a point. At 4.45 p.m. we sat down to a vast meal – with fizz!! After it old Louis started a kind of race game in which he gave as prizes tiny gold dollars, gold coins (of which I got a fat Indian one) and a beautiful watch for Lee the guide! [Illegible] was not in it for lavishness. George Dessler then demonstrated with a marvellously happy smile about two dozen odd mechanical toys – he evidently loves his work! A very amusing day – *quite* a new experience. Came away with a presentation bottle of fizz.

Monday 23 March 1942

Finally fixed up to go to a quarter at Fort Myer. Thanked General Marshall accordingly.

Lunched with Nelson, Heavy Tank Mission, over here for a visit. He is in charge of English Electric. I sat next him at the Association of Construction Engineers dinner the night of the Abdication when father's portrait was presented to him – a very nice fellow. Dined with Monnet, Macready [also on the visiting Tank Mission but soon to become the long-serving Head of the British Army Staff in Washington] and Campion being the other guests. Sat talking with Macready and Campion till 2.00 a.m. in our flat. Macready seems a bit worried about morale at home and in the Middle East – no clear loyalty of people at home now for *England*. Production has to be spurred by a call for help [aid] to Russia! There had been trouble in a Regiment of Scots Guards in the Tower [of London] – many of whom had pictures of Stalin over their 'cots'!

Tuesday 24 March 1942

Dill had a meeting with Salter, Bailleau and Self to discuss Self's idea for a Coordinating [Supply] Council in Washington under the Ambassador with

Dill as vice-chairman, and all the missions represented. Salter evidently a bit suspicious of Self's motives. JSM meeting followed. CCS meeting in the afternoon – very successful as the Munitions Assignment directive went through. Also agreed that the Combined Planning Staff should examine the 'Invasion of the Continent' plans and reconcile their ideas. Smith told me just before the meeting that the Australians are making mischief between Churchill and the President over the despatch of a US Division to Australia in return for the retention of the 9th [Australian] Division in the Middle East. Curtin *is* [illegible expletive]. Dined with Joan Mainprice at Mays. Dill left to meet Lady D. at New York.

Wednesday 25 March 1942

Nipped out to Fort Myer with Smith and Bourne and picked our quarter – a small semi-detached quarter for a subaltern. It is certainly attractive there – swimming pool quite close. We shall have to get a good deal of the furniture though and provide our own servant – so it won't be too cosy. Had a very busy day then getting off a heap of signals to the COS. [Admiral] Little very troublesome and pernickety. Dined with Donovan. Met Mrs D., a dull party. Bill kept me talking afterwards till 1.00 a.m.

Thursday 26 March 1942

An easier day – actually got away at 7.30 p.m. Geoff and I brought Joan Mainprice back for a noggin. We then started to look at an enormous crate of toys sent by Louis Marx – about $50 worth! By the time we had had them all out and packed them up again it was 9.00 p.m. – and then Ralph Foster arrived and the process was repeated. At 10.15 we adjourned for hamburgers to the [illegible hamburger joint] – very slick place – all stainless steel – cooked before your eyes. Marvellous equipment.

It is quite plain that London and ourselves are at complete cross purposes over the Pacific Command set-up. This confusion largely caused by (a) the failure in London to realise that the US COS are not responsible to anyone but the President in person and not to a Ministerial body; (b) the fact that the US COS had never seen a copy of what the President sent to the PM on the subject till yesterday. He [the President] had got it all muddled up too. Sent off a long LETOD [private telegram] to try and explain.

Friday 27 March 1942

Dill back, full of praise for US hospitality. They had met Lady Dill [at New York] with a band and filled his house with flowers for her. Went over and saw Eisenhower and suggested he send one of his chaps [strategic planners] over with Geoff to London for a week, which he agreed to do.

I am afraid Evill and [General 'Hap'] Arnold [Commanding US Army Air Forces] are not clicking at all. Their temperaments are too different.

Dined with Leslie Chance at [illegible Washington eatery] and discussed Self's proposal for a Coordinating Council [for Supply questions]. The whole trouble is that Self has lost the confidence of the civil missions who think he is out to create a job for himself. If that be true his usefulness is at an end.

Saturday 28 March 1942

Normally had the day off, but went in till 11.00 a.m. to discuss with Dill Self's proposal for the Coordinating Council. Explained my fear about Self's loss of the [civil] missions' confidence, which I think Dill appreciated. Went out with Smith to Fort Myer to see the Quartermaster about our quarter. Geoff busy on a good world [military] appreciation which he has drafted as a basis for discussion with the US Planners.

Lunched with Monnet, and Brand [chairman of the British Supply Council]. Monnet showed me a copy of a memo proposing a *continued* Priorities Board [for the allocation of munitions], consisting of a representative of the President and of the PM, with the power to summon representatives of all the Combined Boards including a Combined Production Board which obviously must be set up. I fear he will have great difficulty over selecting the right two men – but the principle is certainly sound and more workable than a very large body with a fixed membership.

Sunday 29 March 1942

Found a foot of snow when I woke up – a sudden change from the nice spring weather we have had. Got down to the office [about two miles away] with some difficulty. Geoff and I lunched with Mrs Tait, who runs the cafeteria at the Embassy – a nice body – lives with her married son and wife. Very pleasant simple home.

Knocked out a draft for a memo to the FM about Self's scheme in the afternoon – wove in a bit of Monnet's scheme, which I think good. [See 24 and 28 March.]

News in of a successful 'Zeebrugge' operation [1918] on the docks at St Nazaire [a raid using the latter-day equivalent of a fire-ship, packed with explosives].

Monday 30 March 1942

Busy day. Had a short discussion with Dill on the Supreme Co-ordination [of Supply] idea, after having dictated a short memo on it (which I did not hand in). I believe Monnet's solution of the two-man committee consisting of deputies of the President and PM is right *if* you can find the right men – a big 'if'! Told Dill I feared Self had not got the confidence of the civil missions. No decision on his position till Lyttelton clarifies his own set-up. Dill talked wildly about going home if he couldn't get his (or Self's) idea on coordination through. He is hopelessly prejudiced against the civil missions. However I persuaded him to withdraw *that* idea.

Lunched with the Halifaxes at the Embassy. [The Hon. David] Bowes-Lyon who is out from the Political Warfare Executive at home is staying with them and we had a talk afterwards. He is a very nice fellow (brother of the Queen). He tells me Bill Whitney is *not* being very effective at home – covering too wide a field, like Donovan here.[41]

A lot of trouble going on over the US having stopped shipment to Australia of aircraft purchased by the Dutch East Indies for cash. The CCS decided a fortnight ago that this should continue to be sent to Australia, but they [the US] have apparently stopped shipment by unilateral decision as the Dutch say they want them in the US for training. I fear we may get much friction over this between Evill and Arnold – the Australians using us as their stalking horse.

Tuesday 31 March 1942

JSM meeting in the morning. Long discussion on whether we should or should not try and get in on all discussions between the US and the Dominions in US sphere questions. Evill feels if we don't, we shall get in a jam over allocations which for the Dominions will continue to be made in London. Unfortunate fact is, however, as Little pointed out, that only the US *can* protect Australia and New Zealand now – though admittedly it was the US's fault that we ever got into war with Japan.

CCS meeting in the afternoon. King and Marshall displayed no interest in the Pacific War Council! Much discussion on the Dutch East Indies aircraft which Australia hoped were coming on to them. Very hard to find out whether they really *had* been stopped by US unilateral action or not – but Arnold swore they had not. Finally agreed that the US would put up their ideas on the disposal of all these aircraft – meanwhile flow to Australia to continue.

A copy of the Supply Council paper on Coordination arrived from Chance. It is a wordy document – very poor – ending up only with a suggestion for a 'Shipping Priorities Committee' of two (one US and one British). I thought this must be Salter playing for 'Supreme Coordinator' but Chance assures me it is not. Asked him to send Salter, and if possible Monnet also, to go and see Dill about it all. It looks as if poor old Self is out, anyhow: the FM told him he could not keep him if he was not *persona grata* with the other missions.

Wednesday 1 April 1942

Spent all morning and afternoon in a JSM meeting going through the Joint

Planners' 'General Strategy' paper.[42] Brigadier Williams the New Zealand rep came in about 12.45. Took him and the NZ Military Attaché down to lunch and introduced them to Smith. Smith showed me the directive for MacArthur and Nimitz [in the Pacific]. King refuses to let me see them until they are agreed by Dutch, Australians and NZ! The JP paper went through fairly well, with little major alteration – Little was more amenable. Had a barging match with him over yesterday's CCS minutes. He wanted to see and OK all minutes in future, but I stuck out for the principle that if the US trusted the [Combined] Secretariat, he must do likewise.

The FM told me Hopkins wants to get out of the Munitions Assignment Board: and that Burns is going to be head of the Ordnance. He had pressed Hopkins to stay on it. The Pacific Council met for the first time under the President – no secretaries present, though Macrae, the President's naval aide, is going to produce a note of the 'highlights' for Smith's information (and ours). A very busy day all round. The FM saw Salter about Supreme Coordination. Salter confirmed what I had said – that the civil missions fear Self would try and run them. Self has certainly been very tactless over all this.

Thursday 2 April 1942

Weekly meeting of Heads of Missions with the Ambassador in the morning. He told us that the Pacific War Council had been a complete waffle meeting. After it, he had a meeting with Dill, Morris, Wilson, Brand, Salter and Self at which 'higher coordination' [of supply questions] was discussed. A busy day.

Friday 3 April 1942

Self had a long talk with Brand and apparently they reached agreement on 'higher coordination' arrangements – the basis being that Self would *not* be an 'executive' but merely a civil member of the JSM. I think this can be a workable arrangement, but I must watch out to keep any civil secretary appointed under our thumb and not Self's. Heard from Dill in the afternoon that Marshall and Hopkins are flying to London tomorrow to put the President's ideas for future strategy before the PM and possibly Stalin too. Poor old Smith had let him see our appreciation and then Marshall told Dill he had got [it] on the Joint Planners' level – in spite of strict instructions from Smith to keep it to himself!! I had an agitated time getting it back from the War Department.

Directions for MacArthur and Nimitz received from the US side *after* they had been OKed by Nash and Evatt [New Zealand and Australian members of the Pacific War Council]. Dill rather huffed by this discourtesy – particularly as they were headed 'by agreement' of all governments concerned.

Joan Mainprice came out at lunch time and finished the household shopping [for his quarter] with me. Geoff 'caught' a coloured maid.

Saturday 4 April 1942

Dill went off at 11.00 a.m. for the weekend. Squared up with Smith about directions that only the constitution [not the strategy] of the Pacific Theatre was 'by agreement'. Telegraphed home accordingly to stop them getting hot under the collar. A flap after lunch with Casey and Donovan in New York. Bill who is laid up with injuries in a motor smash has apparently cooked up some very grandiose scheme for American 'SOE' [Special Operations Executive] in the Middle East which he sold to Casey in New York. Casey was urging that an officer should be sent down at once to see Dill and rush it all through the CCS on Tuesday. I told him to hold hard and let Donovan put up his scheme to the US COS first. I am afraid Bill is rapidly cooking his own goose by lobbying round. His 'executive [i.e. Presidential] order' putting him into the COS organisation is held up by State Department influence. Smith is getting completely fed up with him.

Went out to Fort Myer after knocking off. Our coloured maid Julia was installed and functioning. She is dead lame and has no front teeth, but will do us all right, I hope. Found all the furniture installed in the place in most lavish style! They have certainly done us proud.

Sunday 5 April 1942

Went to the Easter morning service at the [Washington] Cathedral: very nice – a fine building; quite good sermon by the Bishop. Packed up kit and took most of it out to Fort Myer at lunch time.

Part III: Washington – Finding a Strategy April 1942 – July 1942

Introduction

By April 1942 significant progress had been made towards establishing the combined organisation in Washington. The achievement thus far was symbolised by Dykes's move out of his rented apartment in the Biltmore and into quarters 13B at Fort Myer, Virginia, in the bosom of the US General Staff. He shared the quarters with the rambunctious one-armed Brigadier Geoff Bourne, then Director of Plans on the British Army Staff in Washington, later General Lord Bourne, commander of the British sector in Berlin during the airlift of 1948–49. The move was made at Marshall's instigation, characteristically downplayed:

> My real purpose in this matter was to lighten both your burdens and those of [Bedell] Smith by bringing you three into the closest possible contact and thus achieve more efficiency towards our common purpose.[1]

Dykes's new neighbours included not only his friend 'Beetle' Smith but also Eisenhower (until his move to London, as Commander of the European theatre of operations, in June), and a central figure in the US Army's strategic planning, Colonel (later General) 'Al' Wedemeyer. The egregious Wedemeyer was a Marshall man whose ambition matched his considerable talent. He was very much the self-appointed guardian of his country's national interest. An uncommon zeal led him secretly to record his own conversations with the British planners, in order to combat the certain danger of being later maligned. According to Wedemeyer, he and Dykes understood each other:

> I saw him frequently in the evenings when he would visit my quarters and have dinner informally with me and my family; and we soon became close friends. Dykes was a well-read and cultivated gentleman who had travelled widely and acquired a *savoir faire* that was both disarming and attractive. As we became better acquainted, our exchanges of views became more and more uninhibited, at times brutally frank. He epitomised British thinking concerning international events, and I hoped that I was expressing accurately America's real interests in the global war.[2]

As Wedemeyer implied, by April 1942 there was a sharp divergence in British and American strategic thinking, exacerbated by the reluctance of both high contracting parties to declare themselves fully. The reluctance was understandable but unfortunate, serving only to increase suspicion, especially on the American side. Oliver Franks has observed wisely that 'in the Anglo-American relationship British policy has to pass the test: can the British deliver?'[3] Finding a strategy during the spring and summer of 1942 set exactly that test.

The search effectively began in early April with the precipitate departure of Marshall and Harry Hopkins for London, to secure British agreement on the proposals embodied in the so-called Marshall Memorandum.[4] Though hedged with a number of provisory clauses, this document canvassed a limited cross-Channel operation in North West Europe in 1942 (SLEDGEHAMMER), in the context of a plan to concentrate US forces in Britain (BOLERO) for a large-scale cross-Channel operation in North West Europe in 1943 (ROUNDUP). The immediate British response was appropriately described by Wedemeyer as 'cryptic', but seemed to represent a commitment to participate in the programme as described.[5] In May the position was clarified as a commitment in principle, pending further study. In early June, the lean and hungry Admiral Lord Mountbatten, harbinger of Churchill's bad news, arrived in Washington to confer privately with the President. He was followed later the same month by the Prime Minister himself, with Brooke, whose contributions were far from reassuring, as Dykes's diary interestingly explains.[6] Nevertheless in late June the Combined Chiefs of Staff reached broad agreement on the fundamental American conception, namely the BOLERO concentration for a 1943 ROUNDUP. Although it was not made explicit – it was not really faced – this appeared to rule out any significant operations in 1942, even SLEDGEHAMMER, except in the grave emergency of a sudden Soviet collapse. The Combined Chiefs considered, and rejected, an alternative operation in North Africa in 1942 (GYMNAST).

Putative agreement at the staff level was instantly compromised by the President and Prime Minister, neither of whom would countenance a year devoid of conspicuous Anglo-American activity. Churchill in particular refused to accept the emerging military consensus that over the next year a North African operation and a cross-Channel operation were mutually exclusive: that GYMNAST in 1942 would preclude ROUNDUP in 1943. As if to rub salt in the wound, he informed the Americans early in July that 'no responsible British general, admiral or air marshal is prepared to recommend SLEDGEHAMMER as a practicable operation in 1942.'[7] This amounted to an absolute veto. Washington recognised well enough that British landing craft and British troops were essential to any operation in Europe in late 1942 or early 1943. Churchill turned once again to an Anglo-American operation in North Africa, cunningly playing on the crucial elements of timing and tactical success. The first landings could be predominantly if not exclusively American, and with luck unopposed; they could be represented to the American people, perhaps even to Stalin, as the long-awaited Second Front; just possibly, they could be accomplished before the mid-term Congressional elections in November 1942 . . .

For many in Washington such arguments were apt to appear disingenuous in the extreme, as Dykes's diary makes very clear.[8] Suspicion of Churchill, and of Brooke, was rife among the military staff. Was it not well-known that the Prime Minister, weighted with the memories of the Somme and Passchendaele, would never cross the Channel without the proverbial band playing?[9] Given such suspicion, it was but a short step to believing that Britain was losing faith in the whole cross-Channel conception, 'going cold on BOLERO' as Dykes put it.[10] If that were so, the US had a ready alternative – the Pacific. Marshall and Hopkins, this time with King, travelled again to London. Dykes returned too. His diary conveys the oppressive atmosphere of crisis. Churchill expostulated to Halifax: 'Just because the Americans can't have a massacre in France this year, they want to sulk and bathe in the Pacific!'[11] Finding a strategy would take a little longer.

Diary
6 April 1942 – 14 July 1942

Monday 6 April 1942

Finally cleared out of the Biltmore after breakfast. A busy day. Telegram in to say that the Joint Planners' appreciation is approved by the COS almost *in toto* – all very pleased. Ellis and Bruverie in about Donovan's wild schemes which he completely misled Casey on [see 4 April]: explained to them the necessary procedure to get the stuff out of the allocation committees. Found late in the evening that Self had taken no action on a telegram from London telling us to hold hard on Russian post-protocol supply discussions. Had to draft letters and a telegram in a hurry on them. He is a very unmethodical worker. Found Julia [the maid] functioning all right at Fort Myer where Geoff and I spent the evening, with Ralph Foster's assistance, disposing furniture to our liking. Looked up the Smiths: Eleanor very hospitable as usual – loaded me up with fruit. Beetle called round later on his return from seeing Dr Evatt [Australian representative on the Pacific War Council].

Tuesday 7 April 1942

JSM meeting in the morning. Some trouble over a Combined Intelligence appreciation of German capabilities, in which our weak Joint Intelligence Committee team had been led altogether too much by the nose by the US team. CCS meeting in the afternoon: King in the chair. Our side had a difficult time over the question of the Dutch-purchased aircraft which the US wished to dispose of entirely without reference to us; but Dill handled it all very well indeed. Beetle as usual was very much on the side of the right, and cooked the conclusions [in the minutes] nobly. Agreed that Evill, Arnold and Towers [commanding the US Navy's air forces] should go into the whole aircraft position as a special sub-committee. Combined Planning Staff given a directive to produce a general appreciation.

Geoff went off to Baltimore, to catch the Clipper for home, in the evening. The place very empty without him. Poor Joan Mainprice in rather a stew, as the people she is p.g.ing [paying guest] with want her to turn out, owing to illness. It isn't easy to find quarters in Washington nowadays.

Wednesday 8 April 1942

Busy day drafting signals after the CCS meeting. Knox from Combined Operations HQ arrived. London evidently think Bill Donovan is the king pin on commandos and raids, as Pug [Ismay] sent him a special letter of introduction for Knox. Sent Pug a signal to say Donovan's stock not very high just now. White, Patsy Field's brother, came in during evening to get the dope for an article on Malta. He is a nice fellow. Got Grindle and Dewing to see him also.

Dill had a meeting with the Ambassador and heads of the civil missions in the evening at which the whole arrangements for coordination [of supply] were apparently satisfactorily settled. Dill has rather pointedly kept me out of all this business. I suppose he realises I am not in love with the whole idea of Self as 'Civil Member' of the Joint Staff Mission. I hope we are not going to have a lot of trouble over all this.

The news is that the Japs have apparently a much superior fleet in the Indian Ocean – situation pretty sticky.

Thursday 9 April 1942

Fairly quiet day. News in that Bataan has fallen – the garrison was very short of food. The FM produced a telegram describing an informal meeting our heads of mission had had with the US COS at the White House with the President last night. Nothing of importance came out of it. News in that HMS *Devonshire* and HMS *Cornwall*, two cruisers, had been sunk by bombs in the Indian ocean soon after leaving Colombo [Ceylon, now Sri Lanka] – a very heavy loss considering our weakness in the Indian Ocean at present. The Japs are certainly devilishly good at the bombing of ships.

Had lunch with Bob Garforth. We are having a lot of difficulties with the Combined Munitions Assignment Board. The tendency is for Washington to try and take over *all* allocations – including those to British Dominions. Dined alone with Ronnie Campbell [Minister at the British Embassy]. We had a long talk on the 'Self set-up'. He agrees with me that all [that is] necessary is a civilian secretary and that Self is too high-level to do the job of ensuring co-ordination. However we must try and make the show work somehow if it is approved at home.

Friday 10 April 1942

A fairly quiet day. News in that HMS *Hermes* is sunk in the Indian Ocean near Ceylon. The situation there is certainly becoming very grim indeed. Dined with Leslie Chance who gave a party at the Woodman [Hotel] as his wife is down from Canada. She is a stout comfortable party, English. Spoke to Jacob on the telephone about the civil secretary needed for the Self organisation. He has Hasler in mind.

Saturday 11 April 1942

Busy day with a lot of papers in to read. Maloney came up with a proposal to require *all* requisitions from Australia to have MacArthur's OK – in order to avoid this continued pestering by Evatt. Considerable disturbance caused by a press report from London giving a very good idea of what Marshall and Hopkins are over in London to discuss. This has been written up into a long article on European offensive prospects – far too near the truth to be published! Cracked off a telegram home, as the US Departments think London has leaked deliberately so that the US would have the blame for having pressed the idea if an unsuccessful offensive was laid on.

Had Pope [Canadian JSM] to lunch. He is a very good chap, but getting elderly in his outlook. Collected Geoff Bourne's car and brought Mac Ross out to dine at Fort Myer. He has been travelling round a lot, looking at tanks. As usual he is rather pessimistic and fed up with his job. The Smiths called in just as we were finishing. Mrs S. nobly sat on for a long time in our icy house – the fireman [boilerman] having failed to keep the furnace going! Then she got on to the Utilities officer and roared him up – the fire was lit up inside a few minutes. They are certainly a *very* nice couple. Got Mac safely back to the Raleigh Hotel – though driving in Washington is certainly no joke.

Got my driving licence in the morning without a test – whisked through by Tizard, head messenger at the Embassy who has a 'graft' at the Traffic Office!

Sunday 12 April 1942

Lay in till 8.45. Picked up Joan Mainprice at 11.30 and went out to Middleburg [Virginia] for the afternoon – a fine fresh sunny day, the country looking much greener than when I was last down that road two and a half months ago. Had supper at a Howard Johnson café on the way back.

Monday 13 April 1942

Fixed up with Pope and Williams [Canadian and New Zealand military missions] to let them see all JSM stuff in a circulating jacket – but not for the Canadian and New Zealand attachés. This will be an awkward business but I think we can make it work. Had a talk with Richard on the secretariat for Self's activities. He feels that no secretary worth a cent would feel he had a job, as in fact Self will be nothing *more* than a secretary – he has no responsibility as head of a mission. On thinking it over I think this is right – though how we are going to tie him in to the show properly I don't know. Saw Knox who has come out as head of the Combined Operations show here in the afternoon. Warned him to go warily in dealing with Bill Donovan's outfit – I fear old Bill has cooked his goose with the US COS by talking far too much with people outside.

John White, Patsy Field's brother, had a very good article on Malta in the [Washington] *Times-Herald* yesterday – written up from stuff he got from

Dewing, Grindle and me. The genesis of it was the party at the Fields' a week before at which Geoff and I had talked a bit on the romance of Malta and what it was going through nowadays.

Went to a Pacific War Council meeting in the evening, and gave them a bit on what is moving on the US Planners' and COS side. Our planners have been given a copy of their paper containing a proposed production directive. This is written from a fairly unilateral standpoint of US needs only, and is written with very little regard for anyone else's needs or for planning production on an *agreed* combined strategic policy. Monnet and Self had already drafted a cable home which went off on Saturday [11 April] pointing out that US production was being more or less arbitrarily adjusted to meet the realities of production. What in fact is required is the process which was visualised in London during the discussions on the Victory Programme; i.e., adjustment in accordance with *strategic* requirements. The trouble is that with Marshall away in London, there is a tendency to say all the time that we can't move toward agreeing on strategy till he gets back.

Tuesday 14 April 1942

Quiet day with no [regular weekly] CCS meeting in the afternoon. Joan Mainprice out to dine. Practice blackout in the evening, with all street lights turned off. At Fort Myer they fired six guns as an alarm signal! – and pulled the main switch. Quite impossible to tell when it started and stopped otherwise – as for the whole 15 minutes sirens blew continuously!!

Wednesday 15 April 1942

Another quiet day. Smith told me they believe the French Embassy are burning their archives and Donovan's organisation report they are shortly going to declare war on us.

Thursday 16 April 1942

Another quiet day.

Friday 17 April 1942

Went over with Strafford [RAF planner] to see Eisenhower in the morning. They had had instructions from Marshall to send all possible help to India in the way of air [support]. Eisenhower as usual flat out to help – but it later appeared that in fact anything that could go would be from our stuff that would be going East anyhow! The truth is they have nothing to send. Busy on the Russian protocol. Burns gave me last night a draft of what he proposed to send to the President. Considerable trouble getting an agreed telegram cleared with [the British] Supply Council. Failed to get agreement with them tonight. Spoke to Stirling [Cabinet Office] on the telephone: they seem to have had very satisfactory talks with Marshall and Hopkins.

Dined at the Dills'. Quite a large party. Sat next to Mrs Gibbs, and a woman called Heida Kaper, secretary to Joe Kennedy when he was [American Ambassador] in London – now a journalist – very intense sort of female. Before dinner I had dashed up to a CTP at Richard [Coleridge's] for 10 minutes.

Saturday 18 April 1942

Fairly easy day, though busy in the afternoon. Went to a party at McDowell's [US Secretariat] – a very hurly [-burly] and noisy affair. We stayed at their place 'warming up' till 8.45 and then went on to dine and dance at the Army and Navy Country Club. Mrs McD. is quite a good sort – insists on 'first names' within five minutes. Others of the party were the Libbys [Admiral King's staff] – he possesses a tall and rather voluptuous wife – no wonder he looks downtrodden between her and Uncle Ernie [King]! Talked quite a bit to a Mrs [illegible] who is a relation of the Astors and related by marriage to the Bowes-Lyons – very keen on 'nutrition' like all American women seem to be!

News in that US planes had bombed Jap cities – it had been due for 21 April – but evidently went off early.

Sunday 19 April 1942

Picked up Joan Mainprice from a breakfast party of the matron of the Elizabeth mental hospital about 12.00 (after being suspected of being a patient by a female in the office as I didn't know the matron's name). Drove down to Rocky Point on the Potomac, rather a nice little seaside place. Had a picnic lunch there and got back about 5.00. Dined with the Popes. Mrs P. is French or Belgian, I think. Others there were Mrs Hastings and Captain and Mrs Sherman [US Navy] – rather a dull party.

Marshall arrived back [from London] with Dudley Pound [First Sea Lord].

Monday 20 April 1942

Busy day, ending up with the Working Committee of the Combined Munitions Assignment Board. Brought Grindle and Jarvis, who is over with Pound, back to dinner and then on to Smith's, where we also met the Eisenhowers. Heard Geoff had left London.

Tuesday 21 April 1942

JSM meeting in the morning. Pound gave us the dope on Marshall's conversations in London. Apparently they are going all-out for a minor offensive in France this summer. CCS meeting in the afternoon which Pound attended.

The chief item was an appeal by the US COS against the Combined Munitions Assignment Board allocation of 29 transport aircraft to Russia. Handy came over in the evening to tell me that the Persians had asked for a US officer as Intendant [superintendent] of the Persian Army! Told Handy the Persians were probably only doing it to try and play off the US against the British and asked him to answer that the State Department had referred the request to [the British] Embassy.

Wednesday 22 April 1942

Busy day. Smith told me he and Eisenhower had been called up last night to see Evatt who wanted to get a formal statement from the President of the American forces that would be allotted to Australia. Smith had to tell him that he wouldn't get that, but promised to let him have a note himself in general terms. Evatt evidently realised that pressure on the political level is not welcome and had drafted a cable home on those lines. MacArthur appeared to be keeping things very close from the Australian Government, evidently not trusting their discretion and censorship.

Saw Eisenhower in the evening and discussed the air reinforcement of India shortly. Our Air Staff say that it is all being done at the expense of our allocations, but I hardly know who to believe. The US story is that there are lots of planes for us held up in this country owing to delays in the [air] ferry service [across the Atlantic]. In these circumstances it is hardly surprising that they want to send *them* off rather than planes allocated to themselves.

Had a chat with Wedemeyer who accompanied Marshall to London [as one of his strategic planners]. He seemed most impressed by all the people he had met and what he had seen. Discussed with Handy again the proposal made by the Iranian Minister for an American 'Intendant' [for the Iranian Army]. They are putting it back to the State Department as I recommended, saying that the British should be consulted.

Called on General Marshall in the evening; but they were out. Then called in on the Eisenhowers. They had just bought themselves a *very* elaborate radio set – one of the best on the market. While I was there a chap called Butcher, and on wife, dropped in. He is something on the Columbia Broadcasting Corporation – quite a good sort.

Thursday 23 April 1942

Fairly quiet day. No news yet of Geoff [Bourne, liaising in London]. Went to HE's [the Ambassador, Halifax's] conference with Heads of [British] Missions in the morning. Dill had had a telegram from Bridges [Cabinet Secretary] about Self – no action, pending a decision on the new organisation for a Minister of State [for war production] to represent Lyttelton here. I told Dill that in this proposal I saw no idea of subordinating him [Dill] to the Minister –

they would be more or less in parallel. I think it should work quite well; Self would presumably move over from us to be his [the Minister's] Permanent Under Secretary.

Dudley Pound gave a small CTP in the evening. Grindle took the Eisenhowers, Smith and myself on to dinner at the Shoreham [Hotel]. A pleasant evening. Eisenhower is very keen to make a trip to England next month, so his wife tells me.

Friday 24 April 1942

Arnold put up a crackpot scheme to attack some French fighters in Dahomey [now Benin, West Africa] with aircraft from the Ranger [aircraft] which are destined for India. Smith got on to it and Dill wrote Marshall to boom the idea off.

Some trouble with Fortier[12] over the Combined Intelligence Committee report on Russian port and railway capacities. He *is* a crashing bore – and quite capable of twisting his facts to fit a foregone conclusion. Another awkward CIC question has been put over by the Combined Munitions Assignment Board relating to Turkish demands for aircraft. Lunched at a party of McGeachy's at the [illegible restaurant], to meet Raymond Clapper, a commentator who has just returned from Chungking [China] and India. Extraordinary how prejudiced Americans can be about India. He complained that we had not industrialised India! I had to point out that Gandhi's chief complaint was *against* industrialisation – also that we had allowed India to start her own cotton industry and had thereby killed the Lancashire trade. Sat next to Mrs Woodford, daughter of Teddy Roosevelt, who is a leader of 'America First'.[13] She is *most* militant and imperialistic now – an unbalanced woman.

Busy afternoon on a US COS directive for BOLERO planning [for the build-up of forces in the UK for an eventual cross-Channel attack]. Spoke to Jo on the telephone. He has fixed up West's promotion to Higher Clerical Officer [West had charge of the files in the JSM Secretariat] if we can get it through the Treasury representative here. Geoff arrived back at 5.30 p.m. having had quite a successful trip to London. Joint Planning is working very well there now he says: but we were caught very unprepared by Marshall's plan for continental operations. I don't think Home Forces had done very much about it during the last few months.

Went with the Smiths to dinner at the Dutch Legation in honour of Princess Julianna and Prince Bernard. I sat next to Mme Van Tetz, an American woman married to a Dutchman, who was quite pleasant; and Mme Stoeve wife of the Dutch Admiral. She and I both felt very conscience-stricken at being given a *whole* young chicken!! The waste of food in this country is simply terrifying. Met Mrs Marshall there, Morgenthau (Secretary of the Treasury) and Mrs Willson, a very shrill kittenish old fixer, wife of Admiral Willson (King's chief of staff).

Saturday 25 April 1942

A very busy day – all Heads of Missions were away for one reason or another, but there seemed to be pile of work in.

Sunday 26 April 1942

Beall came round with the Packard which I am thinking of buying, about 11.00. Got her cleaned up and then set off to give her a trial run. Picked up Joan Mainprice and went out eastward to Chesapeake Bay. The dogwood trees in the woods along the roads are very lovely indeed. Most of the coast there is 'Hayling Island' at its worst [a byword for third-rate English seaside resorts], but we found one place called Randell's Cliff where there are just five or six bungalows and a path down to a long narrow sandy beach which was very pleasant. The car behaved well and I shall certainly buy her, even though the tyres are poor.

Monday 27 April 1942

A busy day. Had a long talk with Colman, lately Military Adviser to Earle Page [Special Australian Envoy to the War Cabinet] in London. He was quite alarmed to hear that the Australians would have to compete alone with the US staffs here without our support at all. Apparently they had all warned the Australian Government of the danger of selling their birthright for a mess of pottage – but Curtin and company would not listen. I think the final result of all this will be greatly to strengthen the Imperial connection in Australia.

Had Angus McDonnell, Ralph Foster, Dick Dewing and C. S. Forester (*Captain Hornblower*, etc.) to dinner. Forester was in the Science VI [form] when I was Captain of the School at Dulwich [College], but I did not remember his face. He is a quiet sort of bird, quite pleasant.[14]

Hitler made a very queer speech from which it looks as if there are considerable interior stresses in the German system between Army and party.

Tuesday 28 April 1942

JSM meeting in the morning, which lasted till 12.30. CCS meeting in the afternoon: Admiral King *not* present. Chief subjects were:

(1) Request by us for 40 transport aircraft in India, which Marshall after some discussion undertook to examine sympathetically. I think he will pull something out of the bag – there are 330 airliners operating in this country, 250 of them on a purely commercial basis.
(2) Planning for BOLERO – staff arrangements and landing craft.

(3) Horne [deputising for King] reported that a memo is going up to the President recommending that the US clamp down completely on all Vichy [French] possessions in the Caribbean.

(4) Munitions Assignment Directive – order of battle appendices. Evill gained his point that the Arnold–Portal agreement [of January 1942, on aircraft allocation for that year] should stand as the basis of assignment, pending the reports of the Arnold–Evill Committee.

McDowell did the minutes, Richard Coleridge being on a week's leave – the result was that it was 7.30 before we could clear them. Had a long talk to Smith while waiting. He foresees a very militaristic and imperialistic spirit developing in America as a result of the war. He quite seriously thinks that America will have to absorb Canada and all the British West Indies even by force if necessary. I doubt America's capacity for going tough and *staying* tough – but he may be right.

Wednesday 29 April 1942

A busy day. JSM meeting in the morning to discuss Nelson's [US chairman of the Combined Munitions Assignment Board] letter about 'revamping' the 1942 and 1943 production programmes. Self was not very effective on it. Talking with him in the evening, I feel he knows there is no real job for him in the JSM and that he is now looking forward to getting out altogether.

Dill wanted me to go off with him for a tour of US troops with Marshall, but with Coleridge away I couldn't make it. The situation in Burma looks very bad indeed. The Japs are thrusting up towards Lashio.

Thursday 30 April 1942

Woke up feeling bloody so stayed in bed. Joan Mainprice came out with my papers in the morning, and called the MO [Medical Officer] to look at me. Beetle Smith called in after tea.

Friday 1 May 1942

Joan and Birley [Supply Council secretariat] came out in the morning. Birley is having difficulties with Self over the agenda for the coordinating meeting fixed for Thursday next. Mrs Smith looked in after tea. Grindle, Montgomery [Dill's secretary], Joan Wakefield and K. Channing stopped in, after playing tennis, for drinks. Got up for supper: feeling better, but not yet *right*.

Saturday 2 May 1942

Staggered in to the office and had a fairly busy day, ending up with a telegram from London giving us the works on the new Russian protocol. Informed Burns accordingly.

Sunday 3 May 1942

Failed to contact Burns in the morning, but discussed Russian procedure with Chance. He came in about 12.30. We went off to lunch at Mrs K's Tollhouse at Silver Spring [Maryland], taking Joan with us, and spent a pleasant afternoon there, returning about 4.45 to the office, to find Hopkins had suddenly blitzed Burns into action during the afternoon: also the FM, who, failing to raise me, had thrown Dewing into the fray. He and Burns with the help of Fraser, who does Russia on the British Supply Council, had produced a draft 'covering note' to the revised schedules and a memo on the executive organisation (which was valuable). Dewing very martyred because no secretariat could be produced within an hour or so. Monnet and Chance were called in later, before Burns sent off his draft to Hopkins – a stupid storm in a tea-cup – quite an unnecessary flap. Got away about 8.10 p.m. and supped at Schenck's with Geoff. His sister and Dennis Smith (*Daily Telegraph*) were the others.

Monday 4 May 1942

Busy day cleaning up after yesterday's mess. Great depression in Joint Planning all round – as we seem to make no further progress at all on combined planning. The US Army and Navy are completely divided, the latter going all out for the South-West Pacific and the former for BOLERO. Until they can reach a clear-cut decision one way or the other, we shall get nowhere – doubtful even if we shall get any landing craft for the UK – all will go to the US Navy's amphibious forces. Warned the FM over the difficulties and then went over to have a talk to Eisenhower and Handy who are fully conscious of the difficulty: but see little means of remedying it. Beetle I found equally depressed by similar considerations, after dinner. He fears we shall get a complete impasse on the air allocation problem too. Got a half-promise from Eisenhower that he would take a trip to London toward the end of the month.

In the morning had a talk with Monnet, Brand, Chance and Fraser, about the executive machinery for dealing with the Russian protocol. Brand [as head of the Supply Council] very suspicious of Burns's proposal that it should lie with Maloney, the Munitions Assignment Board executive, but I explained this was only because that was the one piece of governmental machinery under Hopkins's direct control! Fraser is very knowledgeable on the subject and is the obvious man to run the show on the British side.

Heavy thunderstorm at midday. Cooler at night. Feeling a bit stronger. Richard Coleridge back after a week's leave looking much better for it. Prearranged code word arrived at 9.00 p.m. to show that the intended occupation of Madagascar was being carried out – we shall know in the morning with what success!

Tuesday 5 May 1942

JSM meeting in the morning. A lot of uninformed talk about the US proposal that MacArthur should OK all Australian requisitions which everyone mixed up with the question of the 'venue' for Australian bids – London or Washington. CCS meeting in the afternoon. Smart, representing Australia, put up a very woolly show on the MacArthur proposal, which left all hands completely fogged. Arnold refused to let any more US transport aircraft go to India, holding out great hopes for the future as usual. Marshall had evidently not been able to do anything about it with him. I fear we are in for serious trouble over all these air questions. Arnold is trying to expand too fast and bitching our programme completely without giving corresponding value. Cleared off all signals home the same evening, and got home soon after 8.00 p.m. Went with Bourne and Strafford to see 'Gone with the Wind' – 9.00 p.m. to 1.00 a.m. and I wasn't bored for a moment. It certainly is a *wonderful* film.

Wednesday 6 May 1942

Very busy day. Fixed up the papers and agenda for tomorrow's joint [British] missions meeting with Leslie Chance in the morning. Lots of signals and other papers to draft. Tommy Brand in at 5.00 for a chat on combined organisations etc. He is a very sane and cheerful person. Finally got finished about 8.20 p.m.

   News in that Diego Suarez [Madagascar] is in our hands. Corregidor [Philippines] has surrendered to the Japs.

   Had Knox's report of a President's meeting yesterday on landing craft production. Somervell [US Army Service Forces commander] held another this morning. The trouble is that London have not yet given an estimate of requirements. We cracked off a stiff JSM telegram home asking them to hurry up.

Thursday 7 May 1942

Long waffling meeting of the Heads of all the [British] Missions under the Ambassador – all about the setting up of a Combined War Production Board. Monnet ineffective – but his point was good, i.e. let it develop from the *ad hoc* machinery set up to deal with the immediate problem of revamping the 1942 and 1943 programmes. Self held out for setting up the organisation *as such* regardless of the immediate problem. Tore off the minutes in the afternoon. Had a great argument with Self in the evening. He was very annoyed because I said a long statistical report by the Combined Raw Materials Board about rubber would be quite indigestible by the CCS. He was also very annoyed because he is shown [in the minutes] as 'also present' at JSM meetings!

The FM held a JSM meeting in the afternoon with Pope, Smart and Williams [representing Canada, Australia and New Zealand] to discuss our strategy appreciation (on which by the way we are making no progress at all with the US Planners). Nothing of interest came out of the discussion. The NZ [military] attachés were apparently peeved over not being invited. It is high time all their attachés were absorbed into their military missions.

Friday 8 May 1942

A quieter day. Got my hair cut at lunchtime at last. Arnold has come across with proposals for aircraft allocation which virtually stop all US aircraft coming to the RAF. Great consternation in the Air Staff. Turned in dog tired – slightly feverish.

Saturday 9 May 1942

Very busy day. Chance and I saw HE [the Ambassador] in the morning to fix up about meeting times for the Heads of British Missions. Some flap on over Russian protocol stuff. E. P. Taylor [Supply Council] had produced a redraft of the covering letter with Burns and they had sent it in to Hopkins. Self thought it should be wired home at once as it differed from the London version. I agreed finally to hold it up till we hear from Hopkins – otherwise we shall get two half-baked drafts on the boil. Wilkinson, MacArthur's liaison officer, came in for an hour in the afternoon, to get me to go through his draft report.

News in of a US naval victory in the Coral Sea. Madagascar has apparently gone off well, though we had 1,000 casualties. Trouble with the Free French authorities in New Caledonia. Went to an Angus McDonnell party in the evening, with the Smiths who I think enjoyed it greatly. Met David Wills [British Press Council public relations] and wife – a good chap.

Saw copies of a letter to the President put up by Marshall posing the issue of the South-West Pacific versus BOLERO – this inspired I think by my talk to Eisenhower last Monday. Marshall stated bluntly that if the South-West Pacific is to win the day, it's only right to tell the British so at once. The landing craft situation for BOLERO is very complex. The War Department has ordered 8,000 small boats *quite* unsuitable for BOLERO. God knows how we shall get all this worked out.

Sunday 10 May 1942

Lay in till 12.30. Tinkered with the car till 4.00 p.m. Craig McGeachy, Angus, Ralph Foster, and David Will round to tea to discuss the new Press and PR set-up which Ronald Tree [Parliamentary Private Secretary to the Minister of Information] is concocting.[15] They all fear that a Press Counsellor will be imposed on them and their valuable *direct* contact wasted. They want my influence with Dill (who has spent the day with Tree) to stop this, and to let Harold Butler who is to come out decide on his own what is the best set-up.

Supper at the Dills': went through a draft letter from Dill to Marshall after, begging him not to let Arnold's air allocation proposal come up to the CCS but be discussed in London.

Monday 11 May 1942

Took the car in to Haley's to get the engine knock seen to. Busy day. Had lunch with Beetle, Eisenhower, Upson (Air), Clark (chief of staff of Commanding General, US Ground Forces) and Galloway who is over here from the Middle East for a short visit. John White called in after dinner. He is off tomorrow to join the Marines as a buck private! He brought with him a Miss Phillip, daughter of the US Ambassador to Rome from '37 to '40, who is working in Donovan's organisation. Beetle and Eleanor also looked in for a chat.

Tuesday 12 May 1942

JSM meeting in the morning. The question of our representation in combined discussions on the revamping of the 1942 and '43 production programmes was discussed with Self. Agreed that Dewing, MacNeece-Foster and Dorling [deputy heads of Army, RAF and Navy delegations in the JSM] should lead our teams. Considerable discussion on the Arnold Committee position [on aircraft allocation], which seems to be going from bad to worse. Beetle told me that King had objected to Arnold going to London and that is now in suspense.

The CCS meeting in the afternoon touched an all-time low. About 30 people present – the US side has grown with every meeting. Business done – nil. Had a long gloom with Beetle about it afterwards. He is moving toward the idea of cutting down CCS meetings to one a month for purely formal purposes with all allied nations' representatives present, and trying to get Dill, King and Marshall to meet to settle the real business. We shall certainly get nowhere on present form. The Planners are also very gloomy. No move forward on any of their work at all – the main difficulty being the Arnold Committee position.

Spoke to Hollis and Jacob on the phone. Jo [Hollis] wanted to get the position of the US Planners in London cleared up. Told him I would shortly be coming over with Eisenhower. Jacob told me he would try and get Lyttelton [Minister of Production] to come over about the end of the month. A long hard day. Getting hotter. Dennis Daley arrived in the evening; he is going to command in Jamaica. Took him back to dinner and got all the news from Home Forces. He says [the fall of] Singapore gave an enormous fillip to training at home which has greatly improved in consequence.

Wednesday 13 May 1942

Persuaded Evill and Dill to get the COS to invite Arnold over to London prior to a return visit by Portal [Chief of the Air Staff], with an agreement signed in Washington as the ultimate end. Beetle put the same idea in a memo to Marshall. Sent this in a signal to Jo too. It seems this is the only way to break the jam, and it would be very hard for Arnold to refuse.

Lunched at the Embassy. Others present besides the Halifaxes were Galloway, [Harold] Balfour (Under-Secretary of State for Air), Wilkinson (Liaison Officer with MacArthur), and Angus McDonnell. Got Wilkinson to make some final corrections to his report to MacArthur. Halifax said the Pacific [War] Council in the morning was even more of a waffle than usual.

Ashley Clark, now head of the Far East Section in the Foreign Office, came in to see me in the afternoon – what could we do to help China? Could we bring more pressure to bear on the US?!! I put him straight on this and stressed our needs in India which the US would not fill. Needled him hard to counter-attack the scurrilous yarns going about regarding our alleged misdoings – the old story of Wavell's refusal of Chinese help, pinching Chinese lease-lend stores at Rangoon etc. Foreign Office people take a hopelessly apologetic, flabby line. I told him to ask for some of Stilwell's reports on the Chinese! Long bleat in from Evatt relayed by the COS at home – can we find out why MacArthur's demands are not being met. He is trying the same line in London as he did here with the President – a mischievous man. Went down with Burns and Wansborough-Jones to see Salter in the evening to get his advice on how to handle a Combined Military Transportation Committee report on the shipping situation. He advises to put it straight to the Combined Shipping Adjustment Board and get the CCS to ask them for their comments – not to suggest that military shipping should in any way be cut.

Dined with Bob Brand [Supply Council]. Tommy Brand, Monnet and McCloy there also. We discussed the difficulties of getting the US COS to face an agreed strategy and the particular problem of the air. McCloy keen to get more done for the Middle East. Stimson [Secretary of War] has apparently turned against it. I stressed the hopelessness of BOLERO if the Middle East and Russia collapse – and the two are interconnected.

Lyttelton announced his intention of coming out – Ian evidently successful.

Thursday 14 May 1942

Went out with the FM, Pope, Irving and Garforth to see the training at Fort Belvoir, the US [Army] Engineers' principal Depot.[16] Lovely big training area there, with fine buildings. The training was very well done – the general impression most favourable. Most impressive *stunts* were:

(1) High-speed, flat-bottomed assault tanks driven by outboard motor which they drove up on to a shingle beach at about 30 knots!

(2) Tank obstacles made of logs which a light tank charged at full speed – the driver temporarily knocked out by a bump on the forehead – but he does that regularly, apparently. Some tank men took a tank over timber trestle bridges to test them to destruction, stopping and starting on the bridge. Interesting to see they use all *wood* roadbeams in their pontoon equipment – aluminium, open pontoons, gunwale loaded.

Also saw the armed forces bridge – steel tracks on heavy rubber floats – but it can't be built without a derrick lorry. Large quantities of very heavy mechanical equipment seem to be carried. Pleasant lunch in a nice mess overlooking the River Potomac. A party of troops doing an obstacle course they had there looked amazingly fit and keen. Most encouraging show. Got back at 5.00 to find a good deal to do. The Arnold letter is making no headway and Portal apparently won't come out here! They evidently don't realise the position at home in the least.

Friday 15 May 1942

Very heavy day. Watson, Morris and Bebb came down to discuss the future of our Joint Intelligence Committee representation. The US apparently do not wish to recognise us as having a *senior* JIC team here corresponding to their senior JIC team – though Noel Hall [Minister for Economic Warfare at the Embassy] negotiated an awkward paper about 'Axis Intentions' single-handed very successfully. Cook has just arrived to head the Army Intelligence staff [in the JSM]. Agreed with them that the present was a bad time to take up the constitutional point.

Redrafted a letter from the FM to Marshall which sought to get Arnold to London as a first step at least. Spent most of the remainder of the day getting out an answer to stupid questions from London about MacArthur's demands for reinforcements. Evatt is apparently trying to get the *COS* to needle the US COS over there! I am surprised they allow themselves to be used by him in this way. Smith gave me all the dope, but I am doubtful how much we can disclose to the Australians. MacArthur has evidently not kept the Australian government fully informed.

Saturday 16 May 1942

Very busy day again. More signals in from London reference Australian bleats. They want us to put definitely to the US COS a request for information as to what is proposed. Went over with Smith to Eisenhower and thrashed it all out. MacArthur had asked for two carriers, three divisions and 1,000 front-line aircraft (all from the US). Finally got a signal drafted after much chat with Smart [the Australian military representative in Washington] which the FM agreed. Much trouble caused by the War Department having received a list of requisitions – they could not sort out what had been demanded in London – all the result of demands being put in to two places at once. No progress on the Evill–Arnold invitation to London till about midnight when a formal invitation arrived from London.

To supper at Schenck's. Met Buxton there who had been in the *Prince of Wales*. He gave a very interesting description of the sinking of the *PoW* and the *Repulse* [on 9 December 1941]. The Japs came right in with machine-gun fire *after* releasing torpedoes, eight of which hit the *PoW*. Three bombs also hit from 12,000 feet. Singapore was definitely *not* a good show, I fear. Panic and confusion everywhere.

Sunday 17 May 1942

Lay in late. Went out to Chesapeake Bay with Joan Mainprice. To supper at the Fields'. Henry Field gave us a very amusing description of an arrival party given by himself and Jack Murchie at which they had taken a camel up to a fifth-floor apartment!

Monday 18 May 1942

No news yet of US acceptance of the invitation of Arnold to London. The President however has given a directive that the Navy Department *are* to produce the landing craft for BOLERO – *and* are to man them. Somervell [Army Service Forces] apparently short-circuited the Navy Department and went direct to the President.

Leslie Chance up for lunch. Fixed up the agenda for a meeting of British Missions on Friday next. The text of a letter covering the Russian protocol was finally agreed by the President after the US COS had tried to hedge it a bit.

Smith told me the US COS are very worried about the Pacific situation. They fear a full-scale Jap attack on the [American] lines of communication. The Coral Sea action was by no means a victory. They lost an aircraft carrier. The Chinese have asked to attend a COS [?CCS] meeting. He [Smith] wants to fix it now that we have purely formal CCS meetings with everyone present including allies, but that the real business will be done at *very* small meetings of Marshall, King and Dill only, with perhaps Arnold and one or two of our Heads of Mission too. Agreement in from Bridges [Cabinet Secretary] that Self should move out from the JSM when Lyttelton's [Ministry of Production] representative arrives. Agreed with Self that he will advise Dill *against* taking in Seal [Deputy Secretary to the Admiralty][17] in lieu. All we want is a civilian assistant secretary *only*, who would work under me.

Dined at the Bensons' [Military Attaché] – present the McCloys, Senator and Mrs Pepper, Mrs Raymond Lee [wife of Benson's US counterpart in London], Mrs Cameron Clark, Dick Dewing, Bernie [Bernard] Baruch [American financier and occasional Presidential emissary]. Quite an amusing party. Rubbed into Mrs Pepper that women in England had a much larger place in public affairs than in the US. McCloy very pleased with some dope I had given him about Malta for a speech.

Tuesday 19 May 1942

JSM meeting in the morning. CCS meeting in the afternoon. Smith told me during the meeting that Arnold *was* going to London. He begged me afterwards to ensure that Portal came back with him [Arnold] to sign up any formal agreement. Went down to the Willard [Hotel] at 6.00 with Self and discussed the procedure for the review of the 1942–43 [war production] programmes with Monnet and Tommy Brand. Much talk in generalities of 'the overall picture'. I begged them to give *current* examples when talking to the JSM otherwise they would never convince. From a War Office signal it looks as if Campion is bringing back with him only our nett requirements. They all feel strongly that if we merely present those, we shall have no right to question *US* requirements at all: they insist we must table (1) overall production [and] (2) overall requirements. This is sound in principle undoubtedly, but they do not fully realise the mechanical difficulties of detail involved.

Wednesday 20 May 1942

Heard our departure [for London] was postponed till 22 May. Arnold and Towers are both going to London, the President having taken a hand in the matter. An appallingly busy day, with an absolute string of people in to see me. Herbert (Director of Censorship) came in to talk about the Censorship of Transatlantic mail. We have that very well taped if only we can get all of it through our hands – but Pan Air are running a direct service to Portugal from Brazil! – which we cannot touch.[18] He is most convincing and has very tellng documentary evidence. Tommy Brand and Chance to dine with me and discuss arrangements for the Lyttelton visit. I am sure a *combined* approach is essential. We *must* get on partnership terms. There is a rising feeling of imperialism in this country which we shall have to face. If we at the end of the war are merely in the position of satellite to America we shall have a bad time. Therefore we *must* play the full partnership game.

Much trouble over Evatt's bleat to the COS. They want us to horn in with the US COS. But Evatt is playing crooked with us – he will force us into a position when we may have to argue *against* Australia instead of *for* her. Smart is very sore at the proposal that MacArthur should vet all Australian requisitions – but I am afraid they will have to accept that, having asked for US 'protection'.

Thursday 21 May 1942

Another *very* busy day. JSM meeting in the afternoon to discuss tactics for the Lyttelton visit – quite inconclusive. Self shot his usual line. Dewing stressed the importance of not prejudicing good relations with the War Department. Agreement on *principle*, I think. Dill left very confused over it all. News in that Macready is to replace Wemyss [as Head of the British Army Staff]. He will go down very well. Did some hurried shopping at lunch time. Dined with John Davies [JSM], and Campion and Lethbridge who have just arrived – more discussions on 'production' adjustment tactics.

Friday 22 May 1942

Packed up my kit, collecting a big heap of letters and parcels for posting at home from various people. Got down to Bolling Field at 11.00 to find that owing to the weather we should not start till early next morning! I think Arnold's office might have taken the trouble to ring up. Only Arnold and Eisenhower had been warned apparently. After I got back to the office, I went over to the War Department to clear up a botheration that has arisen in the SNOWPLOUGH outfit [a specially selected US–Canadian force, originally trained in snow warfare for projected operations in Northern Norway], between Brigadier Duncan and Pyke [British commander and tame but eccentric scientist].[19] The latter is sulking in his tent and has sent in his resignation to Mountbatten [responsible for Combined Operations]. It looked at first as if Duncan was in the wrong. But with Knox's agreement, I wanted to get the US view on the subject. Saw Moses [Assistant Chief of Staff in the relevant branch] who told me that Duncan is fine and Pyke impossible. Fortunately missed being button-holed by Pyke who walked unseeing past me twice!

Decided to spend the rest of the day as a holiday. Took Joan to see a flick, 'Joan in Paris' – very good (Free French & British prisoners v. Gestapo stuff), and to dinner at 'Mrs K's Toll House' – where we were unwise enough to choose soft shelled crab. They are *not* good – the shell is the consistency of shrimps – thin – and the whole animal is fried in batter. I believe you are supposed to eat them whole, but I object to the skin.

Saturday 23 May 1942

Up at 5.00 a.m. Went down with Eisenhower to Bolling at 5.45. Took off at 7.15. The party consists of: Arnold, Towers, Evill, Eisenhower; Clark (chief of staff, US Ground Forces), Anderson (staff officer to Towers), Beebe and Vandenberg (staff officers with Arnold), Fraser (RAF). The aircraft is a stratoliner (without pressure gear, extra petrol being fitted instead) made by Boeing. Holds about 16, very comfortably fitted up. The captain is Bryan, now in the Army Air Corps, though the rest of the crew are still wearing [the civil airline] TWA uniform. Had breakfast of scrambled eggs and bacon and coffee soon after leaving. The country is not particularly interesting till you strike the Hudson River Valley. Reached Montreal about 10.00. Bowhill, who has Ferry

Command, was out to meet the party – his eyebrows as good as ever, about one and a quarter inches long.

Eisenhower, Clark and I borrowed a Royal Canadian Air Force car and nipped into the outskirts of Montreal from the aerodrome – about a 20 minute run. The country looks extraordinarily like Northern France, buildings and cultivation being in the French style. Notices are all in French and English, population being 65% French Canadian. I had no idea that Montreal was such a big place – one million inhabitants. We went up to the hill on the north-west side in the residential area, but it was cloudy and thick so we could not see much. The gardens were very pretty, tulips, lilac and rock plants at their best. That part had a much more English appearance than Washington!

Got away again at about 11.50 a.m. and touched down at Goose River in Labrador at 4.20. It is a desolate spot with no human habitation anywhere near. The country is sand, covered with moss and lichen and spruce trees – just like what I thought Labrador would be, in fact. There is a mixed RCAF and US outfit, with a few RAF people too. Arnold said afterwards that the RCAF and the US don't get on well, and he thinks the RCAF are not pushing ahead fast enough. They have built a few barrack huts and one hanger, so far: runways are gravelled with some sort of building fluid poured on. In winter they have to be kept cleared of snow by blowers. It was very cold then still, but all hands on the station seemed very cheery, in spite of their isolated life – or because of it, perhaps! Took off from there at 6.00 p.m. (Washington time) and after having some food, bunks were made down and we turned in. At 12.30 a.m. however I woke with 'descending pains' in my ears to find we were just about to land at Gander (Newfoundland). Apparently we had (a) struck a certain amount of icing conditions, (b) heard from the UK that Prestwick landing conditions would be very bad indeed – so the captain decided to return.

Sunday 24 May 1942

General Brant (US commander) met us and we were all taken off to the US Officers' Club for some hot coffee. We then turned in in the officers' quarters – fairly recently erected? – but a bed and blankets were very welcome. Woke up about 8.00 a.m. – pouring rain and the whole place a sea of mud and builders' mess – all aerodromes seem like that, but this one more than ever. Had a light 'brunch' about 11.00. Brant told some amusing tales of the little complications of life in Newfoundland with one US commander, three RCAF and one or two British all on a co-operative basis – to say nothing of the local Newfoundland authorities. The latter were very upset recently by a US military policeman firing his revolver in the air while trying to stop a fight between US Army and Marines. They wanted to arrest the MP for discharging firearms in the street.

After lunch, Eisenhower, Clark, Vandenberg, Beebe, Anderson and I and three or four of the US officers went down to the 'Skeet Gallery' – or clay pigeon ground: single-barrel, pump-action shot-guns; a high trap one side and a low trap the other; seven stands laid out in a semi-circle. Twenty-five shots go to a match (one 'free' one on 24). We had a lot of fun at it. I managed to hit something under half. The Officers' Club is a fine big timber building, H-shaped, with three enormous rooms, one of them being a games room with table tennis, pool and darts. As usual in US messes, there were two or three ladies in the place, nurses and stenographers, I think. After some fried chicken ('in the rough'), we embarked and got off about 3.00 p.m. (Washington time). By this time it was beautifully sunny. The country looked rather like parts of Connemara [Ireland] in some ways – lots of small pools and lakes, very green and beautiful colouring. Shifted my watch on six hours to make it London time and had supper about 12.30 a.m. just as it was getting dark.

Monday 25 May 1942

Slept like a log all night. Turned out soon after 9.00 a.m., when Northern Ireland came in sight. Arrived Prestwick at 10.50 a.m. Passed straight through Customs etc. as a formality then went in for breakfast where I was surprised to find bacon, egg and butter without a hint of rationing. Heard after breakfast that owing to the weather we could not leave till 6.00 p.m. Met a staff officer of 4 Division who were trying to do a Combined Operations exercise which had been cancelled after two days' vain wait for the weather. He took Eisenhower, Clark and myself along to Hawkesworth, now commanding 4 Division, who talked very intelligently for a bit and then passed us on to see [load-carrying vehicles of varying tonnages] unloading and berthing after the exercise. On returning to Prestwick found it was impossible to get through to London tonight. The RAF managed to get us sleepers on the night train from Glasgow to which we drove by car. Lovely rainwashed sunny evening.

Tuesday 26 May 1942

Arrived London about 7.00 a.m. William Stirling and a large British and US reception committee met the party. Went to the Cabinet Offices and had a bath. Then to William's flat for breakfast. Saw Jo [Hollis], Bridges, Ian [Jacob], Pug [Ismay] in the morning, lunched with Ian. Met the Joint Planners and gave them the works in the afternoon. Planning for the ROUNDUP organisation [to plan the Allied invasion of North-West Europe in 1943] is under hot discussion. The CIGS objects strongly to the Joint Planners' idea of appointing a Supreme Commander now – at present the organisation is completely nebulous.

Caught the 6.34 train down to Camberley. W. met me. Lovely to be home again.[20] She has done marvels with the garden with the help of the children.

Wednesday 27 May 1942

Caught the 9.01 up. Saw Lyttelton at 11.00 and told him the set-up. Impressed on him American determination that the Service Departments must control production. Lunched with Bill and Rosemary Elliot [RAF Director of Plans] and Mrs Davison [wife of his Washington colleague]. Saw Kennedy [Director of Military Operations] in the War Office; Chief of Combined Operations [Mountbatten] at 7.45 and gave him the works on the Pyke situation [see 22 May]. Dined with Bridges, Poynton and Norman. Had a long talk with Pug, Ian and Jo after dinner. Discovered that the PM had renewed an assurance to Australia that if invaded there, we would cut our losses in the Middle East and send all help: pointed out this was quite contrary to the COS agreement to the JSM's appreciation [on future strategy]. Pug dictated a minute to the COS on the point. Sat up with Jo till 2.40 a.m. talking.

There has apparently been much criticism of the COS organisation lately in the Press and Parliament. A White Paper was issued describing it. The COS themselves took no interest whatsoever, but Jo put in a very good memo to Pug pointing out that they should take stock. The main suggestions followed our old ideas – i.e. that more should be decentralised to the Vice-Chiefs of Staff and the Directors of Plans, thus allowing the COS time to think big.

Lawrence Burgis [Cabinet Offices] has had trouble with Willie [mercifully unidentified] who has become cunt-struck on a very doubtful lady on the staff!! Willie tried to get Burgis shifted out, on promotion. But Jo told Bridges the full story which shook him considerably. I gather relations between civil and military in the Offices are not good, Burgis being our only link now. Bridges is disappointing – not strong enough to act on his own without interminable consultation.

Thursday 28 May 1942

Eisenhower, Chaney [Marshall's representative in London] and Somervell came along at 10.30. Ian discussed production programmes with Somervell, as it has been decided he shall go over with Lyttelton to Washington on 31 May for discussions with Nelson [chairman of US war production board]. I tackled Eisenhower on the ROUNDUP command question which the COS wanted to discuss with him. We all went in to the COS at 11.15. Eisenhower was very good and plumped for a Supreme Commander. Both he and Somervell made a very good impression. He made it clear that Chaney must be considered as having full powers of decision.

At 3.00 p.m. saw Hambro and Keswick about South American SOE [Special Operations Executive]. They do not agree with Bill Stevenson[21] that there is nothing to be done there. Undertook to warn Smith accordingly. They will let me have a note to take back. Went to a Combined Operations meeting with Eisenhower and Clark at 4.30. The CCO [Mountbatten] put over the [cross-Channel] assault problem very well. He wants authority to supervise *all* training of the assault force which I believe is right. Eisenhower and Clark all for that. The CCO certainly has *drive*.

Went down to Camberley by car. Found Dick's [his son's] bike, which I had borrowed, had disappeared from the station – but found my own there – left from before Christmas!!

Friday 29 May 1942

Caught the 8.11 train up. Had a go at Bridges on West's promotion which he is being sticky about. Saw Wemyss, who is to be Military Secretary instead of returning to Washington. Macready will take his place: apparently P. J. Grigg [Secretary of State] is ousting Macready. Saw the CIGS [Brooke] at 3.15 p.m. and gave him 10 minutes on Washington form before Eisenhower arrived. Took Eisenhower on then to Kennedy [Director of Military Operations]. Simpson [Kennedy's deputy] there too. Had an interesting chat – on DMO organisation, separate air forces, etc.

Took tea with Miss Partridge and the telephonists – Miss P. is getting married next week, and she was giving a party to all the old hands, Pug included. Then took Eisenhower on to see [Churchill's underground] Central War Rooms, and up to discuss BOLERO and Nevins [US officer attached to the British planning staff].[22] We found Findlater and Stewart [Army Director of Plans] in with Stirling and got the BOLERO questions fixed up at once. Agreed with Eisenhower that Nevins should live with the Joint Planners but make no written reports home to Washington. Dined with Jo and Stirling. Sat up late talking to Desmond Morton [Churchill's crony and intelligence adviser] about the Free French. To bed at 2.15 a.m.

Saturday 30 May 1942

Discussed the Joint and Combined Intelligence Committees with Capel Dunn [Cabinet Office]. He sees great difficulty in getting our people to disclose sources to the US JIC. Looked over Miss [Joan] Bright's [Special] Information Centre.[23] Fixed with her and Stirling to send us a weekly DOTEL [informal telegram] to say what is afoot in London – also her vade-mecum, to be kept up to date. Lunched with Kingsley [Dykes] and Ian, who is leaving for Washington with Lyttelton tomorrow. Spoke to Geoffrey Neville about publicity arrangements [in Washington], having failed to make contact with Harold Butler.

Tried to fix up to return a bit later, Dill having suggested I might stay a little longer. Found the prospects were not very encouraging so replied I would return on Monday [1 June] as arranged. Caught the 5.24 down to Camberley. Dick's bike still missing, but if it does not turn up the old porter will fix him up with one of the derelicts, some of which are in quite good condition.

Sunday 31 May 1942

Got up late. Dick arrived from Wellington [College] about 8.15 – looking very well and much grown. We dodged around the garden a bit, cut out a huge old dead lilac, and then started to burn all the remains of the holly he had taken out last holidays – got a huge fire going. Eisenhower and Clark arrived at 1.15. We had a very nice lunch and they were as usual charming. I think W. liked this. The place was looking quite at its best, as it was a fresh sunny day. A Home Guard exercise was raging all round the garden at the time!

News in of a raid on Cologne by 1,000 bombers in two and a half hours!

Monday 1 June 1942

W. came with me to the station to catch the 8.11 to town. Heard at 10.20 that we should *not* be able to get off at 12.00! Went round to see Cavendish-Bentinck [Chairman of the Joint Intelligence Committee in London] about the Combined Intelligence Committee. I gather Godfrey [Director of Naval Intelligence] was very upset because Noel Hall met the US JIC *alone* for the paper on 'Axis Intentions', without a sailor! I told Cavendish-Bentinck that the method of negotiating agreed papers must be left to us – the result is all that matters; also that the RN representative in the Washington JIC was very weak anyhow. Impressed on him our difficulty over disclosing sources. Godfrey says Wilkinson (US Director of Naval Intelligence) accepts the accuracy of our Alpha sources such as Y [signals intelligence from decoded German traffic]: but I explained that cuts no ice with the War Department – G2 [Intelligence branch] must send over their own man to be convinced. Brooks came round then to discuss the Political Warfare Executive. I warned him not to let his representative in the USA get mixed up with the Embassy as he would then cut no ice with the Service Departments. They have apparently agreed to split the world into areas for PWE purposes, Japan being left to the USA. Brooks does not think they are competent to run it properly, but I insisted that we must let them do their own show in their own way.

Met Field at lunch in the Rag [the Army and Navy Club in Piccadilly]. He told me that the ABDA HQ had worked very smoothly – particularly on the Intelligence side. He had no use for Bungy [Edward] Playfair [later the official historian], who he considered very slow on the uptake. Percival as a commander in Singapore was useless. He spoke very highly of Pownall and Dewing. Singapore, all round, was a very melancholy affair.

Went out to Northolt [West London] with Stirling at 5.00 to get away at 6.00, but found the weather was still unfavourable, probable ETD being 9.30 a.m. tomorrow. Libya operations seem to be going well.

Tuesday 2 June 1942

Warning [for the flight] from the Air Ministry came at 8.15 a.m.; reached Northolt at 9.15. Mountbatten, Harriman [Roosevelt's emissary], Slessor [Assistant Chief of the Air Staff (Plans)] and Hindley (Air Ministry civilian) have joined the party, Fraser and Jackson being left behind to follow later. Jack Slessor seems fairly content with the Arnold discussions. Had a long talk with Mountbatten, after lunch at Prestwick (which we left at 2.00) and in the plane. His energy has undoubtedly developed his show enormously, while Home Forces have apparently completely failed to produce the necessary drive. It is clear to me that you want *one man* to drive all this stuff along, as Sinbad always said. Paget [commanding Home Forces] seems much too busy on training exercises and takes the line that ROUNDUP is a perfectly normal military operation with a few slight naval complications at the start. I am convinced Mountbatten is right that he must be responsible for the whole of the training of the assault force. Home Forces would make a balls of it. I admire his drive and unselfishness immensely.

Wednesday 3 June 1942

Reached Goose Bay [Newfoundland] about 4.45 a.m. London time (nearly 15 hours in the air). Touched down at Bolling Field about 7.45 a.m. Washington time. Very low cloud, which made our chance of getting in pretty doubtful. Richard Coleridge came up to lunch to give me the form. Went down to the office in the afternoon. Found Joan Mainprice looking very fit after a holiday in Canada.

Lyttelton and Ian Jacob had arrived the previous night. Angus Nicholl was down from New York where his ship *Penelope* is refitting. Gave Ian and him dinner at the [Washington] 'Rag'. Angus was in very good form and *most* interesting on all his adventures in the Mediterranean. All his ship's company have apparently signed a [?]memorial asking for the VC for him.

Thursday 4 June 1942

Busy day getting back into the swim. CCS meeting in the afternoon (preceded by an excellent lunch) to meet Mountbatten, who gave an excellent discourse on what is being done at home on the training and development of Combined Operations technique. Marshall gave a stag dinner party for him at his home in evening. King, Towers, Arnold, Eisenhower, McNair, Clark, Beetle, Dewing, McNeece-Foster, myself present as guests: a pleasant evening.

Preliminary news of the naval outcome off Midway Island [in the Pacific] is very encouraging.

Friday 5 June 1942

Busy day. Bebb asked me to address the Joint Intelligence Committee on various things. I gather Cook who has just arrived as Army Intelligence [officer] is being a little trying. Ian and I dined with the FM. Also present were General and Mrs Burns, and Smith. A pleasant evening.

Saturday 6 June 1942

Spent a large part of the day flogging away at the conception of the combined order of battle as a preliminary to combined production. Bourne and company [on the British planning staff] had evidently *not* sold the idea to Handy. Had a go at him and Eisenhower first. They are very suspicious of the Nelson–Lyttelton [civilian production] combination.[24] Carried on with Smith and Vittrup [US Secretariat], Jacob backing up, all afternoon. Think I have got them convinced. JSM meeting in the morning to take some of Paddy Beaumont-Nesbitt's papers about publicity arrangements: also the draft reply to a Chinese proposal for a Supreme War Council. The Americans seem to be getting pretty tired of the Chinks!

Went with Ian and Smith to an Angus McDonnell party – very good fun as usual. I was stuck with Mrs Pettigrew at first – a 'keen American hostess'! Disengaged after a bit and sat with the Surles's and Kirbys. Mrs Surles told me she has two grandchildren and a son who is a major. She looks a very young 40! She is a very good sort. Ed Kirby has become a colonel! Had a crack with the McClays [Shipping Mission] too – nice people.

Sunday 7 June 1942

Definite news that two Jap carriers sunk, two damaged at Midway.

Took Ian, Ralph Foster and Joan Mainprice out to Chesapeake Bay to bathe, after lunch. Very pleasant afternoon. Ian and I went on to supper at Mrs Raymond Lee's. Pleasant company; sat with Mrs Lee, Ronnie Campbell [Minister at the Embassy] and Mrs Bacon, a prominent lady in the political world – amusing and vigorous. Had a long crack with an elderly female, now working as an adviser to the War Department, who has done a lot of Arctic Exploration!

Monday 8 June 1942

Busy day. Beetle told me that Admiral Leahy will almost certainly become a super-Chief of Staff for the Americans – a Pug Ismay, but senior instead of junior.[25] Our COS are trying to get the US to allow some Liberator bombers (which have been sent to the Middle east specially for [action against] Romanian oilfields) to be used to help get in the next Malta convoy. We had to wire back to London to get a better case.

Went to the Commonwealth Munitions Committee – a long waffle. McNeece-Foster [deputy head of the RAF Delegation] in the chair – poor as chairman. Discussed our civil establishment arrangements with Self who is due to leave at the end of the week. Asked him to fix Hayward to stay on.

Tuesday 9 June 1942

It looks as if the US have put down four Jap carriers at Midway!

Marshall agreed to the use of the Liberators for the Malta convoy – but only for a definite attack – not merely for demonstration purposes, which I feel is right. Lunched with Ian and Tommy Brand. Discussed the [British] 'civil forces' [in Washington] – Bob Brand is for strengthening the British Supply Council chairman by giving him a proper staff.

JSM meeting in the afternoon – meeting with Evatt after it. The FM very patient. We got nowhere really. But it is clear that the Australians are feeling rather like orphan children *vis-à-vis* the USA. It is their own fault – I have little sympathy. We shall have to tell the US that the UK are sending three fighter squadrons to Australia – *and* that the PM has renewed the assurance that we should let the Middle East go if Australia were attacked.

Wednesday 10 June 1942

CCS meeting at 11.00 a.m. – nominally restricted attendance – but the US Navy turned up in full strength plus aides – also McNarney [Marshall's deputy]!! Beetle *furious*. We had our own team only, less Dewing, plus Mountbatten for one or two items. I left Beetle to it. Rather a day of frustration for various reasons. Heard in the evening that the US Planners have jibbed at producing the order of battle for production until the air question is settled – and *that* makes virtually no progress at all. Eisenhower's appointment as Commanding General, European Theatre announced by Marshall. He will leave us very soon which makes me sad. Clark goes with him as a Corps Commander.

Dinner for Lyttelton in the evening – all the JSM, the Supply Council, and his party. He made quite a good speech – and broadcast after very well – an attractive and forceful personality.

Thursday 11 June 1942

A fairly quiet day. The Planners came to a full stop on the overall order of battle. The US side won't play till they have settled the air figures and they are still very far from that. Had words with Admiral Little who complained because the Secretariat had put a memo by Admirals Reeves and Dorling [JSM], addressed to the CCS, to the Combined Planning Staff [i.e. one level down in the hierarchy]!! I was unrepentant. He also objected because we had expressed a view to London on the question of the status of the Combined Munitions Board! A tiresome old man – who has received the GBE in the Birthday Honours!![26]

Got my nose and throat looked at in the War Department Clinic – very thoroughly! Dined with the Smiths: others present – Jacob, Foster, C. S. Forester – a very pleasant evening. Forester said he had only spent a few weeks in Spain. All his detail [for the Hornblower books] he got from Baedeker and a dictionary of seamanship.

A great blow – Smith tells me he is going to London in July as Eisenhower's chief of staff. I shall miss him terribly.

Friday 12 June 1942

The Libya battle does not look quite so good. The War Office send us absolutely no news at all – blast them.

Ambassador's meeting with the Heads of Missions in the morning. Had a chat with Angus McDonnell after. He speaks very highly of old Ralph Foster who has apparently persuaded the [radio] 'soap opera' writers to insert pro-British stuff.[27] Dill/Lyttelton meeting in the afternoon following one between Hopkins, Nelson and Lyttelton with the US COS. He [Lyttelton] said the US COS were very forthcoming. Dill curiously suspicious of Lyttelton – apparently poisoned by Self, which is a pity. Marshall has suggested to Lyttelton to send a [US] armoured division to the Middle East.

Bought a Palm Beach suit.

Saturday 13 June 1942

Fairly busy day. Went up to the Embassy to a small CTP in the evening to meet a bunch of British and US 'war heroes' (commando men, pilots, air gunners etc.) who are being fêted as part of a publicity show for Defence Bonds. Talked to an air gunner who had been on *81* raids over Germany: also to Hall, who lost an arm at the Vargos commando raid.

Dined at the Dills'. Jacob, Macdonald-Buchanan and Montgomery [Dill's ADC and secretary] also there. Went with them to a [base]ball game – Chicago v. Washington. The standard of throwing and catching is *amazingly* high – a good game to watch – Washington beat Chicago, by one run, the real winning hit being off one of their men's heads. It knocked him silly, but he got a 'walk' to the next base for being 'beaned'. This put their man on third base *home*!

Sunday 14 June 1942

Lay in late. Went to Chesapeake Bay; bathed and lounged on the beach. Supper of 'crab cakes'. The weather changed during the day and became delightfully cool and fresh.

Monday 15 June 1942

Fairly easy day. The news from Libya looks bad. We are having to withdraw. Self left for good.

Tuesday 16 June 1942

JSM meeting in the morning. A long [illegible] by the Admiral [Little] on the paper by Dorling and Reeves pointing out the need for an increased proportion of escort vessels to merchant ships. News in of the appalling fiasco of the American heavy bombers against Ploesti oilfield [Romania]. Only 13 got away from Egypt; doubtful if any dropped their bombs anywhere near the target; four of them came down inside Turkey. The state of training said by Tedder [Air Officer Commanding-in-Chief, Middle East] to be very poor. On the other hand the remainder seem to have done well against the Italian fleet in an action brought on by the Malta convoy operation.

CCS meeting in the afternoon quite peaceful. US representation has risen by now to nine, including the Secretariat.

Dined with Evill at a party given for Air Marshal Jarrod (Training) – a pleasant party. Sat next to Thornton (the Air Attaché) who bores me, and Vandenberg [on Arnold's staff]. I take to him more on closer acquaintance.

Wednesday 17 June 1942

News in that the PM, Pug, the CIGS [Brooke], and Guy Stewart [Army Director of Plans] are probably arriving by air tomorrow. Many arrangements to be made. Coleridge and Hayward [of the Secretariat] most helpful as usual. The FM told me Little had been arguing the point with him over his [Dill's] position as Head of the JSM. I fished out his directive and gave him a pep talk on the subject! Old Little *is* a nuisance.

The Combined Production Board laid an egg for the CCS at last, but owing to a mess-up by Nelson's people we did not get their paper till 9.30 p.m. Took it round to Smith and he got Marshall tentatively to fix a meeting for 2.30 tomorrow. Pity we have to rush it so, as the US COS will think *we* are trying to bounce them.

Practice black-out at night.

Received a letter from the Military Secretary to say I had been promoted substantive Colonel [though acting Brigadier] from 5 April, with seniority from 1 July 1941. A sad thought that I shall *never* have a command now.[28]

Thursday 18 June 1942

Spent the morning making final arrangements for the PM's arrival etc. CCS meeting at 2.30 to meet Lyttelton and Nelson who presented a paper from the newly constituted Combined Production and Resources Board. It was quite a good document, but unfortunately the CCS had to be called at very short notice to take it, as Lyttelton leaves tomorrow. King churlishly refused to attend at all. Marshall declined to take any final decision at all pending further examination. Lyttelton and Nelson put up quite a good show, and generally speaking all went off quite well. We had quite a lot of trouble to get out presentable minutes, though.

Went down with Jacob to Anacostia [airport] to meet the PM's plane at 7.30 p.m., thereby missing a birthday party given by the Smiths for the Coleridges' boy. The plane arrived almost dead punctually at 8.00 p.m. The PM, Pug, the CIGS, Guy Stewart, Thomson [Churchill's naval aide], Martin [Principal Private Secretary], Kinna [shorthand writer], Inspector Thompson [body-guard], and Sir Charles Wilson [physician] accompanying. Halifax, Lyttelton, the FM, Macready and Marshall down to meet them. The PM looked very fit, I thought. After dropping Pug at Ronnie Campbell's where he is staying, Ian and I went on to the Mayflower [Hotel] and dined with Guy Stewart.

News from Libya definitely *bad* – we have probably lost Tobruk. Losses on the Mediterranean convoys were very heavy indeed – and only two ships got into Malta after all.

Friday 19 June 1942

CCS meeting at 12.30. The CIGS explained they had come over largely owing to the President's conversation with Mountbatten [earlier in the month] when he [Roosevelt] had said he was worried because US troops would not be engaged with the enemy on any scale this year. He feared a Continental operation next spring would be too late and was turning toward North-West Africa as a possible let-out this year. Brooke said the British staffs had been looking at all these possibilities, and also at operations in Burma this year. The general impression he gave was certainly that BOLERO [building up forces in the UK for an eventual cross-Channel attack] had dropped back in the batting. I could see Marshall, Eisenhower and Smith were considerably perturbed by this. Dill and Brooke and Pug went over for more talk with Marshall and company after lunch. Smith came up to me, very worried. Pug returned about 4.00, and after Smith had left I got from him that the CIGS did not in the least intend to write down BOLERO and that the afternoon's talk had confirmed this. This improved the situation considerably.

Pyke, the 'abominable snowman' wasted an hour of my time in the evening with a scheme for tunnelling into the glaciers of Norway and thereby making them impregnable fortresses for guerrilla bands. Shot him out when Pug and Smith appeared with Eisenhower's write-up of the afternoon's talk, which is to be discussed at another CCS meeting tomorrow.

Dined with the Smiths – sumptuously as usual (chicken, crabmeat salad, strawberries and angel cake!). News from Libya definitely bad. Tobruk is once more besieged and we are where we were last autumn once more.

Saturday 20 June 1942

CCS meeting at 11.00. They discussed the record of the previous afternoon's talk in the War Department and agreed to put it up as a CCS paper to the President and PM, after some expansion – general gist being that BOLERO should go ahead: if the Russians crack it will at least secure the UK; a change of plan for the next offensive theatre can be made about September. They are dead against GYMNAST [an invasion of North-West Africa] this year as too great a dissipation of forces. Pug anticipates a major explosion from the PM when he is confronted by this document. But all the CCS were solid in the view that they should stick closely together and present a united front. The CIGS expressed himself as very relieved to find such unanimity of opinion. The atmosphere at the meeting was thus much easier than on the previous day.

I whacked off the minutes and then Smith and I drafted the CCS memo. Pug came in during the process. Smith gave him a piece of gum to chew!! Pug accepted it, but soon got rid of it – I feared it would stick to his fingers, but fortunately that was avoided. Smith asked him to let me go and be the liaison officer [with Eisenhower's new command, with Smith as his chief of staff] in London – but got no change of course. I fear they will return to the charge on this; I must do my best to head them off – and they will have to produce a suitable man at home. Smith and Eisenhower are curiously nervous about London – just like two boys off to a new school. I shall certainly send Richard home with Smith for a few days.

Herbert called in for advice as to how to tackle a censorship problem London has stuck him with – due entirely to a balls-up by the Foreign Office allowing commercial traffic to be opened up, unwisely and apparently without consulting the Censors. Advised him to tell London to get on with it themselves – it was too small beer to put up to the CCS.

Sunday 21 June 1942

The PM arrived back [from Hyde Park, New York, the Roosevelts' home] during the morning, but Richard was taking the first watch so I went with the Fields and children to bathe at the Archibolds' place which is a big estate out on Reservoir Road – the house built exactly in the style of an Italian villa – all surrounded by grass and trees, and a quarter of a mile from the road – a lovely place. Had a sandwich lunch with them on return and then went back to my quarters to change and go into the office for the rest of the day. But there was complete peace. The PM, Dill and the CIGS had had a private huddle attended only by Pug. A combined one was billed for 9.00 p.m., but no secretaries required.

News in that Tobruk has fallen – apparently with many prisoners lost. A bitter blow, that.

Went to supper at the Fields' – very pleasant out in their garden – a large crowd there. Had a long talk with [George] McGee [later Ambassador and Middle East expert] who is one of the US men on the Combined Raw Materials Board. We discussed the need for a truly combined and objective outlook if anything really useful is to be done.

Monday 22 June 1942

JSM meeting at 10.00 a.m. Fairly busy day. Ian and I went round to the Eisenhowers' after dinner. Found them supping in the kitchen, having had a lot of people in during the evening. Gailey (Ike's PA) and wife there also. He was delighted with the interview he had had with the PM that evening.

Tuesday 23 June 1942

Went down to Bolling Field at 8.30 a.m. and saw Eisenhower and Clark off by air for London. I was *very* sad to see him [Eisenhower] go – I shall miss him a lot. Meetings going on hard all day about (1) the possibility of moving a US armoured division quickly to the Middle East; (2) shipping and escort vessel construction (meeting at the White House, under the President).

Ralph Foster came out after dinner and showed us some of the [radio] 'soap opera' scripts introducing pro-British propaganda lines. They are extraordinary slush – *but* they reach about 20,000,000 listeners a day. Ralph has been very successful in getting in on that business, but it has to be kept *very* quiet, to avoid a violent US reaction.

Wednesday 24 June 1942

A fairly quiet day, as all the great were away at Fort Benning [Georgia] looking at troops. The Combined Military Transportation Committee flogged out another answer to the problem of getting the US 2nd Armoured Division to the Middle East – without touching BOLERO convoys. It would not arrive before October at the earliest.

The PM and party arrived back about 7.15 p.m. Went back to the office at 9.45 after dinner with Ian, Guy, Sir Charles Wilson, Lethbridge and Garforth at the Mayflower. Found Salter had been ordered by the PM to produce a better shipping answer for the Armoured Division. Tried frantically to dig out Wansborough-Jones and Grindle [JSM transportation and naval planning], but only succeeded at about 11.30 p.m. JSM meeting ordered for 8.45 a.m. and CCS for 9.30 a.m. (No orders for the latter reached Smith at all except through me!) Finally got a shipping answer out about 12.30 a.m. which Pug, Salter and Wansborough took along to the PM at the White House [where he was staying]. A hectic evening's work.

Admiral Cunningham arrived [replacing Little as head of the British Admiralty Delegation]. The news from Libya distinctly bad. We have only about 170 tanks left standing: very little artillery. Auchinleck [Commander in Chief, Middle East] feels unable to hold the Sollum line and prefers to fall straight back on [the Mersa] Matruh position, hoping to weaken Rommel thus by over-extension. There can be no doubt we have had a resounding defeat. The supremacy of the German 88 mm self-propelled gun and of their tanks has been demonstrated.

Thursday 25 June 1942

JSM meeting at 8.45 a.m., mainly concerned with the Middle East reinforce-ment versus BOLERO problem. Considerable alarm displayed at a note I had written yesterday, based on what Smith told me, to the effect that the US COS did *not* consider the Arnold–Portal Agreement [on aircraft allocation] in any way firm until the Planners and Transportation had reported on it. Got the FM to rattle off a quick note to Marshall asking the straight question. At the CCS meeting Marshall made it clear he would *not* have any cut in July BOLERO [troop] movements which carried all the advance parties. He offered instead to send 300 tanks and 100 self-propelled guns. This looked pretty good and at a subsequent JSM meeting it was decided to close with it if the PM agreed. They were to be sent in two sea trains – though it subsequently transpired that these could not handle the vehicles, so we shall have to provide the ships! The US certainly make *very* rash promises – I wonder how many of these vehicles will actually be forthcoming.

Very disturbed by Smith's reaction to the FM's note to Marshall about the air agreement. He said they [the US military] would feel we had bounced them by letting a copy go up to the President through the PM before the US COS had OKed it. Checked up at once with Evill who said Slessor had been assured by Arnold he was putting a copy to the President on the 21st. It later transpired that Arnold *had* done so, but had not confessed this when the agreement had been heavily criticised by the US COS. Only when driven into a corner did he admit it. I am afraid he is a *complete* twister. Anyhow the US COS now accept the agreement which is satisfactory. A slight irony was that Marshall and company were giving Hap Arnold a birthday lunch – complete with four trumpeters to sound off 'Happy Birthday to You'!! They are an astonishing race, peculiarly childlike in many ways.

Closed up fairly early and went down with Ian to the Mayflower to pick up Guy Stewart and Sir Charles Wilson before seeing them off. At dinner we warned them of the habits of the Secret Service people who arrange departures from the White House. They had brought their baggage down, but left their small kit in their rooms. As a result, they found themselves without it, and *with* their heavy baggage. Guy had no hat, jacket or anything! His own damn fault. Arrived up at the Embassy, which was the rendezvous, at 8.15 p.m. to find the CIGS fuming because there was no sign of a White House car at all! Finally an enormous limousine arrived about 15 minutes late (complete with radio telephone!) which took the party off in a cloud of dust to Baltimore. Very sorry indeed to see Ian go. It has been great fun having him here these three weeks, and I shall miss him a lot.

Friday 26 June 1942

Meeting of the [British] Heads of Mission with the Ambassador at 9.30 a.m. Halifax said the PM had told Litvinoff [the Soviet Ambassador] very definitely that all the questions of a 'second front' had been told to Molotoff [the Soviet Foreign Minister] on paper in London, and he would not discuss it further. No CCS meeting held to clear off our agenda, as the US COS would not meet in afternoon and ours were at the fortnightly Embassy meeting with the Dominions Ministers and Civil Mission Heads at that time.

Took Richard Coleridge to lunch at the Club. He agrees with me that Geoff Bourne has got a bit over his oats and is thereby losing his touch with the US Army officers. Went to a small CTP at Angus's [McDonnell] to meet Marlene Dietrich. She is not a particularly spoilt person, quite human, and with a sense of humour – not very strikingly good looking – it shows what good photography can do! Had to leave after a very short time, as I was due at [Bob] Brand's to dinner, with Chance and Tommy Brand. Much discussion afterwards on the need for strengthening the position of the Chairman of the Supply Council and forming a proper secretariat for it, as an outpost of the War Cabinet Secretariat.

Saturday 27 June 1942

Went out with the Smiths for a day's trout-fishing. Set off at 8.30 a.m., in a warm Scotch mist, and picked up the Manns on the way out to Catortin, about 10 miles beyond Frederick in Maryland. We went to a fishing lodge on the slopes of the extreme north end of the Blue Ridge Mountains, owned by a Mr Brewster, who is a tax lawyer and professional lobbyist – a very likeable fellow all the same. His place is a small stone bungalow set in a dense woods, beside a mountain stream. The house is very comfortable with all modern conveniences. Staying with him was Paul [surname omitted], a modest little man who is one of Washington's biggest building contractors, and a great friend of the Smiths. They fixed me up with a rod and waders and we got in an hour before lunch. I met one, but lost him. After lunch we put in about three hours – I got three, and threw back three more small ones – *great* fun. I was loath to leave, about 7.00 p.m.

Got back about 9.00 p.m. and had supper with the Smiths.

Sunday 28 June 1942

Easy day in the office. Lunched with McDowell and Holmes at the Army and Navy Club. Called in at the Coleridges' in the evening to leave them some trout. Found young Firestone (of Firestone Tyres) and wife there and two friends of his. Then went on to supper at the Fields'. Sat next to Mrs Archibold – an imperious old woman. George Wainwright showed some stereo lantern slides in colour – viewed through Polaroid glasses – very lovely effects.

Monday 29 June 1942

JSM meeting to go through the CCS agenda in the morning. Arnold is trying to make trouble over the temporary diversion of Spitfires from Australia to the Middle East – though the three squadrons in question were a free gift on political grounds from us – and he can't talk after diverting heavy bombers from India to China and from BOLERO to the West Coast [of America] without reference to us. Had a talk with Smart [the Australian military representative in Washington] in the evening. He wants to send the new Arnold–Portal Agreement to Australia. Asked him to hold hard temporarily, till we get London's OK. I urged on him the need to get his planners closely in touch with the US Planners over this question of the strategic deployment of forces. Beetle was as usual most helpful over it and told Vittrup [US secretariat] to arrange that they win there.

Tubby Lethbridge in to dinner. We called on the Wedemeyers [US planner, living in neighbouring quarter at Fort Myer] after it, and Beetle came round to see Tubby later, as he [Lethbridge] is to be Director of American Liaison in the War Office.

News from Egypt little better. We are falling back from Matruh, but casualties light.

Tuesday 30 June 1942

Slack day. Got my hair cut at lunch-time. We are still drawing back in Egypt, and are now on the Fuga line. The US, particularly the President, very windy, and fear Rommel may capture Cairo in 96 hours. I hope he *won't*. Thank God the *Queen Elizabeth* is safely through the [Suez] Canal from Alexandria. Bob Brand brought a telegram he proposed sending to Lyttelton suggesting a chairman of the British Supply Council *as well as* a representative of Lyttelton's on the Combined Production and Resources Board. The FM very contemptuous and suspicious that Brand is trying to keep himself in a job.

Wednesday 1 July 1942

Very busy day. Much chat with Pope [Canadian JSM] who is very steamed up over the idea (which appears in the new Arnold–Portal Agreement) that the US COS are responsible for deciding the strategic requirements of Canada! I explained that Canada must have either the US or the UK as a sponsor in CCS matters and for home defence she obviously came under the US. London very foolishly has not sent full copies of the agreement to the Dominions and are evidently dithering as to whether they should or not, as they won't answer an enquiry on the subject.

News from Libya little better at all. We are back on the Alamein position. The US are all most pessimistic and enquiring as to our plans when Alex and Cairo are captured. This defeat is going to make our task here extremely difficult. They [the US] will be even less inclined to fall in with our ideas than ever. Handy and Street [Marshall's men] whom I saw in the afternoon were very nice about it, though. I couldn't help telling them a bit about our position after Dunkirk to show that we at least had been through worse times already. Handy is not ready yet to consider taking an officer into his staff in exchange for the US officer in the London Joint Planning Staff.

Ellis (of SIS) [Secret Intelligence Service] called in with [Montgomery] Hyde to talk about Special Operations Executive [work] in South America – I am afraid it is a bake [evidently an unfavourable verdict]. Allen and Clark of the Combined Production Board Staff came up to talk to the Joint Planners about liaison arrangements.

Thursday 2 July 1942

A hard day. News from Libya looked no better and there was a rumour (unconfirmed) of the Alamein position being broken and parachutists on the [Suez] canal. JSM meeting at 10.30 a.m. Harold Butler who is the new Press Minister attended and made a good impression. At 12.00 there was a meeting of the 'Military Representatives of the Pacific Powers'. Marshall, Cooke (acting for King), Dill and Chou [Chinese representative] gave off the situation in their areas. This went on till nearly 2.00 p.m. – our nice lunch arranged for 1.00 p.m. was spoiling. Chou produced a map marked in Chinese – which no one could recognise at all. A very boring procedure altogether. After lunch the ordinary CCS meeting at which Marshall raced them through 13 items in 30 minutes! I never saw anything done so quick in my life! But of course we had considerable difficulty in sorting out the minutes afterwards.

Poor old Beetle in a hell of a stew because he can't find a [British] COS paper I lent him – thinks it may have got accidentally burnt, with some secret waste he was clearing away.

Friday 3 July 1942

A busy day again. Got Smith to realise the need for tying up together the Secretariats of the various Boards with the CCS Secretariat. Had Piercey (Combined Production and Resources Board) and Birley [Supply Council secretariat] out to dinner and discuss this angle.

Libya news looks more reassuring.

Saturday 4 July 1942

Quieter day. Went to Ronnie Bramwell-Davis's [JSM] wedding to Miss Hoblin – a nice girl serving in the WAAFs. A good show – large attendance with quite a few Americans in one of the Cathedral Chapels. Saw Sir Philip Mitchell about the Fiji agreement with the US: then went up with him to the NZ Legation where the FM and Commodore Parry joined us. Nash [New

Zealand representative on the Pacific War Council] gave Mitchell a run over the situation there. He [Nash] is a nice little man. I like him and Mrs N. very much, with their simple genuine ways.[29]

Dined at the Bensons' house as Paddy Beaumont-Nesbitt's [JSM] guest. Sat with him and Margaret Griggs, a Chinese expert working for Bill Donovan with whom I had a long crack afterwards. I fear Bill's ideas of what he is going to do, now that his 'OSS' [Office of Strategic Services] is designated a supporting agency of the US COS, are a bit too big to suit his new masters.

Beetle found the missing [COS] paper OK.

Sunday 5 July 1942

Took Joan Mainprice out to the Potomac and paddled up the canal in a very rickety and leaky home-made boat. Good fun. Went to a CTP at Arnold's at 5.30. Had a long crack with George (Ferry Command) and Mrs G. She is a nice little person with three small children who kept trying to edge into the party! Went along to the Smiths' afterwards with the Chous. She speaks English just as well as her husband. Then on to supper at the Fields'. Had an interesting talk with David Cohn about post-war problems.

Monday 6 July 1942

Rather a busy day. Went with Geoff Bourne to a private view of 'Next of Kin' to give an opinion on whether it was a suitable film for American consumption. It is *wonderfully* effective propaganda for British consumption, on security, but *I* think it shows us up as a bit *too* foolish.

Tuesday 7 July 1942

Smith and I held a meeting with Piercey and Gregg of the Combined Production and Resources Board secretariat to fix up arrangements. Left with Bourne and David Cohn by road for Charlottesville at 5.00 p.m. Went via Warringon, Skyline Drive, Stanardsville, arriving 8.30 at Farrington Country Club where we were staying the night – a lovely place in a most beautiful park. We were too late for dinner there so we went to a 'diner' for ham and eggs. Much amused at the artistry of the young fellow cooking who 'tossed' the fried eggs from his frying pan like a pancake. He made a boss-shot with one lot – and just ditched them to waste!! Shades of rationing.

Wednesday 8 July 1942

Went round the University [of Virginia] with David Cohn in the morning. Very beautiful buildings – red brick and white stone pillars: it was designed by Jefferson (who had a passion for serpentine garden walls) – all very spaciously laid out with plenty of grass and trees. We clocked in at the office of the Institute of Public Affairs, being met by a Miss Anne Yates, a very efficient secretary, and Hale, the boss, a dismal-looking cove, but quite pleasant. We then went up to Monticello, Jefferson's house on a hill about two miles out – a lovely old place with a lot of original furniture etc. in it.

Before Geoff delivered his talk on the 'New Strategy', Paul Thompson, a US Army Engineer, spoke on the 'New Tactics' – a lot of good stuff in his talk, though he was not easy to hear. Geoff was *good*, and very attentively heard. Audience of about 300, mostly old trout, as usual at such affairs. Major Silsbee, Army Air Corps, was the last of the three main speakers. He read a very boring paper at about 180 words a minute. Then followed Lovett, Public Relations Navy Department, who put out some violently pro-US Navy stuff (e.g. the US Navy were doing all the Russian convoys, with *some* help from the British). Finally Nickerson [military historian], who produced statistics to show that the expectation of life in the Army was far higher in this war than the last – very boring.

Had a mint julep with the McGees before dinner at 6.30 with the [illegible]. Large party. I sat next to Mrs Crow whose husband I met in Athens with Bill Donovan and opposite a Miss Wright – quite pleasant. We did *not* go to the evening session but went out instead to see a Mrs Derby with whom David Cohn was staying. Lovely old home up a [illegible] about two miles long. Her son is 'missing' in Bataan, poor soul. On the way back called in at the Alumni Hall where a general piss-up was in full swing – argued the point on Munich, Spain etc. – great fun. Topped off with a swim at 1.00 a.m. with the McGees. A very good day.

Thursday 9 July 1942

Left at 7.20 a.m., having been called late. Owing to a broken fan belt, did not arrive in the office till 11.15. Very pleasant drive up. Found Richard had had a very busy day indeed, over air transport of vital stores to the Middle East. Swarms of people to see me and much paper.

Friday 10 July 1942

The Germans are pushing hard on Voronezh [USSR]. Still quiescence in Egypt. Some stir caused by the PM wiring to suggest GYMNAST [the North West African operation] to the Americans. Smith told me that some suspicious souls, headed by McNarney [Marshall's deputy] I gather, say we are suggesting this because we have cooled off on BOLERO. This is what we feared and Dill had wired off yesterday as soon as news of the idea came in. Reported all this by LETOD to London:

> Understand most confidentially that Dill's opinion proved quite correct. The belief *is* held by many that Britain is going cold on BOLERO, and that these suggestions for side-shows are

smoke-screens to conceal this cooling-off. Jacob will remember how the CIGS's mention of possible side-shows at his first meeting with the US COS led many to believe that we were trying to wriggle out of BOLERO [see 19 June]. Although reassured by his later remarks the following day, this suspicion has again arisen. You will also remember that the leakage from London at the time of Marshall's visit was construed by some as an attempt to pass the responsibility to the US COS.[30]

On the previous evening Richard and I had had a long discussion with Smith, Vittrup and McDowell [US secretariat] on the Combined Production and Resources Board design for the 1944 [Anglo-American] order of battle [as a first step towards estimating the munitions necessary to equip the forces raised]. They [the US officers] are completely unconvinced that it is possible to make any estimate at all and intend to plonk down a requirement for a seven million [man] army complete with 100% reserves etc. everywhere. (This is based on hypothetical needs in case of a British defeat.) We could do little to convince them – though they accepted the proposed directive. Warned Jacob we must expect trouble over this.

Saturday 11 July 1942

A quieter day. The FM went off to Canada for three days. The Germans claim to have crossed the [River] Don [USSR]. Little more news from Egypt; we seem to be gaining ground in the north of the El Alamein position and Rommel is pushing ahead in the south of it.

Called in at an Australian CTP for a short time. They have a very nice place indeed at the north end of Connecticut Avenue in completely rural surroundings. Met a Mrs Southern there whose husband is Chief of Staff to MacArthur. Went down in the evening to the Morrisons at Welbourne, dropping Joan Mainprice at Middleburg on the way.

Sunday 12 July 1942

Had a delightfully lazy day. Mrs Morrison as hospitable as ever: she asked Joan Mainprice out to lunch and to stay the day when I told her she was at a loose end. Richard told me on the telephone in the evening a telegram for the FM had come in from the PM who apparently completely fails to realise that in US eyes GYMNAST and BOLERO are mutually exclusive.

Monday 13 July 1942

Left Welbourne about 10.00: went by [?side] roads to Front Royal: thence westward a few miles on the Strasburg road, then over the northern section of the Skyline Drive – very lovely. Home via Sperryville and Manassas. A glorious hot day, at a leisurely pace which gave me time to look at all the things I wanted to. Called in on Richard on return and found he had summoned the FM back. Apparently the President has seized on the idea of a Pacific offensive and it looks very much as if BOLERO is going to be thrown out of the window altogether! London can't say we didn't warn them!

Tuesday 14 July 1942

Met the FM with Richard at Bolling Field just before lunch. Went back to lunch with him. He saw Marshall about 4.00 after a US COS meeting. Marshall confirmed all that Coleridge had got yesterday from Smith. The FM sent it all back to the PM urging on him the imperative need to *convince* the Americans of our steadfastness to BOLERO.[31] Spent the evening with the Smiths after dinner. Beetle thinks that Marshall possibly raised the Pacific War as a bogey to frighten us, but didn't really mean it. Now however he finds, rather to his surprise, that several people *like* the bogey! The FM agreed that I should go to London at once.

Part IV: TORCH – Conception and Birth
July 1942 – November 1942

Introduction

Dykes himself called the last of the shorthand notebooks in which he scribbled his diary 'TORCH – conception and birth'. It is a fitting title. The diary opens with the dramatic meetings in London in July, in which Dykes participated, to try to strike some kind of Anglo-American strategic bargain. But the compromise document produced by Marshall, King and the British Chiefs of Staff ('CCS 94' in the diary) was no more than a delusion.[1] A limited cross-Channel operation in 1942 (SLEDGEHAMMER) was duly discarded, though not without a fight; Dykes offers a fresh perspective on the internal American debate, in particular the critical role of Bedell Smith. The option of a large-scale cross-Channel operation in 1943 (ROUNDUP) was retained, by simply postponing until 15 September 1942 a final decision on an operation in North Africa. This last operation, formerly GYMNAST, was now rechristened TORCH. Once ratified, TORCH would be executed not later than 1 December 1942.

As was to be expected, both the September and the December dates were quite unacceptable to Churchill and Roosevelt. Moreover there was misunderstanding between the Combined Chiefs of Staff themselves about what had been agreed and why. It was clear to the British that the postponed decision on ROUNDUP was a palliative for the loss of SLEDGEHAMMER. It was clear to the Americans that the decision not to do SLEDGEHAMMER permitted further transfer of resources to the Pacific. The British assumed the document to observe, the Americans assumed it to flout, existing strategic agreements. 'They were all at cross-purposes in London,' recorded Dykes. 'If the correct military decision was to go for TORCH they ought to have said so.'[2]

Washington's 'Pacific drift', perceptible but hitherto contained, threatened to burst into a fully fledged 'Pacific alternative': in the words of the controversial Marshall/King memorandum to the President, 'to force the British into acceptance of a concentrated effort against Germany, and if this proves impossible, to turn immediately to the Pacific with strong forces for a decision against Japan'.[3] This was uncompromisingly rejected by Roosevelt as US Commander-in-Chief. Not surprisingly, those involved later claimed that the Pacific alternative was merely a ploy, a gigantic bluff. Most historians have believed them.[4] Dykes's papers provide further evidence on this most sensitive question. It is interesting to find that Dykes and Dill, probably the best-informed Britishers in Washington at that juncture, both took it seriously – as indeed did the President himself, who went so far as to suggest altering the record 'so that it would not appear in later years that we had proposed what amounted to abandonment of the British'.[5]

And so it was left to the famous 'transatlantic essay contest' between Churchill and Roosevelt finally to resolve the issue, in early September, in favour of TORCH.[6] Finding a strategy had taken five months of maddening, exhausting, military diplomacy. It can be no coincidence that Dykes's diary entries during this period become increasingly fraught, sometimes despairing, sometimes vitriolic, sometimes just weary. We glimpse Field Marshal Slim's parodic allies made flesh:

> They are so difficult to understand, so unreasonable; they approach quite straightforward problems from such extraordinary angles. Even when one agrees with them on common objectives their methods towards obtaining them are so queer, so very queer. They even introduce consideration of their own national politics and hangovers from their past history, none of which have the faintest bearing on the matter of immediate issue. Their most annoying characteristic, however, is that among all the arguing and haggling is the astonishing way they seem quite incapable of recognising how sound, how wise, how experienced are our views; how fair, indeed how generous, how big-hearted *we* are. They even at times credit us with the same petty jealousies, narrow nationalistic outlook, selfish manoeuvrings, that obviously sway them.[7]

Yet Dykes did not entirely lose his sense of balance. Forwarding to London a report produced by the US Joint Intelligence Committee in late August, he attached a brief covering note. 'The American is a wonderfully naive person,' he wrote, with undisguised affection. 'He reminds me of the small boy who says he has killed hundreds of Red Indians in the shrubbery!'[8]

The diary culminates in the long-awaited birth of TORCH in November 1942, an event attended with a mixture of suppressed excitement and high anxiety. On Sunday 8 November, the day after the first landings had gone in, Dykes lunched with 'Wild Bill'

Donovan and talked about old times. In the afternoon they went to a football game. In the evening, at a small supper party, he heard on the radio that 'we are in possession of Algiers and Oran. Some scrapping on the Casablanca front. Spain seems quiet. It looks like a big success. Thank God.'[9]

Diary
15 July 1942 – 13 November 1942

Wednesday 15 July 1942

Got a quick air passage home fixed up during the morning. Geoff Bourne was *very* keen to go – he rather fancies himself as the one and only person who can put the American Case! At 12.10 when I was still in with the FM I got a message to say I should have to leave at 1.10, but fortunately this was later put back to 2.55. Dashed back to Fort Myer and collected a bag before lunch. Richard and Geoff came down to see me off from the National Air Port [Washington]. Very comfortable journey to La Guardia airfield in New York where I was met by an official of American Air Lines and taken in for a drink in their 'Admirals' Club'. Got away from New York at 6.15 arriving Montreal 8.30 where I was met by Patton of Ferry Command who took me out to the Ritz-Carlton where I am staying the night. Met Gordon Monro who used to be in M.O.1 [a Military Operations branch in the War Office] on the Montreal plane – he is now with Malcolm MacDonald [British High Commissioner; son of Ramsay] in Ottawa as a representative of the Treasury. Montreal shops look *completely* peacetime – almost more than Washington ones.

Beetle Smith after a conference in the War Department in the morning thinks that a Pacific offensive is beginning to drop back again in the batting.

American airline passengers are an interesting study. The businessmen are all very much alike – dressed in Palm Beach suits with woven straw Homburg hats carrying a spotty silk [illegible] band and all clutching a zip fastener portfolio: majority with correspondent shoes. One or two elderly and wealthy dames to be seen. Otherwise the females are more popsies – plenty of tits and peroxide. The 'air-hostess' is a great feature. They are very smartly dressed in a kind of uniform, well turned out and very efficient. They seem to be kept pretty well on the go all the time – serving meals, filling up immigration forms etc.

Thursday 16 July 1942

Met Archer (British secretary of the Combined Raw Materials Board) in the hotel at breakfast. He is going over to London for a month or so. Patton picked me up soon after 8.30 a.m. together with one of our pilots and a Norwegian pilot. A beautiful fresh sunny morning as we drove out to Dorval aerodrome. Went into the Medical Officer's place to get my oxygen mask fitted – then on to draw my parachute and flying kit. Patton very helpful indeed. Took off just after 10.00 a.m. in a Liberator which has been converted for freight and passenger work. Wilkins, a British Airways man, is the captain, total crew being five. I am aft with the radio operator and a young Canadian aircraft inspector who is taking a passage to Gander. Flying at 9,000 feet – lovely blue sky and sun with fleecy white clouds below – quite cold though. Wilkins tells me he was till very recently on the England to Sweden service, but that has now been taken over mainly by Norwegian pilots. He expects a good crossing, without the need for flying at oxygen heights.

The W/T [wireless/telegraph] operator, a North Midlander, registers acute disgust at the lunch provided. '[Illegible expletive] noot bootter and cheese again!' The caterer is apparently a woman who has studied diet and is convinced that these foods contain all the vitamins etc. that airmen want. But the W/T operator grimly wonders if she can keep her husband going on that diet!! Apparently the food on the return journey is honest meat, and plum cake! That is what makes the crews so particularly savage, when there is absolutely no shortage at all in Canada.

Came down at Gander about 2.45 p.m. (Washington time). Had a meal at the 'Eastbourne Inn' – a mess run by Ferry Command which is free for all transient personnel – all hands pile in, pilots, engineers, flight crews, WAAFs – an interesting place. My crew are all BOAC men [British Overseas Airways Corporation]. Met Cottle, the Group Captain, and got him to send off a signal to Hollis giving my ETD from Gander. Cottle tells me he hears from Brandt that Marshall's party are all passing through tonight – so I shall only just get in ahead of them. Got off from Gander about 5.00 p.m. Washington time (9.00 p.m. GMT). These Liberators are very comfortable – *very* little vibration and noise.

Friday 17 July 1942

After a very good flight at about 9,500 feet, we arrived at Prestwick at 9.30 a.m. (London time). Had a cup of tea and cleared Customs: then set off in a communication aircraft about 10.10. A very bumpy journey down, very low cloud and rain all the way. Arrived Hendon at 1.00 p.m. where William Stirling met me, and took me in to the Rag [Army and Navy Club] for lunch and a shave.

Saw the CIGS in the afternoon and Pug. Told them of the American feeling that we were lukewarm about BOLERO; of their dislike for GYMNAST etc. Pug surprised me by saying that he thought our COS should get the PM's OK before putting anything to the US COS – rather than present a united front with them. I told him that if *that* was the line, the sooner we broke up the

Combined Chiefs of Staff set-up and reverted to our arrangements with the French, the better. I think he saw the point.

Got the car from old Finch in the War Office and got down to Camberley about 8.30 p.m. Found all well there.

Saturday 18 July 1942

Attended COS meeting at 11.00 and gave them the form, stressing the American feelings (a) that some landing could be made on the Continent this year if we really put our backs into it; (b) that GYMNAST [North-West Africa in 1942] and ROUNDUP [North-West France on a big scale in 1943] are mutually exclusive. I gathered that they themselves had by no means made up their minds as to the right course. Portal is out for GYMNAST; Brooke wants to go ahead with BOLERO but *plan* for GYMNAST; Pound offered no opinion.[10]

Beetle Smith came in during the afternoon. Jacob, Hollis and I had a long talk with him and pointed out the strategic advantages of GYMNAST and the dangers of a ROUNDUP. If Russia collapsed, it would be a disaster to have a considerable force on the Continent, to be chewed up when the Germans moved back west: it might be that even if Russia were only neutralised. GYMNAST if successful, on the other hand, would be the best insurance for the Middle East if things went badly with Russia. Even in the event of a complete German failure on the Eastern front, it might not rule out a ROUNDUP late in 1943. *But* GYMNAST must include Algiers and Oran [Algeria] at least – not merely Casablanca [Morocco]. Beetle reacted fairly well to that idea, and said he thought the US COS might accept it, if our people put it over firmly enough. He thought the Pacific idea was definitely *off*.

I gather from Pug that the PM was rather hurt by Dill's reference to Chapter III of [Sir William Robertson's] *Soldiers and Statesmen* [excoriating the Dardanelles operation of 1915] in his telegram despatched just before I left.[11]

Caught the 5.24 train down to Camberley.

Sunday 19 July 1942

Spent a very pleasant day doing odd jobs in the garden and about the place. Dick [his son] came over from Wellington before lunch, returning after supper. It was a lovely sunny fresh day. W. certainly has the garden in great order. Taffy [the dog] distinguished himself by gashing his paw badly, necessitating a large bandage round the 'fetlock'.

Monday 20 July 1942

The PM querying whether the 'Combined Chiefs of Staff' can have any existence except in Washington! The British and US COS met the PM with Hopkins at No. 10 at 12.00 for the opening meeting at which the PM outlined the various possibilities. They then continued in a private huddle with only Mountbatten and Pug present from 3.00 till nearly 6.00, with apparently no progress. The US COS have not yet accepted the impracticability of a SLEDGEHAMMER [a smaller-scale operation in North-West France] this year, which all our people *have*. This is rather at variance with what Beetle told me on Saturday – that Eisenhower *had* accepted this. But opinion is at present *so* unformed that it is impossible to be sure of anything at this stage.

Took Beetle to lunch at the Rag and had to take Libby [King's staff officer] along too as Marshall and King stayed to lunch with the PM at No. 10. Libby is a dull and unattractive fellow – I couldn't get a private word with Beetle all day.

Dined together with Guy Stewart, Jacob and Price [Cabinet Office]. Guy disturbed me considerably by saying that examination of the practicability of GYMNAST was by no means complete. Had a long talk with Pug and Jo afterwards. We can see no light at all yet. They say the PM was terribly hurt by the Dill telegrams to say that the US COS wished to meet with ours *alone* and wished to be excused from accepting his invitation to Chequers for the first weekend. He felt that they were trying to form a 'united front' against him etc., etc.[12] Pug dislikes Dill and I had to defend the FM vigorously, saying that he had to put the US point of view. I must say I think if they felt all that, they should not have allowed the signal to go to the PM. Jo suggested it would help Dill with the PM if he occasionally sent him a 'Private' [telegram] with a little background information. The PM apparently loves them.[13]

Had a word with Robert Sinclair in the morning. He leaves for Washington very shortly, and wants to borrow Hayward [JSM secretariat] to 'settle him in'. I agreed to this of course. He is a nice fellow, and should do well in Washington. It has been decided that Bob Brand shall remain Chairman of the British Supply Council; Sinclair will decide after he has been there a little while whether he can take the job on or not.

Slept in the Cabinet War Rooms.

Tuesday 21 July 1942

Saw Ritson (Treasury) with Burgis about Hayward's promotion. He is going to let Humphrey Davies settle it with me in Washington. Showed Beetle the Cabinet War Rooms. More discussions with Beetle on GYMNAST etc. No conclusions have been reached on the US side. They *may* simply offer to secure the UK; send about two corps to the Middle East; and direct most of their attention to the Pacific. Beetle says that political pressure at home may *force* some action by American forces this year – and if it can't be in Europe it will have to be in the Pacific. Beetle took Ian, Stirling, Jo and myself to lunch at Claridges – the food amazingly good considering rationing!

Discussed GYMNAST with the Forward Operational Planning Staff. They seem fairly optimistic as to its practicability – and a report from the JSM has come in to say that [illegible] declares that there is a complete organisation ready in the French Army [in North-West Africa] to welcome an American expedition. Also had a good chat with the Joint Planners (Lambe, Guy [Stewart], and Bill Elliot). They are not yet firm in their minds. The one thing necessary seems to be to reinforce the Middle East as hard as possible, at the expense of BOLERO. Whether GYMNAST should be launched or not must depend on the Forward Operations Planning Staff report (apart of course from American acceptance of the idea!).

No activity much in Libya. In Russia, it looks as if Rostov will fall this week.

CCS meeting at 11.00 in complete privacy as before. The point at issue is *still* SLEDGEHAMMER – I gather they have not yet got on to major strategy [i.e. Europe or the Pacific, France or Africa] at all, but only on whether or not it is practicable to land and stay on the continent [in 1942].

Went down to Camberley for the night.

Wednesday 22 July 1942

Another CCS meeting in private at 11.00, at which the US COS discussed their memorandum pressing for a landing on the Cherbourg peninsula [of North-West France] before 5 October – with the object of (1) raising Russian morale, (2) getting a toehold for a subsequent ROUNDUP and (3) taking an offensive somewhere and thereby raising our own morale. Our COS pointed out the certainty of being pushed out or hemmed in, with the bad consequent effect on the morale of the Russians and the occupied countries. They refused to be shaken. The party met under the PM and Hopkins at 3.00, and the PM reinforced their [the British COS] arguments, repudiated the suggestion that we had given a firm undertaking to Russia to do SLEDGEHAMMER, and reaffirmed the intention to do ROUNDUP [the bigger-scale operation in North-West France] when favourable conditions occur. Marshall admitted SLEDGEHAMMER was off till *October*, but pleaded for ROUNDUP preparations to continue. King questioned whether ROUNDUP would *ever* come off!! (He *would*.) The Cabinet formally confirmed our refusal, so the Americans had to accept it and report home, as the President had ordered the SLEDGEHAMMER issue to be settled definitely before any other ideas are discussed. Hopkins is rightly anxious that no word of the *disagreement* should be allowed to leak out. We must keep a 'united front'!!

Went round to Claridges to see Beetle Smith at 7.30 and found Eisenhower, Clark and Gross with him. Poor old Ike is terribly fed-up with our refusal. Although he had felt, before leaving Washington, that SLEDGEHAMMER was probably *not* a sound move, he is looking at it now from the *tactical* point of view, of the landing primarily [as distinct from subsequent operations] – which is of course a practicable proposition. Our COS gave a dinner party for the US team, which may have helped to soften the blow a bit – they had cheered up quite a bit by the end of the evening. Beetle took the opportunity to tell Mountbatten that *Pyke must go!* I sat next [to] Vandenberg, who is having a pretty easy time as the air staff officer, and Gross (Transportation) [on Eisenhower's staff]. Gross had been very much impressed by the Russians in Moscow, though was struck by the gloom and fear in the place.

I had a long crack with Beetle afterwards. He is relieved that SLEDGE-HAMMER has been cleared out of the way, never having felt that it was really on. We discussed possible planning arrangements for GYMNAST, in case that is accepted. Had a talk with Jo on return to the Cabinet War Rooms. Urged him to get the Joint Planners to knock out a short paper on the merits of GYMNAST.

Had a long talk with Holmes and Stevenson in the morning about Dominion representation in Washington. Pointed out that, as in the case of the Arnold–Slessor Air Agreement, they might often get stuff in CCS papers which the Dominions Office [in London] were not sending to the Dominion governments. Agreed to let the War Cabinet Offices know what we were doing in this way in case of doubt, and pressed on them the need for Dominion Office telegrams to be repeated to us in Washington.

First news in of Auchinleck's attack in the Western Desert. The first objectives seem to have been reached by the infantry preparatory to the tanks going through.

Thursday 23 July 1942

Got off a full report on yesterday's decisions to Washington. Discussed GYMNAST planning arrangements again with Jo, Price and Stirling in the afternoon. We agreed it was important to get a Supreme Commander appointed as soon as possible, who must be an American to minimise French antagonism. Went up to the Ministry of Economic Warfare and had a talk with Vickers (Intelligence) about Bebb and the Combined Intelligence Committee in Washington. Asked him to leave Bebb there as otherwise Combined Intelligence might languish! He agreed that it might be necessary to keep [in place] rather a high-powered chap to do a comparatively small job.

A quiet day – the Americans apparently mulling over GYMNAST on their own.

Friday 24 July 1942

Went round to the Turf Club to have a talk with Oliver Stanley [Secretary of State for the Colonies]. He foresees a lot of domestic political trouble if Russia cracks or even if she does not and we don't open a 'second front' – mainly through the PM's intransigent attitude over the organisation of his own Cabinet. While there Beetle rang me up to say the US COS wanted a meeting at 12.00 – and he badly wanted a chat with me first. Went up to Claridges and rode down to the Cabinet Offices with him. Apparently the US COS don't altogether like *Pug* producing minutes of the meetings with the PM without one of their own people to crosscheck. Marshall wanted to make some amendments in the record. They wanted the 12.00 meeting to be a formal CCS meeting, with Beetle and myself to take a note. He showed me a memo they are tabling. They propose to keep SLEDGEHAMMER alive and to continue BOLERO and [?ROUNDUP] planning. But if there is clearly no chance of doing SLEDGEHAMMER at least by 15 September, they propose GYMNAST on a combined basis. They will wish however to take out a considerable number of air groups from the BOLERO force for use in the Pacific – and also to send a US armoured division to the Middle East in lieu of one of ours, in War Supply [i.e. British allocated] shipping.

Our COS accepted it with a few minor additions and amendments. Smith and I produced a revised version (aided (?) by Libby, who had oiled in to the meeting uninvited!). The CCS met again at 3.00 p.m. and we got a final version. Pug made trouble over it being a CCS paper at this stage – and we had to produce a version without that heading for our COS to take to the PM at 4.40. Beetle took him [Ismay] up pretty sharply on the contention that the CCS could only function as such *in* Washington, pointing out the text of the document establishing the CCS organisation. Pug got round that by saying that the PM was chairman of our COS [not strictly true] and that they could not therefore commit themselves till he had OKed a paper. Beetle unconvinced, but resigned! The PM accepted the paper and put it through Cabinet at 6.00 p.m.

Ian, Beetle and I dined together at Scott's, all feeling a good deal more cheerful. Beetle told me that he had had a hell of a job selling GYMNAST. I am quite sure that without him the party would have ended in a deadlock. When Ian and I got back we had a huddle with Jo and George Price on how the very complicated planning for GYMNAST (now TORCH) is to be worked. I was disturbed to find a good deal of belly-aching by the Joint Planners on the whole conception [of a North-West African operation]. Guy Stewart seems to be the nigger in the wood pile. It is obviously *vital* that any backing out should be done by the US side this time [after the British had, apparently, 'backed out' of a 1942 operation in North-West France]. Our people have certainly been slow. By this time a general outline plan should have been ready.

Saturday 25 July 1942

CCS meeting at 10.30 when arrangements for command and planning were discussed. No difficulties arose – the Supreme Commander for TORCH is to be US. To avoid competition between TORCH and ROUNDUP the same man is to be put in command of both. When and if a decision is taken to mount TORCH, he will take it on, leaving ROUNDUP to be carried on by someone else – probably the SLEDGEHAMMER commander for the time being, who will be British. Marshall and King seem fully determined to go full out on TORCH. No discussion on the personalities of the commanders themselves yet, but the British and US COS will see each other at Chequers [the PM's home] in the evening and they may fix something up then.

Beetle showed me a long signal from the President who had evidently had a sharp attack of strategy the previous evening. He was for combining GYMNAST with operations against Dakar [Senegal] and GOK where else. It had been written obviously before he had received the CCS paper giving their agreed proposals for TORCH. Hopkins sent him a message to ask him not to throw any spanners in the works by cavilling at points of drafting etc. His acceptance had not come through though by the afternoon.

Beetle and I lunched with Tubby Lethbridge (now a Major General). After that we cleaned up the draft minutes and Beetle left for Claridges to get packed up as they are all leaving tonight. Jacob was to see him off from Euston in the PM's train which will pick up Marshall and King from Chequers on the way up to Prestwick. They are due to take off from there tomorrow, calling at Iceland on the way over. We felt on the whole we had done a pretty good job. I sincerely hope no appalling snags will appear in the course of detailed planning which is to be centred in London under the Supreme Commander.

Had a long cag [talk] with the Chief of Combined Operations [Mountbatten] on the phone. As a result of some fairly plain speaking from Marshall (and even more so from Beetle) he is withdrawing Pyke and letting the SNOW-PLOUGH scheme carry on under Wedderburn and a man called Petter who is a designer, just flown over. He wanted to include in a note to Marshall a long extract from one of Pyke's waffles which accused all and sundry of 'intellectual dishonesty'. I managed to dissuade him from that, as being likely to do himself no good in the War Department generally. Judging by Beetle, Mountbatten's stock has slumped a bit in American eyes since his visit to Washington [in June, to confer privately with the President].

Caught the 6.24 train down to Camberley, travelling with old Parkin who is now a staff captain in Q.1 (Accommodation) [a Quartering branch of the War Office]. He has left censorship. It would have been far better for him to have stuck to his proper job as Librarian at the Staff College, where he would have been far more use. No chance to get anything for Winnie's birthday other than a book by Somerset Maugham, which I picked up at Waterloo Station.

Sunday 26 July 1942

Pottered around at home. Tidied up the flower garden paths and edges, and put the scythe in working order. Caught the 6.11 p.m. train up, Winnie seeing me off at the station. Met Father [a Justice of the Peace] at the Club at 7.40 and gave him dinner. We had plenty of time for a good chat. He told me he had just won a law suit against Roy, promoter of the Carbide Company, for his fees (£750).

Carver picked me up in a car at 8.50 p.m. and we all went off to Euston together. I got away to a smooth start on the 9.30 p.m. train for Prestwick.

Monday 27 July 1942

Very comfortable journey up. A perfect fresh summer morning when we arrived at Kilmarnock [Scotland]. The local train to Prestwick had gone but I got a lift. The RAF Embarkation Officer, met me and got me quickly through the various formalities. Got the BOAC Station Superintendent to warn Montreal to get me an onward passage. Had a long crack with the Medical Officer, a nice little Scotsman. Wrote letters all the afternoon and evening sitting out in the lovely little garden at the back of the mess. A *perfect* summer evening – very clear and fresh.

Took off in Liberator AM 262 (Captain Allen of BOAC as pilot) with a full load of returning ferry pilots, Polish and American, at 10.10 p.m. Flew at about 8,000 feet. Not a comfortable journey as we were close-packed and it was very difficult to sleep. I had a seat 15 inches wide and three feet long to sleep on. By resting my head on a ledge about two feet away I managed to get some sort of rest. Sat up in the aft compartment till pretty late talking to Oppenheimer, a very nice fellow – an American ferry pilot whom the US government allow to remain on the job working for RAF Ferry Command. BOAC apparently run their Liberators on a commercial basis for freight and service passenger transport. They certainly ought to try and fix them up a little better, as their ferry pilots have quite a hard life. Travel in a bomber with a full passenger load is certainly a grim and squalid business – such a mass of flying kit, parachutes, Mae Wests [life jackets] and junk of all sorts.

Tuesday 28 July 1942

Touched down at Gander at 4.00 a.m. (Washington time), i.e. 12 hours for the trip. Met as usual there by Mike Jefferson, 'the Mayor of Gander'. He is a Texan who seems to have some vague sort of a job as a 'despatcher', but whose primary function is to keep up the morale of the ferry crews. He has a great fund of Rabelaisian wit and meets and sees off every single aircraft – runs a system of fines for pilots out of which he collects a 'beer fund' for the maintenance crews. It is a queer hard life at Gander. We had breakfast in the cafeteria which apparently supplies it free for all – rather like the bunk house on a ranch – but a very good breakfast indeed.

Took off again at 5.30 a.m.; spent about an hour circling over Montreal above thick cloud. Touched down at last at 11.30. Jackson, the Station Superintendent of BOAC, met me and fixed me up for onward passage. After a wash and shave took him to lunch at the airport restaurant. He was 11 years with Siamese Airways – a good chap of the rather pushful Canadian type. Left for Washington at 2.10 p.m., missed connection at New York by a few minutes, but American Air Lines kindly fixed me up on the 6.00 p.m. plane. Arrived Washington 7.30 p.m. Richard met me and took me out to supper with them. Very hot and close in Washington.

Wednesday 29 July 1942

A very busy day. JSM meeting in the morning at which I had to explain and expound CCS 94, the CCS paper [on Anglo-American strategy] produced in London during the recent conversations.[14] They were all very critical of the apparent contradictions in the paper, but I think I put the thing in its right perspective. The FM sent off a telegram to the PM giving the conclusions of his talk with Marshall and urging the PM to fix up the question of command with the President at once. I am sure that is essential. Got him to remove a suggestion that Mountbatten should run SLEDGEHAMMER as it might embarrass the COS to have that put direct to the PM. Also got him to put in a little soft soap. (This was achieved about 10.30 p.m.)

Dined with the Smiths and went on with them to see Mrs Eisenhower who is doing the forlorn widow act in a very luxurious apartment in the Wardman Park Hotel. American women are not used to separation from their husbands, it seems! In the talk there I gathered that Beetle thought very poorly of Eisenhower's staff – it seems to want a lot of strengthening.

Thursday 30 July 1942

The FM telegraphed Dudley Pound suggesting Cunningham [then with Dill in Washington as head of the British Admiralty Delegation] for the naval command of TORCH. At the CCS meeting in the afternoon (at which Admiral Leahy presided for first time) TORCH was discussed. It was obvious that the US COS had come to see that a decision on the operation must be taken *now* if we are to be in time. Leahy said the President thinks it *is* all decided already. It is clear to me that they were all at cross purposes in London. Marshall said that it was the *British* COS who were so insistent on keeping BOLERO and ROUNDUP going that they wanted the date for deciding on TORCH to be postponed till 15 September!! His recollection is quite wrong as I checked afterwards by my London notes. It is, as I suspected, that they are being forced by the logic of events to realise that an immediate decision is necessary. The trouble in London was that our people felt the US COS were so keen on ROUNDUP that they did not want to kill it out of hand by pressing for an immediate decision for TORCH.

Beetle was much distressed that it should have turned out this way – if the correct military decision was to go for TORCH they ought to have said so. As it is, acceleration of the date will probably be forced upon us by the President and PM with consequent weakening of the CCS position. Incidentally he said Marshall and King had been brought very close together by the London trip which is a very good thing: also that poor old Stimson [Secretary of War] fought the President *against* GYMNAST while Marshall was away, believing that to be Marshall's line. When Marshall came back with the news of the complete change of front to TORCH, Stimson's face was completely blackened – he may even go so far as to resign, as he had a furious row with President over it.

We had a quick Joint Staff Mission meeting after the CCS meeting to knock off a telegram home urging the COS to press the US COS for an immediate decision. The FM saw the President in the evening, who was pretty gloomy about Russia, Litvinoff [Soviet Ambassador] having just been in.

Dined with Chance and Tommy Brand. Saw Beetle again late. He was very worried about planning difficulties in TORCH. His orders to join Eisenhower are suspended, but he feels Eisenhower badly needs someone to take a grip on his staff.

Friday 31 July 1942

Telegram in from the COS asking us to urge the US COS to decide *now* for TORCH and not wait till 15 September. Before we could do anything about it Beetle told me that the President had already decided in this sense. An agreed telegram was sent off to this effect, copy to Eisenhower. At lunch time we got news that the PM was going off with the CIGS to the Middle East at once to meet Smuts and Wavell and also Stalin, if he would fix a rendezvous! Poor old Dill had to postpone his visit [to England] fixed for tomorrow, thereby missing his son's wedding. The old PM certainly does get about a bit!

TORCH is catching on well here, though it will take a little time for the US Planning Staff to reorient themselves.

Saturday 1 August 1942

Richard Coleridge went off to London by stratoliner [aircraft]. Missed seeing him off through going to Bolling Field in mistake for National Air Port! JSM meeting at 12.30 to produce a revised draft of the Combined Planners' 'Strategic Hypothesis for 1944' which Macready and Cunningham objected to. Further meeting at 5.30 p.m. to pass the new draft and my covering telegram. The new document is certainly much better as it hopes for some positive progress during the next 18 months – but will the US accept it?

Dill went off to New York for three days in the afternoon. Had the Fields, John White, [Admiral] Noble and Ros [Mrs] Coleridge to dinner at Fort Myer. Auchinleck reports that he is definitely *stopped* in the Western Desert. The Germans are pushing ahead south-east of Rostov [USSR].

Sunday 2 August 1942

Flew up to Quonset Airfield [Rhode Island] with Strafford and Oulton [JSM] in the morning leaving Anacostia at 9.45 in one of the aircraft lent to the RAF

Delegation [at the JSM] by the US. Took the controls for part of the way. It was rather murky and visibility was poor. At Quonset is 52 Squadron of Coastal Command (Hudsons) under Wing Commander Leggatt who are being lent to the US for anti-submarine work at Trinidad. I had met Leggatt last in Gibraltar when travelling with Bill Donovan [in early 1941]. The squadron is mixing in very well with the US squadron there: half are leaving for Trinidad tomorrow. Commander Greer who commands the US squadron gave us lunch in the mess. Left Quonset at 4.15. Had a very good view of West Point, New York city and Annapolis [Maryland] on the way down. Gave Strafford dinner at the Army and Navy Club when we got back. Quonset is built on reclaimed land – a very fine place in Rhode Island where carriers can berth alongside. The whole place has been constructed within the past year, and is beautifully fitted up. The married officers' quarters are frame houses from a little village which was, *in situ*, moved bodily to the new sites!

Monday 3 August 1942

An easy day. Went down and had a long crack with Sinclair in the afternoon. Impressed on him the importance of the Combined Production and Resources Board squealing at once if the first rough estimate of 1943 requirements is beyond their capability – this will be the best way of getting requirements re-estimated on a rational strategical basis.

Had a long talk with Smith on TORCH planning, security and the cover plan. He is very set on the idea of cleaning up Japan once we have cleared North Africa as he does not believe we shall defeat Germany in 1944 if we spread ourselves into a new theatre in North Africa! Called in for another talk with him after dinner. He thinks he will probably be off [to London, as Eisenhower's chief of staff] about mid-August.

Tuesday 4 August 1942

Some progress evidently being made in TORCH planning, to judge from a COS telegram relating a meeting with Eisenhower. In the evening two more signals came in giving the British COS estimate as 7 October as the earliest possible date for Torch, and their reasons for going in so early even if not *fully* ready, in order to forestall the Germans. A signal also in from the PM, in the Middle East, to the President asking for Harriman to accompany him on his visit to Stalin in Moscow. The PM evidently feels the need for a little moral support.

American military intelligence apparently anxious that the Germans are preparing a striking force in France either to invade England or to counter in Spain. Suggested to Smith that this if true might equally well be designed to counter an invasion of France.

Had a chat with Lubin who is most anxious to get the Combined Munitions

Assignment Board to adopt a more objective line. He showed me a report indicating that the Air Corps had grossly underestimated when ordering spares for aircraft. He also told me that Clay on the [CMAB's] Ground Committee is fanatically pro-American as opposed to pro-United Nations – but that he might be brought round to a better frame of mind if judiciously soft-soaped socially! What a world it is! Had a talk with Handy, who I fear is still *very* far from convinced about TORCH. I hope he will play up all right.

The Germans are pushing on south of the Don, obviously aiming at the Caucasus oil, rather than a destruction of the Russian Army.

Wednesday 5 August 1942

Busy day. A lot of visitors. Dill saw Marshall who is apparently anxious that the Germans have a hidden striking force which they may use to invade the UK, when it is denuded for Torch.

Thursday 6 August 1942

Very busy day. Several urgent signals in requiring action for the CCS meeting. Our COS did not like the strategic hypothesis proposed by the JSM and preferred the Combined Planners' one, with some amendments. The command of TORCH was also raised, and a draft directive for Eisenhower proposed. JSM meeting at 10.30. CCS at 3.00. King in a very fractious mood. Leahy seemed to be expressing doubts as to the feasibility of TORCH. Dill and Cunningham remained for a private huddle on command (to which Arnold and McNarney stayed, *uninvited!*). A signal was sent off by the President to the PM confirming Eisenhower [as Supreme Allied Commander for TORCH]. The US COS have apparently got rather cold feet over TORCH – they are beginning to realise their inexperience in the face of the difficulties. Finished up about 8.20 p.m.

Friday 7 August 1942

Another very busy day. The Planners had a very stormy meeting in the afternoon with the US Planners over the strategic hypothesis [for 1944]. Two disturbing factors came out of it: (a) that they think CCS 94 [the document produced after the July talks] has changed the basic strategic concept of making Germany the main enemy; (2) that they are by no means enthusiastic about TORCH.

Saturday 8 August 1942

JSM meeting in the morning to discuss the situation disclosed by yesterday's Combined Planning Staff meeting. A telegram drafted and despatched. The FM very worried by it all. He wrote a private letter to Marshall telling him we were disturbed to find their Planners not enthusiastic [for the North African operation]. Grim telegram in from the Middle East (very private for the FM). Auchinleck is pushed out to command a new command covering Iraq and Persia if he will accept it: Alexander takes over Egypt and Palestine: Montgomery takes 8th Army *vice* [instead of] Gott who was to be appointed but was shot down in an aircraft yesterday. Anderson takes Alexander's place in TORCH. I fear the latter will be a bad blow to the Americans. Certainly the situation is pretty grim just now. The Germans are stepping ahead toward the Caucasus.

Had lunch with the Fields to say goodbye to Noble who is off to Ankara [Turkey] as Naval Attaché. Went for a few minutes to a CTP at Tom Hammond's. Then on to the Bensons' [Military Attaché] to dine. Sat next to a Miss Martin, a portraitist – a very intense and rather boring female; opposite Mrs Walter Lippmann and next to Major Towers, Air Corps Ferry Command, recently returned from the Middle East – very pro-British. Had a long talk with [the columnist] Walter Lippmann afterwards – quite a good chap.

Sunday 9 August 1942

Went in to work in the morning – pretty busy. Went to a flick in the afternoon with Joan Mainprice – 'Tortilla Flat' – very good I thought. Screeching wet till the evening. Seven and a half inches of rain has fallen during last 48 hours! We had three inches of water in the basement last night.

Monday 10 August 1942

Busy day. The US have been carrying out a combined operation against Tulagi and Guadalcanal in the Solomons [Pacific islands]. Apparently things have not gone too well, and they have lost three heavy cruisers and other ships from dive bombing, though the troops got ashore all right.

Saw a very good colour film of the Midway battle [June 1942] taken by US official photographers.

Tuesday 11 August 1942

Quiet day. Not much news in from the Solomon Islands. The Germans seem to be driving on hard towards Stalingrad and the Caucasus. Eisenhower's directive approved by the President and US COS, as amended by us on Sunday. Got my hair cut at last.

Wednesday 12 August 1942

Leahy told the FM that four cruisers had been lost in the Solomon Islands show, including HMAS *Canberra*. They seem to have cleared up Tulagi all right though. Had a busy day – just before I left the office a signal came in from the COS proposing two piddling amendments to the Torch directive. Dictated off a bender[15] which the Heads of Missions liked very much – they discussed it at a party given by Evill for H. P. Lloyd, who is just back from Malta. Later, on a point raised by Macready, the FM began to weaken. I took a redraft round to him at 11.00 p.m. He first drafted a new signal altogether and then decided to send nothing, but try the amendments quite casually on the US COS tomorrow. He may possibly get away with that. Their piddling points are an awful nuisance to us though and do the British COS no good in American eyes.

HMS *Eagle* reported sunk, presumably on a Malta convoy.

Cunningham is most worried about King's attitude to TORCH – fears he won't play very wholeheartedly. He has apparently asked for a very big naval force.

Thursday 13 August 1942

JSM meeting in the morning. Dominion Representatives in to discuss a US paper on the Dominion Air Forces. The US COS have still failed to put up an assessment of the *strategic* requirements of the Dominion areas which must be the first step to any determination of Dominion expansion plans.

CCS meeting in the afternoon. The FM put over our COS amendments to Eisenhower's directive very painlessly. Just after we came out of the meeting we got a telegram from the COS wanting amendments to a shipping order of priority which we had just approved – after hearing nothing from London for five days! I don't think it matters much. A very busy day. Dined with a Mr John Davenport and Miss McEnery of *Fortune* [magazine] who are writing up an article on supreme control in war. Educated them on the fallacies of the All-Supreme Commander, and on the subject of higher coordination generally.

Geoff Bourne arrived from England about 11.00 p.m. having been held up at Prestwick by weather for several days. Planning for TORCH is on a rather hit-and-miss basis I gather, particularly on the US side. Eisenhower has not yet got a very strong team except for Gruenther, his deputy chief of staff [later Supreme Allied Commander, Europe].

Friday 14 August 1942

Beetle Smith in a very edgy mood. They have had a signal from Eisenhower outlining his plan [for TORCH]. He intends to go for Oran-Algiers (no mention of Bône) and to strike at Casablanca from the land side. Marshall evidently feels this is on too narrow a front and too small a scale. I suspect they feel we are not producing enough naval strength. God knows we are pulling out everything we can for the show. Old Beetle got very shirty when I told him of Bourne's report that their planners had denied they had any plan for an assault on Casablanca at all! It is obvious he *detests* Bourne. I can't quite make out what is amiss. This is certainly one of our difficult periods!

Marshall has sent a curious reply to Dill in answer to his letter asking if the US COS still held to the previously agreed strategic concept of Germany as the principal enemy. There can be no doubt that they are turning more and more to the Pacific – and I gather they are sending more troops for the Solomon Islands – some are going from New Zealand. *And yet* Bourne says Pug speaks of Dill as a scaremonger for having reported the tendency!

A very busy day – hot and close. The long-awaited Malta convoy received a hell of a pasting. Only about five ships got in and we have lost several warships. If TORCH does not succeed Malta will be starved out.

Saturday 15 August 1942

Busy day. Had a rush at the finish to knock off a note for the FM on the development of the American swing to the Pacific.

> The effect on the Americans of the receipt of the COS telegram which summarised the Prime Minister's telegram to the President suggesting an American GYMNAST plus a British JUPITER [an operation in Northern Norway], plus full-scale preparations for ROUNDUP, was to rouse in some minds the suspicion that GYMNAST was being suggested because we were cooling off on the whole BOLERO idea. The COS telegram was the first intimation which we had ever received that the COS were turning their minds towards North Africa.

> On 13 July we heard from Smith that the President had received a memorandum from the US COS concerning the proposal for an American GYMNAST. In this apparently they had recommended the Pacific as an alternative theatre if BOLERO was not approved. The President had immediately called for details of their proposal. Smith was very concerned about this as he was afraid that it marked the real danger of switching all American effort towards the Pacific. The Americans were too set against GYMNAST which in their view was quite incompatible with any form of ROUNDUP.

> In default of any guidance from London you emphasised the need in a telegram to the Prime Minister [15 July] for convincing the American COS on their arrival in London of British adhesion to the ROUNDUP conception. In a subsequent telegram [16 July] you reported that as a result of a further talk with Marshall the President had apparently rejected the US proposals for full-out operations in the Pacific as an alternative to BOLERO. On 21 July Smith told me that as the US COS had made no progress with our COS about SLEDGEHAM-MER it was possible that they might simply offer to send sufficient troops to the UK to ensure its security and to send about two corps to the Middle East to reinforce that front. The remainder of their effort would be devoted to the Pacific since political pressure in the US would force some action by American forces this year, and if it could not be in Europe it would have to be in the Pacific. He told me that he gathered General Marshall was extremely concerned at the possibility of irresistible political pressure of this nature.

> The following day, 22 July, the US COS were formally told that the British Government would not agree to SLEDGEHAMMER. The disappointment among those I discussed this decision with (Smith, Eisenhower and Clark) was intense. The next day the Americans were engaged in producing CCS 94 ['Operations in 1942–43']. This document was produced mainly by Smith, who had a great deal of difficulty in putting over the idea of TORCH at all. CCS 94 was discussed on 24 and 25 July and finally accepted in its present form.[16]

Bourne told the FM that Pug had criticised some of our telegrams as 'alarmist' on this subject. Very foolish of Pug to talk like that, but I am afraid he has a personal zid [animus] against Dill.

Went round to the Fields' at 8.00 to go on to a dinner party with them. Dinner was at the Adlai Stevensons'. He is in the writing line somehow.[17] The party was mainly given for young Bingham who is the editor of a paper in San Francisco and is going over to London on [Admiral] Stark's staff for public relations. He is the son of Bingham who was US Ambassador in London some time before the war. Sat next to his sister at dinner – she is older than him – breeds horses in Kentucky – very keen on hunting – knows the Morrisons well and often stays there.

Sunday 16 August 1942

Got up early to see the FM off [to England], but the departure was postponed. Went down to the airport at 11.45 – still held up. Lunched with Dill and Macdonald-Buchanan [Dill's ADC]. Left them at 3.00 as the plane was still not ready: they had had to change one engine.

Tinkered at the car in the evening after getting back from the office. Dined at the Fields'. Pleasant party. Richard Coleridge [on a liaison visit to the UK] returned by train from New York, late at night.

Monday 17 August 1942

Beetle showed me in the morning a signal from Eisenhower giving his personal estimate of the chances of success of TORCH. He rates it at less than 50%, owing to the difficulty of clearing up the country quickly after the initial landings. I have an uncomfortable feeling that on that the US COS will ca' canny [go easy]. One of our troubles is that London and Washington are forming their opinions on different sets of data. Eisenhower has only sent in so far his *draft* outline plan, the British COS remarks thereon and his own comments on their remarks. But he has *not* yet produced his final outline plan. Signalled Hollis asking him to try and get identical documents exchanged. All this 'off the record' stuff with one lot of COS and then the other, but never the same to both, will get us into bad trouble. Beetle agrees with this.

Coleridge told me he thought Jo and company were very ununderstanding [*sic* – ?not understanding] of the position here. I am afraid they may find themselves living in a fool's paradise. It worries me a lot.

Dined at Craig McGeachy's. Leith Ross, John Foster, the Raymond Clappers, Lippmans, Miss Ward (*Economist*), Miss Tollemar (David Bowes-Lyon's secretary). The latter and I tried our best to persuade Mrs Clapper that it was *not* a good thing to evacuate all our children from England to America – not with much success, I fear. The Americans are *terribly* depressed about the war just now.

Tuesday 18 August 1942

Easy day. Beetle seemed much more optimistic about the chances of TORCH with the US COS. Very interesting telegrams from the PM to the President describing his meetings with Stalin in Moscow. He evidently had a pretty sticky passage, but kept his end up well.

Wednesday 19 August 1942

News in of a large-scale raid on Dieppe. Not a push-over by any means, we gather. The TORCH atmosphere is improving on the US side, I think. News of the Middle East command changes has caused comparatively little stir here. A busy day.

Thursday 20 August 1942

JSM meeting in the morning. A long discussion about Strategic Deployment [of forces] tables. Evill and the Air Staff are very worried about the continuous drain of US air forces to the Pacific, which Arnold is apparently quite unable to withstand. During the meeting Smith called me out to go over with him to Hull [Marshall's staff] who was writing a brief appreciation on TORCH for the President. Unfortunately we got there too late, but left the Joint Planners' and Joint Intelligence Committee appreciations for his edification and got him to send a telegram to Eisenhower asking for his shipping requirements.

Cunningham was summoned to the White House with King in the afternoon. The President insists that the North Russian convoys start again at once, TORCH or no TORCH.

Beetle has definitely got his orders for TORCH HQ [in London], leaving about 30 August.

Friday 21 August 1942

King in a most cantankerous mood at the CCS meeting – chiefly private US fights! We came through all right. Cunningham did his stuff very well.

Dill [in London] sent Marshall a personal message to say our COS did not want to raise the question of allied strategy, but merely to place on record their view that the previous agreement [Germany first, then Japan] still held and to reserve their position. When I took this to Marshall he pointed out the paradox and strongly advised leaving things alone.

News in of Dieppe [raid]. We apparently lost 2,000 in prisoners and other casualties out of a total of 6,000 engaged. Not a howling success, but it will put the wind up the Huns, and is very good experience.

Had Patrick Davison and Inglis Jones [JSM] back to dinner. Geoff came in for food at 9.00 to find we had eaten most of it! A pleasant evening.

Saturday 22 August 1942

Rather a busy day. Had long talks with the Admiral [Cunningham, acting head of the JSM], Macready and Evill on what reply we should make to Dill's message [on agreed Anglo-American strategic priorities]. As I see it the issue is whether Pacific diversions will prejudice TORCH or not. If *not*, then it would be better not to create a lot of friction by raising the main issue. A successful TORCH would engage large numbers of US troops and air [forces] automatically. Evill finally admitted that *so far* there was no evidence that we had reached this point. So I sent a private telegram to Dill giving our views.

> After showing your message to the Heads of Missions I handed it to General Marshall yesterday afternoon after a somewhat stormy CCS meeting at which Admiral King had been cantankerous. General Marshall said that to place on record the views of the COS at this juncture would start the fight straight away. If the British COS wished to raise the question at all now they must expect it to develop into a major argument on fundamental principles.
>
> From King's remarks at the CCS meeting yesterday, it is clear that there is a fundamental difference of opinion on grand strategy. We have not enough evidence at present to assert that diversions to the Pacific would in fact prejudice TORCH. Should it become necessary for this reason to raise the issue, the Heads of Missions feel that it would best be done on the Prime Minister–President level. This would give most chance of avoiding acrimonious discussion on all staff levels and would probably ensure that the short-term requirements of TORCH were fulfilled. It may of course be that the result of the Prime Minister's visit to Russia and the Middle East will necessitate raising the issue anyhow.[18]

I had to get this finally fixed up at the Admiral's CTP which he was giving for Admiral and Lady Curteis. (Curteis is coming out as C in C Western Atlantic.) Went on from the CTP to supper with [Admirals] Dick and Patterson [JSM], who also collected Admiral and Lady French, Geddes (Shipping) and wife, Galbraith and Admiral Bellinger (USN – an anti-submarine specialist). A very pleasant evening – after supper we played stupid round games like Buzz Fizz and the 'giant sneeze'! Quite amusing.

Sunday 23 August 1942

Had lunch at Silver Spring [Maryland] with Joan Mainprice and went to the pictures in the afternoon – otherwise lazed.

Monday 24 August 1942

Very pessimistic telegram to the CCS from Eisenhower. He doubts whether the resources allotted to him make TORCH a practical proposition. I wish he had said what more exactly he wanted to make certain of success. The telegram certainly gives the impression of cold feet. The naval implications as usual are the trouble. I wish he had put his troubles positively instead of merely negatively. I fear we are going to have a lot of difficulty over this business.

Keswick who is with Special Operations Executive here now and was in Chungking for eight months came to see me. He tells me Donovan's show [OSS] has no organisation at all in China and that they are very maladroit with the Chinese. I think it is only a question of time before the US are in just as bad odour with the Chinese as ourselves.

Tuesday 25 August 1942

A disastrous day. We had a COS signal in the morning to say that after looking at Eisenhower's final outline plan [for TORCH] they had decided that the forces were too light and that they now thought we should accept a later date and go for Casablanca concurrently. It meant getting more naval forces from the US. We were to make no approach, as the PM was going to do it direct to the President. The outline plan arrived [from London] by hand of General Doolittle in the morning. Got copies to the US side at once. About 6.00 p.m. we received a memo from the US asking us to put home a revised draft directive for TORCH, giving Casablanca and Oran only as the objectives – to be gained as bases from which to conduct a later offensive against Tunisia (800 miles eastward). This is a shattering blow. I fear our COS have bitched it by swinging back to Eisenhower's original plan after previously heading him off it. The US COS gave no reasoning, nor did they ask for any discussion. Cunningham *furious*.

Cunningham told me earlier in great confidence that the First Sea Lord [A. V. (later Lord) Alexander] had told him that if his proposal for supreme British Naval Command in the TORCH area was OK by the PM, he would ask for Cunningham as the C in C. That would have been fine. But GOK what will happen now. Are our COS trying to bluff more naval support out of the US? I was rather hurt that Beetle Smith told me nothing of what was coming though we were discussing the thing a few moments before. He came up later rather contrite. I tried to show him how hopelessly unsound the plan would be and I think he realises it, and feels that King *could* produce more naval force if he really got down to it. The only course open now is for the PM and one or two of our COS to come over here and thrash it all out. I wonder if he will.

We gather that you [the COS] consider (a) that we are fault in not having referred a matter of high importance to you before deciding on your behalf at the CCS meeting, and (b) in particular that we have acquiesced in greater importance being placed by the Americans on the offensive against Japan at the expense of the European theatre.

As regards (a) you will appreciate that with only one regular weekly meeting of the CCS, we are placed in the most invidious position if after nearly one week we are unable to report either your approval or disagreement. As regards (b) undue emphasis on the Pacific was vigorously resisted by our planners in the Combined Planning Staff meeting. We have left the Americans under no illusion as to what is our interpretation of CCS 94 with regard to WW 1 [the Germany-first strategy paper agreed at ARCADIA].[19]

Dined with T. V. Soong [Chinese Foreign Minister]. Geoff Bourne and a Dr Reichman were the other guests. Soong and Reichman (a League of Nations man) cross-examined us on the possibility of patching [reopening] the Burma Road. We explained our Middle East difficulties. He [Soong] was quite reasonable.

Lovely fresh sunny day. Went up the Washington Monument in the lunch hour. Fine view of the city from the top.

Wednesday 26 August 1942

JSM meeting at 10.00 to discuss what action we should take on the US proposed directive for TORCH. Went up with the Admiral [Cunningham] to see Halifax, who advised a signal home to give the background. Went to lunch with the Admiral and drafted one which I got off about 2.30.

> I am deeply disappointed at the way the whole concept of combined planning at this end has broken down over this whole [TORCH] business. It is, I think, largely due to internal difficulties on the US side. They do not like to air these in public, and hence prefer, not unnaturally, to settle their domestic dispute and issue a short memo on their conclusions rather than discuss the whole case in open court with our Heads of Missions. Nevertheless it is only by the latter method that free expression of opinion can ever be given and all the various aspects of a problem properly considered.[20]

From enquiries made from the White House about a signal later in evening, we gather the PM has gone into action with the President. Had a long talk with Aurand, Smith and Deane [US secretariat] in the afternoon. Smith has advised Hopkins to set up a Director of Requirements in each [Service] Department (like our Assistant CIGS), to avoid the anomaly of Somervell deciding both requirements *and* production.

Dined at Lady Dill's. The other guests were the Bundys, the Burdons, Mabel Brook & Geoff Bourne. [Harvey] Bundy (Special Assistant to the Secretary for War) is a very good chap. After they had left Nancy Dill, Mabel, Geoff and I played consequences – very amusing. Nancy D. seems only too glad to be 'young' with the FM away![21]

15Thursday 27 August 1942

Signal came in from the COS giving their views on the new proposed [TORCH] directive. Got this circulated as a CCS paper. The Admiral [Cunningham] told me that he is warned to take the Naval command in TORCH which is very heartening. He is nominally to be called home for consultation about [naval] escorts etc. Beetle tells me that on present form the President is likely to stand fast and not produce more naval forces for TORCH. It certainly looks as if the whole thing is going to be a flop.

Went to a large CTP at the [US] War College Club given by Beetle to meet the Deanes [Smith's successor]. Carver [Cabinet Office] arrived from London in the afternoon. Gave him some dinner and then went on to Bill Donovan's where I found the Halifaxes, Smiths, Sheehans and a Mrs O'Donnell who has a job in OSS. Vincent and Diana Sheehan are very attractive people. Bullitt arrived just at the same time as I did.

The PM's telegram to the President arrived in the evening, pointing out all the difficulties and dangers of doing Casablanca and Oran only, without reaching out for Tunisia.

Friday 28 August 1942

Heads of Missions met the Ambassador at 9.30. JSM meeting at 11.00 to settle the line of action at the CCS meeting in the afternoon when TORCH is to be discussed. At 12.00 we had a Pacific Powers party – nothing of interest. Marshall apologised for the undue prominence given in the US headlines to their small contribution at Dieppe and in the air offensive [against Germany].

The CCS met at 3.30 after the US COS had had a meeting with the President. A good discussion on TORCH, in which King showed himself as the immovable obstacle. The US COS are scared of being cut off inside the Mediterranean; and of a grand US effort being a public failure. Unless Casablanca can be tackled concurrently they won't touch it at all. King said that *unless ordered* he would send no ships from the Pacific at all. The US COS are clearly not interested in the Middle East aspect and look on the whole scheme only as a means of getting a bastion against the invasion of the USA from Africa. No conclusions reached – the President will send his own reply to the PM. Got off a signal home and finished the minutes about 8.30. Brought Wicks back to dinner. He tells me that the accumulation of trucks over here owing to the shipping shortage is becoming very serious. Yet Salter always says that shipping *can* be found for finished munitions.

King's attitude of refusing to discuss the Pacific as part of the 'overall picture' is very disturbing as it shows the complete failure of *combined* planning. One strong man with a small brain has sabotaged the whole system. Beetle and I feel very low about it all.

Saturday 29 August 1942

Got off another signal home in the morning drafted by the Joint Planners suggesting that the PM should urge the disastrous strategic consequences of the American plan. In the afternoon one arrived from the COS to say they had discussed the matter with the PM and Eisenhower and were now examining the possibility of doing Casablanca, Oran and Algiers only – Bône and Philippeville [now Skikda, Algeria] were too risky, and failure at several points would be bad. This was again another complete change of front. It certainly is very difficult here to be at all positive and consistent when they keep changing the line at home.

It does look from this end as though we are not quite clear what we want to do. First Eisenhower was boomed off Casablanca because there were not enough naval forces for the job. Then the COS said that they were very doubtful whether the expedition would succeed on the lines proposed in his revised plan. Now, after laying enormous stress on the vital importance of getting to Tunisia very quickly, they say that Bône and Philippeville are not much good anyway!

I fully realise how very difficult it must be at your end, and I can assure you that we are having a bellyfull here too. Our real difficulty is that we can never press any line very strongly because we are not convinced that it will not be reversed in the next signal from home. For example,

we are not clear at all as to whether you would accept the limited Casablanca–Oran idea in the last resort, or whether you would say that it is worse than nothing at all.
The Admiral [Cunningham] put up a magnificent show at yesterday's CCS meeting. The minutes give a somewhat colourless picture, but he gave away *nothing*. King was obviously determined not to discuss the problem any more than he could help. The most distressing feature is that neither his own people nor we are able to induce him to consider the 'overall picture' and come out into the open with what his problems are in the Pacific. This is fully realised in the US Secretariat, but there is nothing we can do about it. I am afraid it is the worst of having in such a high position a man of great strength of character with a very small brain. He certainly is a bastard.[22]

Beetle told me King was prepared to produce one battleship but nothing more. We must wait in patience for the President's reply to the PM, but meantime valuable days slip by. Had the Coleridges and Birleys [Supply Council secretariat] to dinner at Fort Myer. The Smiths were to have come, but Eleanor is in bed with a bad cold.

These are grim and anxious days.

Sunday 30 August 1942

Went swimming with the Fields in the morning, and stayed on for a sandwich lunch there afterwards. Went to a party at John Davies's in the evening for Donald Campion who is leaving shortly. Had a long chat with Aurand. He tells me he is being 'promoted' out of the Combined Production and Resources Board. He suspects strongly it is because he takes too objective a view – and not sufficiently an American one. This is very disturbing news indeed. I feel the whole idea of the 'combined approach' is fading right out. Sat down when I got in and drafted a note, saying I felt that the time had come for a real show-down with the US COS.

Monday 31 August 1942

No news in of what the President's reply to the PM will be. I am feeling very blue indeed about the whole position as time is slipping by so fast. Passed my note to the Heads of Missions who discussed it for two hours in the afternoon. I am to make a memo of it for Cunningham to take home when he goes. A very gloomy day.

Had lunch with McGee, and Milton who is trying to work out a Secretariat system for the Combined Production and Resources Board, and wanted to learn all he could about our secretariat system in London – an interesting chap. Went to a CTP for Leith Ross given by Stopford. Had a long crack with David Wills and Hutton (Food) about the article which appeared a day or two ago in the [Washington] Post disclosing that the US were insisting on taking their own special food for their troops in the UK, cost what it may in shipping.

Tuesday 1 September 1942

The COS sent us a résumé of the President's wire and the PM's reply: we got the former in full in the morning and the latter in the evening. The PM presses hard for *three* landings [Casablanca, Oran, and Algiers]. About 6.30, Beetle dashed up to say that the US COS were agreeing to this and drafting a reply for the President stating in full what troops etc. they were prepared to contribute. The President is curiously insistent on 'all-American' landings. Thank God it looks as if we are going to get somewhere at last – but it is pitifully late. I am awfully sorry for Eisenhower – he *has* been buggered about.

Wednesday 2 September 1942

Signal in from the COS ordering us to withdraw and cancel [at Churchill's instigation] all copies of their signal of yesterday! Telegraphed Stirling to tell him that it had been invaluable in preparing the ground yesterday before the US COS met the President. Why *won't* they realise how important it is to keep us in the picture – and quickly at that.

> The COS telegram has been duly withdrawn in accordance with instructions received late last night. But I think you should know how valuable it was.
>
> We did not get hold of the President's telegram to the Prime Minister until 11.00 yesterday morning. I had had a glance at the American copy about 10.00. As soon as the COS telegram came in I discussed it with Smith. He went into action hard and the result was that by the time the US COS were summoned to the White House to discuss the Prime Minister's telegram their staffs and particularly the War Department staff had had time to brief them. Without that previous warning, the US COS would probably have gone over to the White House and when confronted with the Prime Minister's telegram and the need for an urgent reply, would have played safe.
>
> About 6.45 p.m. we got our copy of the Prime Minister's telegram. The [US] staffs were trying to draft a reply to it without ever having seen a copy of the telegram. You must realise that the White House entourage are extremely cagey and jealous and will not let copies of these signals out of their hands. Marshall came back from the White House and told Smith at once to try and get hold of a copy of the message. Fortunately it had arrived just before and I was able to lend Smith our copy on which to work. If he could have been given a copy an hour or two earlier they would probably have got off a reply last night instead of this morning, thereby saving most of a day.
>
> When Smith arrives in London in a few days time he will doubtless talk to you about this and enlarge on what I have said here. He admits quite frankly that their system of circulating signals is quite hopeless and they have to depend on us for a great deal. That is why it is of such vital importance that we get early copies of the Prime Minister's signals. Smith said to me that a great deal of trouble has been caused by the fact that their staffs frequently have to draft replies to signals which they have never seen. They get only a rather garbled gist on the telephone or a recollection of one of the Chiefs of Staff who has had parts of it read to him by the President.
>
> I hope therefore that the originator of the COS telegram will be applauded as a saviour of his country and not damned as an indiscreet staff officer. [Marginal annotation by the recipient: 'It was worth it!!']²³

Had a look at the War Department part of the draft reply from the President. It looks pretty good to me, except that it appears to tie Eisenhower down in the allocation of US forces between the three landings. Beetle assures me this is not intended. Warned Stirling accordingly. Beetle has been an *enormous* help over all this business.

Broke off after a very busy day to go to a New Zealand party to meet old [Peter] Fraser, the PM. Fraser looked very well and was very friendly. Went on to the Smiths' to eat chop suey, cooked by Beetle – very good too. They are a grand couple. I gather from Beetle that Geoff is distinctly *persona non grata* in the War Department just now. He apparently caused great offence there a short time ago by picking up some publication off Gailey's desk while waiting to see Handy or Wedemeyer [Marshall's staff], no doubt from sheer thoughtlessness. But it has had a very bad effect. I shall have to talk to Macready about it – we can't afford to have any friction points just now.

The news from Egypt looks good. We seem to have stopped Rommel's attack for the time being.

Thursday 3 September 1942

JSM meeting in the morning. Decided to send off a telegram to the COS warning them to get a world appreciation prepared as we shall certainly have to take up the major strategy issue as soon as TORCH has been launched. Got it [cleared] through the Heads of Mission OK.

> It seems now quite clear that the major question of our basic strategic policy will have to be tackled with the Americans as soon as we see the outcome of TORCH. The issue will be whether our main offensive effort next year is to be concentrated against Germany or Japan.
>
> If we are not to be caught unprepared for high-level discussion of this nature, which would presumably take place in November or December [1942], it is essential that there should be in existence a well-documented world appreciation on which our case would be based. The final aim must be to produce an agreed strategic policy which means exactly the same to both sides. We suggest very strongly that for tactical reasons it would be unwise to start with the assumption that our basic agreed strategy remains unchanged, and merely to produce reasons to support this. It would be better to show quite clearly that we are approaching the problem with a completely open mind.[24]

The President's reply to the PM came in during the evening. It is terribly restrictive, e.g. he insists American troops do all the first assaults leaving no combat ships for us at all. As they have no troops properly trained in assault landings this is taking a very big risk. However Murphy [US Chargé d'Affaires preparing the way with the French] thinks it will be a push-over as far as the French troops are concerned. Finished off a memo on the present deficiencies of combined planning which Cunningham intends to take back to London with him.

> The truth is that in spite of much good will and many excellent personal relations from the highest level downwards, we are not achieving in the Combined Chiefs of Staff and Combined Planning Committees that frank discussion on difficult matters of policy that is indispensable to the proper conduct of affairs. This attitude of mind is the biggest obstacle we have to overcome. Orders from the highest quarters will not produce good will and a real desire to cooperate; it may well be that the removal of some incompatible personalities will be found essential.
>
> Somehow or other we must work out between the two nations a common aim. For a short time

we had something like it in BOLERO, and things went comparatively smoothly while this plan held the field from April to July. Now we lack a common aim. It will emerge only from the clear definition of combined strategic policy, interpreted in the same way by both sides. Once this is achieved, it will be merely a question of give and take on both sides and of reconciling our different outlooks as to the way this aim should be reached. It may be too much to hope that we shall walk exactly in step with the US, for though they have the same basic tongue as our own, they differ from us widely in outlook, temperament and methods. But if we cannot walk in step, we must at least travel the same road and not take divergent courses.[25]

The naval staff here are completely in the dark as to what US naval forces are to be provided [for TORCH]. King's paragraph in the President's reply merely said that none would be provided other than those available in the Atlantic and others whose completion is being expedited – a nice helpful remark. I am surprised he got that past the President. Cunningham is going to tackle him tomorrow. King has apparently completely repudiated his assistant chief of staff who had worked out an agreement with Patterson [JSM] over the split of escort vessels between the UK and the US. He *is* an old shit – he simply won't play at all.

Dined with Bill Donovan. While I was at Bill's, Admiral Cunningham rang up to say that he hears that Dill, Eisenhower or Clark, Ramsay and Mountbatten are coming over to try and get this TORCH plan squared up, leaving tomorrow! Rang Beetle and told him Cunningham would have to cancel his air passage on Saturday!! Beetle says *he* will go! Bill D. has a queer idea that we should do TORCH by getting the French to *invite* us in: I think this is unduly optimistic, though I agree we should exploit SOE to the full in all this.

Friday 4 September 1942

Repeat of the PM's reply to President's signal came during the morning preceded by a DOTEL which gave us the form. As I thought, they are badly scared by the overweighting of Casablanca compared with Algiers (three and a half to one) in combat-loaded troops. Beetle assures me however that this is more apparent than real. The Americans apparently fear that Eisenhower will be overborne by the PM and they therefore insist on most weight being given to Casablanca. The PM also asked that Eisenhower or Clark, Mountbatten and Ramsay should come over. The President refused to have Eisenhower or Clark back and gave a very tepid acceptance to Mountbatten.

Eisenhower, prompted by the Admiralty, had sent to ask precisely what US naval forces were being provided. Marshall had to go and screw it out of King; but in the evening Deane showed me a draft Presidential telegram saying that three battleships, one [aircraft] carrier, two auxilliary carriers, some cruisers and 40 destroyers would be sent. Beetle told me that they had just had news in that another US carrier has been put out of action in the Pacific and a big combat-loaded ship sunk. However King is sticking to his bargain – so far.

CCS meeting in the afternoon. More about Dominion Air Forces, but the Australian, New Zealand and Dutch East Indies representatives spoke up well – Goddard (NZ) particularly. Quite useful conclusions were reached.

The difficulties of a 'Combined' combined operation certainly are terrific. All my worst fears that I had last January when a combined GYMNAST were first mooted are more than fulfilled. The President is now dictating Eisenhower's plan. The PM, I am sure, is giving plenty of advice too – poor old Ike! Meanwhile precious days slip by and planning slowly proceeds with continued wild goose chases. I must say I think we should be very ill-advised ever to try and repeat this performance but GOK how we shall ever do a combined ROUNDUP. It would strain good will on both sides to the utmost. I only pray that French opposition will be so light that TORCH will succeed in spite of the assault being carried out entirely by untrained US troops.

Saturday 5 September 1942

Very busy day. Finished the revised draft of a memo on Combined Planning, and got off several signals home. The PM telegraphed the President to say all was well and that they were pushing ahead hard with the plan [for TORCH]. I hear the US are pushing off one regimental combat team to the UK post-haste, so they seem to be playing up well. News in from London that [Admiral] Ramsay [Flag Officer Commanding Dover][26] only will be coming over with some subordinate naval and combined operations planners. No word of Dill's return [from London] in spite of yesterday's warning order.

Finished about 7.30 and took Joan Mainprice to see 'Mrs Miniver'. It certainly is a good film and seemed to impress the audience.

Sunday 6 September 1942

Saw dear old Beetle off [to London] at 9.00 a.m. at the National Air Port, by stratoliner 'Cherokee'. Julius Holmes and Burgess [US secretariat] went with him. A sad parting for me. Took Eleanor [Smith] back and stayed for a cup of coffee with her. She feels his leaving very much as they have no children.

Monday 7 September 1942

A quiet day. Ramsay's party are still at Prestwick having made a false start and returned with engine trouble. Went down with Strafford and Grindle [JSM] in the morning to look at one of the new Lancasters [bombers] at Bolling Field. They are fine aircraft – a better job than the [B-17 'Flying'] Fortress, I should judge.

Evill has fixed up to go to Ottawa on Wednesday and is going to take me with him for a few days in Canada. Rang up Gordon Monro [British High Commissioner's staff] and warned him I was coming. Dined at the Embassy. Walter Monckton [Director General of the British Propaganda and Information Service, Cairo], Bill Donovan, McCloy and a Major Lockett were there beside the Halifaxes. A pleasant party. Much talk on the value of the air offensive. McCloy is sold on the daylight bombing idea. The Americans find it hard to understand that Rouen is quite a different thing from the Ruhr! Bill was all for throwing out de Gaulle who he thinks will become more and more a thorn in our sides. He certainly *is* a problem child.

News from the Middle East is good. Rommel seems to have been pushed right back with very considerable losses in tanks and equipment. The consignment of Sherman Tanks has arrived in Egypt and been unloaded in record time. Stalingrad still holds. Halifax gave us an amusing account of his tea party with Mrs Roosevelt and the Russian guerrilla girl who claims to have killed 309 Germans.

Tuesday 8 September 1942

A quiet day. No sign of Admiral Ramsay and party yet. Evill came in about 4.00 and told me that the weather tomorrow would almost certainly be too bad to fly up to Ottawa and suggested we should go up by train at 6.00 p.m. instead. Got my kit packed and caught the train comfortably. Arrived New York about 10.30 and went across to Grand Central Station. Could see nothing of the city as it is very dimly lit now. Had a drink on the Montreal train with Wing Commander Roberts who is returning to England from a job in the USA. We were joined by a little sergeant air gunner RAF who is American and joined up with the RAF three years ago. He is over here now for a spell of duty. It is amusing to see an RAF uniform with USA on the shoulder! He refused to revert to the US Services.

Wednesday 9 September 1942

Arrived Montreal 8.30 a.m. on a very cool grey day. Went with Evill to Bowhill's [RAF Ferry Command] flat and met him and Lady B. who is a Flight Lieutenant in the WAAF. A nice person. They left us to have breakfast. Went out to Dorval aerodrome about 10.30. After doing some business with Bowhill, we had a look round the station. They have very good arrangements for briefing the ferry pilots – a big map with all the navigation aids on it, and all the convenient stars for star sights shown for each bit of the flight. Also very good form-at-a-glance records of crew availability. Went out to lunch with Bowhill at the River and Forest Club – a very nice small country club house on the St Lawrence close to the aerodrome. Had some excellent sherry! The place was completely empty except for ourselves. Flew over to Ottawa in a Hudson in low cloud and rain, arriving about 3.00 p.m. McKean who heads the RAF Training Liaison Mission met us, and ran me in to the Chateau Laurier Hotel. Walked down to see Gordon Monro in the afternoon – through pouring rain. Ottawa streets might be those of an English town in the Midlands, in this rain – quite different from Washington – not nearly so grandiose. It is far more like England than America.

Thursday 10 September 1942

Called on General Stewart [Chief of the Canadian General Staff] at 10.30 and stayed talking to him all morning. He is rather keen to try the experiment in Canada of having one supreme commander with an independent joint staff, having the three COS each running their own show. They have apparently decided to drop the idea of being represented on the Combined Munitions Assignment Board – they are going to allocate their own production in Ottawa, more or less as they do now. He is bothered at the prospect of Canadian troops not getting any fighting till late next year at the earliest. I gathered he is not privy to TORCH so could say nothing about that. He is a very attractive personality.

Friday 11 September 1942

Got up late. Went up the Peace Tower in the Parliament Building – a fine view of the city and surrounding country as it was bright and sunny. Lunched with Stewart and his deputy (Gibson), a non-Regular [Army officer] – quiet sort of chap, but I should think quite good. Went out to the High Commissioner's office in the afternoon and had a long chat with Malcolm Macdonald on his verandah in the sun. He said the Canadians were very huffy so far as the JSM is concerned. He made one interesting point about Anglo-American co-operation – that *we* must take the greatest care to foster close relations with all the European countries if we are to have any hope of being able to balance the US and Russia at the peace table and after.

Richard Coleridge called up to say that Dill was on his way back. They have apparently had a spot of trouble over today's CCS meeting – the Combined Planners' papers seem to have been bitched up by that bloody little man Cooke [US Navy chief planner][27] who doesn't attend Combined Planning Staff meetings and then throws his representative overboard.

Caught the 5.45 train to Montebello [Quebec], and put up at the Siegnory Club. It is a *vast* imitation of 'ye olde logge cabin'. The main lounge etc. is shaped like a circus tent, supported on a stone chimney (taking in six huge fireplaces). All done in round timber, except the floor joints which are the same timber carefully axed to make them look as if they were cut from the rough. The whole thing is unutterably phoney. I am shocked to see the number of young male servants, orchestra etc. The inhabitants are almost exclusively big businessmen – and very dull at that they look.

Saturday 12 September 1942

Went out for a two and a half hours' ride (on John Peel) – a very good hack. The trees are just beginning to turn – some of the colours are marvellous. They must be a sight in a fortnight's time – every colour from blood red through the pinks to yellow and brown. Raining all afternoon. Walked down to the village later – *completely* French in appearance. The shopkeepers hardly understand English at all.

Feeling mouldy. I have got a cold coming on – or passing over! To bed early. I am fed up with this place, it is dull, pompous and boring. No doubt better weather would have given me a better memory of Canada – but I leave it with no regrets. I should have liked to see it outside the city and this suburban monstrosity of a so-called Club.

Sunday 13 September 1942

Left after a late breakfast, by the 11.10 train. Walked down to the station – a lovely fresh sunny morning. Picked up my tickets and had lunch in Ottawa. When I joined the 4.10 train for Montreal I found old Mackenzie King [Canadian Prime Minister], talking to an old lady who was making the journey. As he got out he asked me to introduce myself. She was Princess Cantacuzele, widow of a Russian, granddaughter of old General Grant. She lived in Russia 20 years. I thought her rather a pompous and imperious old lady to start with but she improved on further acquaintance. She is practically blind. We discussed the war and many things. She is very bitter against FDR [Roosevelt] and the New Deal – I felt she classed them almost with Lenin, Trotsky and Stalin!

Monday 14 September 1942

Arrived Washington 1.30 p.m. Richard met me at the station. I gather he has had quite a sticky time while I have been away. Trouble with the Combined Planners owing to Cooke throwing overboard his representative on two papers for which he had not attended Combined Planning Staff meetings. Deane was asked to put the point to Leahy, but it ended in *him* being told to see Cooke instead of Leahy taking direct action. Curtin [Australian Prime Minister] has sent in a long bleat to the President which he turned over to the CCS for an answer. The Combined Planners met yesterday to concoct a reply. Curiously enough the US Planners reaffirm our basic strategic policy as first priority for the defeat of Germany. The FM had arrived back on Saturday. He wanted to send a very optimistic telegram on this point [of strategic priorities], but I pointed out that Cooke had perforce to stop all BOLERO landing craft: so we toned it down a bit. Admiral Ramsay arrived in the *Queen Elizabeth*.

Feeling rather depressed and fed-up with everything.

I am afraid that we have given you the impression that both you and Richard have become too 'American minded'. That you acquire something of this in Washington is, of course, inevitable. All we have seen is the first glimmerings of it and tried to apply the corrective. Perhaps we have done this too drastically.[28]

Tuesday 15 September 1942

Had a long talk with the FM on combined planning in the afternoon. He does not seem disposed to take much action on the memo which I got through the Heads of Missions [see 3 September], but will discuss the idea of a Combined Strategic Committee with Leahy and Marshall. He seems rather fed-up with Geoff Bourne – it is time Geoff went home before he loses his glamour. Deane is keen on the idea of a high-powered Combined Strategic Committee, I find. The Combined Planners have reached a deadlock on the landing craft question. The US view is that if ROUNDUP is off, production should be switched from landing craft to escort vessels.

Wednesday 16 September 1942

Busy day. A telegram from the President to the PM said that Bourne was holding up detailed planning of the arrangements for the US to take over the Persian railway! The fact is that the US planners insist that control of traffic should be in *their* hands and not of our C in C – an impossible position for Wilson [British commander in Persia and Iraq] of course, and one which we could not accept. Telegraphed a full statement of the position to the COS.[29]

Thursday 17 September 1942

JSM meeting in the morning. Rather a gloomy one as we are up against the US on nearly every paper that comes up. Took Abraham to lunch. He had a long crack with Wedemeyer [Marshall's planner] about the Persian Railway control difficulty and has I think got him to produce a reasonable solution, which we shall be able to accept.

Spoke to Deane about the State Department's proposal for a big US Mission to the Middle East. He seemed very surprised and was going to find out how the State Department had butted in, particularly as they said in their *aide-mémoire* that it was the US COS scheme – which Deane says it is not. Also saw Handy and tried to get him to be reasonable about Persian Railways and about landing craft despatches to England. He seems very bothered about the Solomons position where the Japs are hitting back hard.

Trouble over a 'clear' [uncoded] cable between United Press men in London and Washington talking about the probability of a show in North Africa coming off. Our censors should not have let it go out from London. This came on top of an equally bad despatch from a London correspondent of the [*Washington*] *Star* yesterday. Cabled the COS protesting. Took Joan Mainprice out to dinner. She seems very floppy and run-down these days and I shall send her up to see a doctor tomorrow.

The Germans reported to be well into Stalingrad.

Friday 18 September 1942

Abraham did some good work with Wedemeyer over the Persian Railway business. He talked to him in the morning and in the afternoon was asked to go over as Wedemeyer was producing a revised draft, acceding to our principles of control etc. Abraham was able to work in one or two vital points.

The CCS meeting was a good one. King quite genial. No solution produced to cover the allocation of landing craft for BOLERO. We had a hell of a job with the minutes afterwards. Deane will not stick his neck out like old Beetle used to.

Saturday 19 September 1942

Got up early and saw Cunningham and Dick [Cunningham's chief of staff] off. Very sorry to see the old boy go. He is a *grand* fellow. Trouble with our planners over Wedemeyer's draft which is certainly verbose and obscure. They produced a redraft which Wedemeyer told Bourne in the afternoon he would not discuss at all – it was take it or leave it! Macready tackled Handy on it and got out a draft telegram of instructions to Wilson, which Handy accepted – though it does not coincide with Wedemeyer's draft. One or two other troublesome things turned up and I got away late.

Sunday 20 September 1942

Rose late. Swam with the Fields – had lunch with them. Went up to see Ralph Foster in the Walter Reed [Military] Hospital. Wedemeyer demanded a Combined Planning Staff meeting at 2.30. When Bourne went over Wedemeyer still maintained that his draft was 'untouchable', but wanted our telegram altered!! He confirmed this on the telephone to the Secretariat in Coleridge's presence! Dined at the Fields'. A pleasant evening; but I am *deeply* depressed over this impasse on the Combined Planning Staff.

Monday 21 September 1942

Saw Deane again over the Combined Planning jam – pointed out the difficulties of Wedemeyer's draft. He agreed and tackled Wedemeyer who agreed to one or two changes. Our planners were naturally very aggrieved that

Wedemeyer will not work through them at all. I fear Bourne is an irritant – though Wedemeyer is being quite impossible over all this. The planners discussed it with the FM in the evening and went over to see Wedemeyer afterwards. The FM intends to tackle Marshall on the subject. We can't go on like this.

> If either side has to come to a planning meeting with a so-called draft paper which they are not empowered, or willing, to alter in any way whatsoever, the whole purpose of combined planning is lost. The object of discussion at such meetings is for each party to bring out points which may have been overlooked by the other, and to clear up doubts and ambiguities. A draft which may be perfectly intelligible to an Englishman may be obscure to an American. Only by going through each point as it arises, agreeing on the object which it is desired to achieve, and then drafting the paper in such a way that it will mean exactly the same to all parties concerned, can useful working documents be produced.
>
> It is interesting to note that in the particular case of the Persian railway paper the final result, after seven days' acrimonious discussion, is to all intents exactly the same as was produced by a combined sub-committee who approached the problem with an open mind. The gradual narrowing of the gap between the US and British [Planners'] positions was not effected within the Combined Planning organisation at all. It was done by roundabout methods through General Macready, Colonel Abraham [visiting British transport planner for the Middle East], and the Secretariat.
>
> Rightly or wrongly, a system of work for the Combined Planners was adopted at the beginning of this year, which is to all intents and purposes a British system. It has broken down, however, because it does not fit in with the American system of staff work. In my view it is the attempt in Washington by the Combined Planners to serve up, on every occasion, a paper which they are certain their superiors will accept in every particular that has caused the combined planning system to break down.[30]

The Germans well into Stalingrad. Munich bombed. Lovely fresh bright day – but I despair of the Combined Planning set-up – very depressing.

Tuesday 22 September 1942

Found that the planners had at last got agreement with Wedemeyer, Handy being present at their meeting with him last night. He had been pretty offensive, though. Drafted a paper to the FM on whole subject of Combined Planning. The snags are (1) overwork of the US Planners; (2) their completely rigid riding orders. Johnny Grindle [JSM naval planner] very understanding and helpful on the whole subject. It is clear however that Strafford and Bourne [RAF and Army planners] enrage Wedemeyer.

> Personalities are a good deal of the trouble. Wedemeyer can be extraordinarily offensive and throw in the teeth of our people Burma, Singapore and other failures, call us the most ungrateful people on earth, and say he always has a witness present when he has any discussion with a British officer, etc., etc.[31]

A long signal in from the PM to the President asking for a forecast of BOLERO movements, and suggesting we discuss with the Russians the possibility of a landing in the Pitsamo area [now Pechenga, near Murmansk, USSR], to offset the disappointment which will be caused by our cancelling all PQ [supply] convoys during the TORCH operation. Got the FM to go over straight away and see Marshall about this.

Wednesday 23 September 1942

A quiet day. Our COS very peeved at US interest in the plans for Burma – they don't like them sticking their noses in!

Thursday 24 September 1942

More trouble on Planning over the question of landing craft allocations. Admiral Cooke wanted to put in a unilateral US paper. Talked to Deane and urged that the Combined Planners should try and get agreement to short-term allocations, and then say that nothing more could be done till the CCS decided the general strategic policy for 1943.

Went to supper with Eleanor Smith and fed on squirrels! Very good – not unlike baby hare to eat. She told me she had always been very doubtful about Deane's capacity to succeed Beetle, but they could find no one else for the job. Wedemeyer apparently had to be pulled up some time ago for undue admiration of the Germans – he did two years at their Staff College! She tells me he is a very temperamental person. We had a great old chat together – a relief to get away from the society blossom type.

Friday 25 September 1942

Deane failed to put over our scheme to Cooke. No CCS meeting. The FM went into action with Marshall to try and get some transport aircraft to take petrol into Malta, the US COS having turned down the request, on a US Planners' report. Patterson also tried the Navy Department with considerable hopes of success for a fast tanker. Old Cunningham handled that job badly. He insisted on putting it to the CCS direct instead of lobbying it first. Considerable mystery about Arnold. I believe the truth is that he has gone [on a visit] to the South-West Pacific, but there are rumours that he is being replaced by Brett in Washington. Deane told me that the President had asked from the War and Navy Departments an estimate of the total air strength required 'to give air supremacy'. Both had replied, uncoordinated – without any consultation of us. Deane did not seem to realise the futility of this. Sinclair got the news from Nelson, but was under the impression that the President was going to issue an immediate directive on the matter.

Went late to a CTP given by Macready. Met Monnet there and told him of our difficulties with the War Department. Urged him to get *specific* cases put up to the CCS by the Combined Production and Resources Board – not generalities. Patrick Davison and Williams (NZ) came back to Fort Myer with Geoff and myself for supper. Williams thinks we try and be a bit too quick with the US – and they don't like being rushed.

Saturday 26 September 1942

The FM gave a press conference in the morning. Had lunch with Harold Butler [new Minister at the Embassy]. He wanted to talk about reconstruction and made some very good points: e.g. we must get our armistice terms decided as soon as possible so that we are not caught short. We shall have a hard job standing up against US imperialism and sentimentalism which in fact will go hand in hand against British interests. We should try and woo China by making concessions (e.g. the return of Hong Kong) *before* they are extorted from us anyhow. Only [Sir William] Jowitt [Paymaster General] is running this stuff at home and has not got the guns. It wants a War Cabinet minister in the lead, with some good *young* staff. The difficulty of course is that all the good men are concentrated on the war – and the PM would blow up at the idea of thinking about the peace. There is a lot in Harold Butler – though I don't know if he has the qualities of a real leader and politician. We found ourselves very much in agreement on all this sort of thing.

A busy day. Vittrup [US secretariat] in confidence told me that the Combined Production and Resources Board's insistence on [munitions] requirements being directly related to strategy was suspected by the US as an intriguing method of working against their building up a big army.

We have consistently pressed the view that strategic needs should be agreed on a combined basis, and that production plans should be framed accordingly. With this end in view we have prepared deployment tables and proposed an assessment of activity by theatres.

The US have never accepted this proposal of ours. They feel that their own requirements in the way of armed forces are a matter for decision by the US Chiefs of Staff alone. They resent our tactics of getting the Combined Production and Resources Board, headed by Nelson, to put over the British idea when the Combined Chiefs of Staff had agreed that it would be sufficient merely to calculate the number of US forces which could be sent overseas on a basis of available shipping only. Having failed in the Combined Chiefs of Staff, we were using Nelson as a stalking horse to achieve the same end.

Vittrup is a very fair sample of American staff officer, and his relations with us in the Secretariat have always been most cordial. It was for this reason that he spoke so frankly to me. I cannot suggest any way of allaying these suspicions on the part of the Americans other than to try, as far as possible, to pin our insistence on relating requirements to strategic needs to *specific cases* of shortages, in which it can be clearly shown that US requirements are out of balance. I do not believe that we shall get any further by continually stating our contention in *general terms*. To do so is liable still further to increase American suspicions of our motives and thereby to increase the difficulties of any combined action, without achieving any useful result.[32]

Vittrup said quite bluntly that he wants the US to be the dictating power after the war – and that means she must be the strongest. We certainly are in for some very difficult times with the Yanks. I should love to get away from here.

Dined at the McGees'. Had a pleasant evening listening to (and singing to) the 'Mikado'. They had a marvellous automatic gramophone. Stalingrad still holding.

Sunday 27 September 1942

Got up late. Took an hour's walk before lunch – *very* damp and hot. About 3.00 p.m. a terrific rain storm passed over, lasting about an hour, which brought the temperature down about 30 degrees in no time. To supper at the Fields'. The usual crowd. Also a Miss Moats – the hardest boiled female I have ever met – now writing a book on her stay in Russia last year. A bitch of the first and impurest water – though, I admit, amusing. Her last remark: 'I don't need any credentials – I've got long hair.'

Monday 28 September 1942

Telegram in from London to say that the TORCH outline plan had never been seen by the COS! in spite of the fact that 101 copies had been issued in London including 17 to British recipients (one to each Service department). Spoke to William Stirling on the phone and told him to get hold of a copy straight away.

JSM meeting in the morning to discuss it. At the CCS meeting in the afternoon, [Mark] Wayne Clark [Eisenhower's right-hand man on TORCH planning] explained the plan. The US COS approved the outline plan, subject to certain nitpicks. King raised queries on the subject of the command of air and naval forces. A fairly good meeting, but we were hamstrung as our COS had not seen the plan. Got through the minutes without any trouble. Clark seemed in very good form.

Tuesday 29 September 1942

An easy day. Had a long talk with Dudley Clarke who is here from the Middle East. He gave me some very interesting information about 'deception' and how they work their 'leaks'.

Wednesday 30 September 1942

An easy day. Traviss, head of the [British Government] Code and Cypher School[33] called in in morning. He seems to be in a great hurry to return, but I impressed on him the need to get fixed up with Strong [Eisenhower's (British) Intelligence officer] the question of the security of US and British cyphers.

Lunched with Monnet and told him of the need to stop plugging 'requirements in accord with strategic needs' as it was only causing suspicion of our motives. He took the point well. He seems convinced that the President *will* issue a new directive on aircraft production, but maintains we should be ready to steer it into the right channels. Crossman, German section of the Political Warfare Executive, came in with Bowes-Lyon. He is plugging a scheme to offer, to deserting Germans and prisoners of war, American citizenship. I doubt if the US will bite, but suggested he sounds out Strong. Crossman says that on all sides they have evidence that the Germans are absolutely fed up with the state of affairs in Germany.

Combined Munitions Assignment Board dinner for Garforth's departure. A very pleasant show. Sat next to Burns and Deane. Deane told me that the Army and Navy could not agree on the question of the scheme for a US 'Directorate of Requirements'. We seem to have agreement with the US on the question of the short-term allocation of landing craft. 'Cross-Channel ships' have had bad luck. One burnt, three torpedoed, two lost through gales. Only three arrived – a grim satisfaction for King! [Addendum: not so bad after all – five out of eight starts arrived.]

Thursday 1 October 1942

JSM meeting in the morning. A very long discussion about the landing craft paper. I drafted recommended conclusions which I hope the FM will put over tomorrow. The COS very annoyed that we let the US COS stick their noses into the Burma problem at all. The CIGS sent a private [telegram] to the FM to say we must keep them out. He *is* a BF [Bloody Fool]. Called in to see C. S. Forester who has just returned from a fortnight in HMS *Penelope*, now working up after repairs. Belben [ex-JSM] is in command. Forester said he had had a grand time: he is now going to write a novel with a Navy background.[34] He told me one curious thing – the US naval authorities would issue no *orders* to Belben about minefields etc. – only 'strong recommendations'!

Had a night out with Dudley Clarke and Leslie Clarkson. Went to the Gaiety – not a very good show – a striptease of sorts, a bad chorus and three average comics. The best turn was one of them doing ventriloquy. Went on to the Trioka after for supper. Good compère-conjurer. We were much amused by one pretty woozy individual who clasped in his arms a girl who had *completely* passed out. The American is quite shameless. The compère made him a kind of butt which he seemed to enjoy thoroughly!! A distinctly tipsy US Naval officer came and sat at our table and, after saying how much he liked us, proceeded to say that the US ought to concentrate on the Japs, leaving Germany to us! I told him that, considering comparative populations, he was certainly picking an easy number for the Americans. It was more than I could stand.

Friday 2 October 1942

CCS meeting went off pretty well. Admiral Cunningham attended [as naval commander for TORCH], having arrived the previous night. Beetle is apparently sick with a gastric ulcer, but is doing very well indeed. The landing craft paper went off fairly well, though the FM did not put it over well. We drew the US COS on Burma and elicited a good deal of information on their plans for building up a Chinese Army Corps in India and another in Yunnan [Province, China] of selected troops.

Saturday 3 October 1942

Took my day off on the Saturday and went down to Harper's Ferry for the day by train with Joan Mainprice. Scrambled up the Maryland heights, and had a sandwich lunch near an abandoned 'farm house' in a clearing. Went up to Eleanor Smith's after supper to see Julius Holmes [TORCH secretariat] who is on a trip over from London. He is very optimistic of the fifth column possibilities of TORCH. They are contacting [General] Giraud and hoping for the best.[35] What a blow-up there will be with de Gaulle! Richard Coleridge told me he had had a very busy day!

Sunday 4 October 1942

A busy day. Fixed up the FM's reply to the CIGS on the Burma business, emphasising that if we do not *add* to the CCS authority and scope, the only result will be to enhance the US COS position and thereby cut ourselves out from consultation. Norman Lee arrived from London and tells me that the CIGS is the nigger [in the woodpile] on all this. He also says that the PM is cooking up an attack on the production programme question in a telegram to the President. I hope his approach will be the right one. Drafted a signal to Jacob, which I will send tomorrow.

Just before lunch a signal came in from Eisenhower giving *his* draft of the directive for the treatment of Vichy ships and aircraft [in Africa, after TORCH] – just as we were clearing one of our own based on a COS telegram! Deane knocked out a draft giving the points of difference which we circulated as a CCS paper. Drafted a telegram on the landing craft business, the planners having produced a quite unsuitable one. Norman Jolley and his brigade major who have been having a run round the US Marines lunched with me. He said they found them quite unwilling to discuss any ideas of ours – they are supremely confident they are right – though they are nothing like so good as they think. The officers are little better intellectually than the troops, though the latter *as troops* are excellent material.

The Deanes had a small party for the Macdowells, Hammonds, Eleanor Smith, Lovetts and one or two others. I stayed about one and a half hours and then went on to John Davies's [JSM]. He showed his colour films – *very* good. After the others had gone, John showed me a draft of a note he has written to try and explain to London our present difficulties with the US, and why we are getting less now than before they came into the war – a *very* good document which I shall send to Jacob at once.

Monday 5 October 1942

The PM's telegram about production arrived. OK, more or less, as it deals with specific absurdities of tanks (87,000 next year!) and ammunition (2,200 million rounds next year). Sinclair doesn't like it though. Busy day getting through Eisenhower's directive on Vichy ships and aircraft.

To supper at Bill Donovan's. Crossman gave us a very interesting talk on British Political Warfare Executive [output] to Germany. He impresses me very favourably. I think our stuff is infinitely more subtle than the Russians', and therefore we get a bad press because it is not realised it *is* propaganda. Yet Berlin ignores the Russian stuff and spends a vast amount of time refuting reports from London.

Tuesday 6 October 1942

Another busy day. The FM was fussed by a letter from Marshall giving a cable from Stilwell who is peeved because Wavell is making trouble about his Chinese Army in India. I roared up the FM to counter-attack. Stilwell does not keep Wavell properly informed at all. Spoke to Deane on the same subject. In discussing 'unity of command' he confessed to me that, in spite of it, the Army and the Navy were fighting like cats in Alaska! – and the command system was hopelessly cumbrous!

Norman back to sup with me. He urges a combined FM/Sinclair memo to the Cabinet pointing out how control of the war must gravitate to Washington – hence we should build up our Washington missions as strong as possible.

Wednesday 7 October 1942

Admiral Stoeve came up for a chat in the morning. I gather the Dutch do not find the US too easy to get on with. Wansborough Jones [JSM] told me they had tried to make a Dutch ship under our charter, lent to them for trooping, sail under the US flag, with her captain subordinate to the Officer Command- ing the Troops!! Richard and I had a further talk with Deane about (a) unity of command, (b) combined planning. From all I can gather their unity of command is nothing more than a shibboleth and seems nearly always to involve a change of command at a critical time. [General] Patton [in London] and [Admiral] Hewitt [on board ship, commanding the naval task force] are still planning the Casablanca [landing] when located 100-odd miles apart from each other. Deane did not seem to think that at all odd!

Marshall is apparently thinking seriously of strengthening the US Strategic Committee with two very senior officers. Deane says Cooke is the real nigger in the planners. The US Joint Planners are continually putting up 'split' [army/ navy] papers.

Hopkins saw the FM in the morning. He evidently fears that the President and PM are getting in each other's hair a bit at present. The PM certainly sent a pretty curt reply to a ball-aching cable from the President relaying a suggestion of King's that PQ convoys should sail in groups of three each with two or three escorts – and hope for the best. As it is we are doing our best with unescorted ships sailing singly – all manned by volunteers – all British of course. Poor devils, they have little hope in the Arctic sea if they are torpedoed. Meanwhile all the USN can do is to sit back and offer futile suggestions like that. No wonder the PM was annoyed. However Dill sent a signal to Pug enclosing a message to the PM begging him not to lose his hair – Pug to alter the wording if he thought fit. Dill also had a long talk with Marshall about Burma. Stilwell is apparently having much trouble trying to goad Chiang Kai-Shek into some activity.

A heavy day, finishing late after cleaning up all the FM's draft signals.

Thursday 8 October 1942

JSM meeting in the morning – nothing of much importance. Had Tommy Brand to lunch, and discussed the PM's production telegram. We do not expect much reaction – Burns and Somervell are drafting the President's reply!

The FM, Evill and Macready met Sinclair, Monnet and Bob Brand in the afternoon to discuss Sinclair's telegram to Lyttelton on the President's new directive for 100,000 tactical aircraft next year. It looks as if all our requirements in accessories etc. will be swallowed up – and owing to the large numbers quality will be sacrificed to quantity. All the other programmes will be upset. Nelson agrees a combined committee should review the new programme and decide the [aircraft] types. Lyttelton is asked to come out at once. The President meanwhile has asked only the US COS to recommend proportions of types etc. It looks as if he is giving up the 'combined' idea altogether. I must say we are certainly on a falling market just now.

Friday 9 October 1942

A Pacific Powers meeting in the morning – a good one. Evill spoke very well on the British bomber offensive in Western Europe and produced some excellent photographs. Sturdee [Australia], who has replaced old Smart, spoke about New Guinea operations. Arnold gave a short waffle on his trip to the Pacific (for which he received a Distinguished Service Medal!!) – and Chou gave his usual dissertation on Jap operations in China. At the CCS meeting in the afternoon our side put over successfully the need for a broadcast warning to all French forces [in Africa], which the President had struck out of the directive to Eisenhower – apparently because he thought it an improper message to deliver to a so-called friendly power through diplomatic channels.

The PM has telegraphed Stalin offering 20 squadrons [of aircraft] in the Caucasus after the next Western Desert battle, and the President has backed it up.

Saturday 10 October 1942

A busy day. Ian writes that the COS are very put out at the way the US COS are assuming power for unilateral decisions: the CIGS would like to abolish the whole CCS set-up. Tore off a short note pointing out that the combined organisations were our only anchor, which Admiral Cunningham is going to take back with him tomorrow. They are being extraordinarily shortsighted in London about all this.

> There are very few things which we are in a position to give to the United States; but we are dependent on them for a great many things. Our only hope of influencing the US Chiefs of Staff is to work through the combined organisations. These may not work as objectively as was hoped when they were first set up; but they do at least give us the constitutional *right* to discuss our needs on equal terms, instead of receiving gratefully such crumbs as may be left from the rich man's table. Moreover, as long as the combined organisations are kept up there is some chance that we shall know what is brewing in American minds instead of being presented, out of the blue, with a *fait accompli*.

> There is a further reason for persevering with combined organisations, exasperating though the process may be. In these organisations British and US officers and officials do learn something of each other's problems, and in the course of time there will be produced a leaven of men who have been trained to think objectively. This leaven may be of vital importance when it comes to the peace table and to reconstruction after the war.

> From a purely national point of view, our greatest triumph has been to secure American agreement to the whole system of combined organisations. The position of the Americans would be far more authoritative without them, since they could then act as despotically as they wished, and we should be compelled to follow their lead with little or no chance of influencing their decisions in any way. In so far as we are dependent on the Americans for resources, we should not be in complete control even in our own theatres. It follows, therefore, that the Joint Staff Mission should be kept as closely as possible in touch with policy and thought in London, and that we should do everything in our power to build up the Combined Chiefs of Staff and other parallel organisations. Only if the Americans feel that they have in the Mission an authoritative body with whom they can deal on equal terms will they be prepared to listen to the Mission's views and be influenced by them.[36]

Monnet came in and discussed the revising of [munitions production] programmes consequent on the new air directive from the President. He thinks it will mean a 40% cut in the Ground Forces programme which will *force* the Americans to abandon their too grandiose schemes. I fear however that Lease Lend will be the first to suffer the cut. He feels that on *that* basis we should be in a strong moral position with the President. Macready had a very sticky meeting today over [the allocation of] 3-inch self-propelled guns. Somervell took the line that all US forces must be fully equipped before we get any *at all* — even though we are the only people who will be up against German tanks! Certainly assignment on strategic needs is right out of the window these days!

Sunday 11 October 1942

Rode with young Buford (Leahy's aide) and wife in the morning: good horse (Lady Low) and a nice fresh morning. Very pleasant. In the afternoon, Geoff, Wansborough [Jones] and I went to watch a pro football match (the [Washington] Redskins v. Cleveland). It is a slow game (two and a quarter hours to get through one hour's actual play) – great skill in the passing and kicking, but much brute force in the rest of it. The intense mechanisation of it all is characteristic of America. However it made an amusing afternoon.

Went to the Fields' for supper. They say that until we employ a $100,000 a year man in film, radio and the press to 'sell' Great Britain, we shall get nowhere. [Henry] Luce [the publisher] has a most poisonously anti-British article in *Life* [magazine] this week. It certainly is a heart-breaking job here these days. I wish I could get clean away out of it.

News in that we have lost three big personnel ships.

Monday 12 October 1942

A pretty busy day. Macready tells me that Somervell is at him to reduce our tank requirements; i.e. all the cuts caused by the President's air directive are going to be passed on to us. We simply hold no cards at all – yet London expects us to work miracles. It is a hard life. Deane, in answer to a request to be allowed to see the directives given to Eisenhower and Maxwell, replies that they are secret and can only be given to us if the President agrees! So much for the Combined Secretariat! – a very different attitude from dear old Beetle. I don't know what we are going to do about it all. I wish to hell I could pull out, but I suppose that is a cowardly attitude to take.

Tuesday 13 October 1942

Fairly quiet day. Wrote to Ian and William Stirling, who is leaving the Cabinet Office today to go on Eisenhower's staff.

Wednesday 14 October 1942

Went to the dentist after lunch and got measured for a new plate, as well as having two teeth filled.

My fears about the two US directives were quite unfounded. Deane passed them over without any trouble. I gather that he didn't like the written request! – it doesn't look well on his files, I suppose. The FM produced a very good telegram home giving the COS the form on 'requirements related to strategy' etc., which I filled out to my satisfaction. He left in a paragraph I drafted warning them never to put on record the view that the US forces were too large, as it might have grave political repercussions afterwards.

The PM has had rather a snubbing reply to his production telegram – the President merely forwarded a draft prepared by his staff – and said so!

Thursday 15 October 1942

Busy day. [General] Davidson, Director of Military Intelligence, is over and gave the Joint Planners and Joint Intelligence Committee a very interesting talk on the general situation. He is pretty optimistic about the Russian situation. Went to a supper party given by Paddy Beaumont-Nesbitt for G.2 [US Army Intelligence branch] to meet Davidson. A good show. Old Scobey, previously secretary of the 'Joint Board' [forerunner of the US Joint Chiefs of Staff] is back as McCloy's military assistant. He fell on me like a long lost brother. Met several good chaps there. Paddy, Macready, Zamoyski [Polish Military Attaché] and I sat up arguing [with one of them] about imperialism till nearly 1.00 a.m. He stoutly denies that the US have any imperialist ideas, but I am *not* convinced.

Friday 16 October 1942

Fixed with Deane beforehand quite satisfactorily some awkward conclusions on the shipment of spare parts for non-standard vehicles and on production programmes. Proposed Armistice Terms [for Eisenhower's use in North Africa] prepared by the US were circulated for CCS approval. Asked London if they had had them and approved: they telephoned that they were not hurrying at all, so we explained Ike was pressing. Time is getting short before Patton's force has to sail.

Quite a satisfactory CCS meeting. Marshall told the FM that things are pretty rocky at Guadalcanal. The US Navy seem to have fallen down badly on the Q. side [Quartermastering, i.e. logistics] – as might have been expected. Patton and Hewitt, his sailor, are not working well together at all [on TORCH]. Hewitt has just written officially to say that he can't land [on the African coast] in darkness – and they are due to sail in about a week. As they are working 180 miles apart, I don't see how they *can* plan properly. The ill feeling between the US Army and Navy is simply *incredible*.

Pouring wet all day. The Potomac is in flood – some of the Navy Department's temporary buildings near the bank have had to be cleared out.

Saturday 17 October 1942

The COS came up with a signal approving Ike's draft Armistice Terms for TORCH, but suggesting the naval paragraph be made less severe. They leave the final decision to the US COS though. A pretty busy day. Went out at lunch time to the Memorial Bridge to look at the Potomac in flood. It is about 18 feet above normal and Rock Creek Driveway is submerged. The current was terrific.

Things look very bad on Guadalcanal. It looks very much as if they [the Americans] will be thrown off.

Sunday 18 October 1942

Took Joan Mainprice out to Great Falls to see them in flood – found I had left my camera behind when I got there which was very annoying. A large contingent from the office there – all rubbernecking too. We got a good walk during the afteroon. The trees are very lovely just now.

Monday 19 October 1942

Busy day. Gather that London approve of [Admiral] Darlan [commander of Vichy France's armed forces] being brought in with Giraud if he will bite, and of the notion that Giraud shall be offered command ultimately in North Africa.

Went to see Alfred Lunt and Lynn Fontaine in 'The Pirate' – a very thin play, though very well acted. Very pretty 'decor'. A pleasant evening.

Tuesday 20 October 1942

Busy day. Marris in about stopping the blockade rumours: he despairs of getting help from the US Navy – but I find from Patterson it is not as bad as he thinks. I feel I am making some progress with Deane.

Wednesday 21 October 1942

Fairly busy day. Long discussion in the evening with the FM and Heads of Mission on whether to recommend the Chief of Air Staff [Portal] to come out with Lyttelton for production discussions and if so whether to press the COS to settle whether they were going nap on the air offensive or not. Finally compromised on rather a luke-warm signal. Richard Coleridge was all for pressing the COS to make up their minds *now* and get the President's air directive moulded accordingly. I fear we should have got no change till after TORCH. Marshall told the FM that there *was* a great deal of anti-British feeling in the [US training] camps – curious that our people who go round have never felt it at all.

Thursday 22 October 1942

Long JSM meeting in the morning. Much discussion of a Combined Planning Staff paper on 'Unity of Command', but we never got on to the subject of 1943 strategy which was the main dish. I discussed that with the FM in the evening: Portal has put in a paper at home asking the COS to make up their minds to go all out for the bombing of Germany; our Joint Planners here warmly supported it. The FM doesn't quite know whether to support it or not: [Admiral] Patterson is dead against it, [General] Macready is half-hearted! We *must* make up our minds what we *want* to do if we are ever to convince the Americans, who are drifting rudderless at present.

Dined with Burdon who is in a Civil Aviation job with the US government. Very interesting party at which I succeeded in getting an all-American party arguing about the colour problem and India. A very amusing evening. Walked along to the Mellon Gallery at lunch time with Wansborough and looked at the modern French pictures.

Friday 23 October 1942

JSM meeting in the morning to discuss the World Strategy paper. The Joint Planners were ordered to produce their own paper, and draft a JSM signal urging for consideration to be given to the Pacific theatre as well as the Western [theatre]. Short CCS meeting in the afternoon. Satisfactory amendments to the Combined Planning Staff paper on Unified Command agreed. I hope our COS will take it. David Cohn telegraphed asking me to stay at Admiral Glassford's [Commandant of US Navy Yard] at Charleston, South Carolina. Fixed up to go down by train tomorrow night.

News in at 6.30 p.m. that our [Montgomery's] offensive in the Western Desert has started. Marshall told us today that Clark had met the French officers in touch with Giraud and re-embarked again by submarine off North Africa. Darlan is at Dakar now. It looks as if it is either going to be *very* favourable or an appalling double cross.

Saturday 24 October 1942

Easy day. Lunched with Monnet, Crowther and Weeks. The US air programme is now fixed at 82,000 combat aircraft for 1943, with an increase of 90 corvettes [escort vessels] and 2.8 million tons of merchant shipping. Monnet came to see me again in the afternoon. He said Clay had told him that we could not give details of our order of battle. I showed him CCS 91 [a document] which completely convinced him that we were guiltless. The only possible conclusion is that Clay does not *want* to learn the details as he knows he could not fail to be convinced! Left Monnet thinking how to get round *this* difficulty. Caught the 7.05 p.m. train for Charleston.

Sunday 25 October 1942

Arrived Charleston (North) about 9.20 where David [Cohn] and Admiral Glassford met me. Glassford is a delightful man – looks exactly like a British naval officer. Mrs G. is a good sort, amusing, rather catty, Canadian or English, tall, slim, fair, 'faded', rather restless. The Commandant of the Navy Yard has lovely quarters next to the yard itself. Walked round the garden after breakfast with Mrs G.; then walked and talked with David. After lunch Glassford took us and his niece Becky Bakewell, a nice girl, down to Charleston in his launch. While he was in the office there, we had a quick look at the town – French in appearance. Unfortunately it was a dull, rather misty day. In the evening, there was a reception at the club for the officers of HMS *Nigeria* – a

6-inch [gun] cruiser repairing after being torpedoed in the last Malta Convoy. (I had to stand in the 'receiving line'!) I found her captain is Paton, late of Plans in the Admiralty! A dull lot of US naval officers and wives with notably few exceptions. Supper in the kitchen – even in the deep south with five servants! Afterwards Glassford and I had a great crack about Wavell and ABDA [now defunct]. He has a very great admiration for Wavell. A very interesting evening.

Monday 26 October 1942

Loafed in the morning. Walked through the Navy Yard with David to HMS *Nigeria* for lunch. There are several LSTs [Landing Ships, Tank] building there. Walked round the golf course with Glassford and David before dinner. A lovely fresh clear evening. Dinner with the 'family' only. A very pleasant day. How lovely it is to dawdle for a bit.

Tuesday 27 October 1942

Went round the Navy Yard in the morning. Had a good look at the LSTs under construction. Only the bow and stern sections are made in the yard, the remainder being fabricated in sections outside by sub-contractors. Two are on the way and two fitting out. The two on the way each had a large gap near the stern, waiting for the sections from a sub-contractor who is late on his contract: but work on the rest of the ship is not held up. They look very serviceable craft to me. *All* construction is welded lap-joint [with overlapping edges]. I then looked over one of the latest US fleet destroyers, *Pringle*. She is like a young cruiser, complete with recce [reconnaissance] aircraft.

After lunch General Moses and wife arrived with his staff officer and wife. They were on their way to the Navy Day parade held on the Citadel parade ground. The Citadel is a Military School [Academy], now some 1,900 strong. The cadets are extraordinarily smart and well turned out. On parade was a detachment from HMS *Nigeria*, who marched very well indeed; a battalion of US Marines; US Army; a detachment of US Navy; the Citadel cadets; and the Navy Yard 'Home Guard'; with a big US Marine Corps band to provide the music. The parade went very well indeed. US troops march without any swing of the arms and with little rhythm or swagger. The Cadets' marching was excellent though. On the Saluting Base were General Sommerall (Commandant of the Citadel), an old boy of 76, but very sprightly; Admiral Glassford; Senator Maynard (who looks like a young horse dealer): Mendel Rivers; [Captain] Paton (HMS *Nigeria*); Lockwood the Mayor and various other dignitaries. It was an impressive show, in beautiful fresh sunny weather. I was touched to hear the American and British National Anthems played at the start of the proceedings and to see the *Nigeria* party lead the march-past.

After the parade, we adjourned to the Charleston Club and imbibed 'Old Fashioneds'.[37] Paton stayed to dinner, and we sat round the fire talking afterwards. A *most* enjoyable day. Glassford broadcast a speech at lunch time calling for real co-operative effort by *all* Services and stressing the Navy's job as servant of the infantry, who had to get to close quarters to beat the enemy – *what* a pleasant change to hear a US Naval Officer talk like that. I am *most* favourably impressed by him, but I gather he is *not* one of King's blue-eyed boys at all. I wish he could get into a position of real influence.

Wednesday 28 October 1942

Loafed and talked with David in the morning. He feels there is a real danger of the US Forces getting control in the country after the war: Somervell is a typical fascist. I wonder if he is right. Went down with the Admiral in his barge (a millionaire's cruising yacht) in the afternoon and looked over their Combined Operations centre in the Fort Sumter Hotel – a great deal of apparatus – teleprinters, magnetic maps etc. – but not yet very active. They still have to ask Washington before they can turn out an Army plane for anti-submarine work!! Still Glassford has got them both in the same room which is an enormous step forward. He certainly has the right ideas. Left on the 8.20 train after dinner.

Thursday 29 October 1942

Comfortable night's sleep. Got to Fort Myer for breakfast. They seem to have had quite a busy time while I have been away. Had a letter from Beetle [in London]. He is apparently *completely* sold on us now! JSM meeting in the morning. Busy day. Took Joan Mainprice out to dinner. The US lost the carrier *Hornet* four days ago in the Solomons.

Friday 30 October 1942

Busy day. CCS meeting in the afternoon – mainly on TORCH stuff. Went to a CTP at the New Zealand legation. Peter Dunn told me that the difference between the atmosphere in the [US training] camps and in Washington is *most* marked. He finds himself up against a blank brick wall here. So do we all. Dined at the Bensons' and went on to a private showing of Noel Coward's film, 'In Which We Serve'. Went down to it with General and Mrs Marshall. They are very nice people, I must say. A wonderful film – most moving. Slow progress in the Western Desert.

Saturday 31 October 1942

Very busy day – a swarm of signals to get off after yesterday's CCS meeting.

Lunched with Peter Dunn. He finds Washington very tough going as compared with the cooperation he receives in all the training establishments throughout the country. Went to supper at Mabel Booth's [JSM] – a pleasant party. The children everywhere dressed up for Hallowe'en which is apparently a great American festival.

Sunday 1 November 1942

Went to the 11.00 a.m. service at the Cathedral. Then on to Eleanor Smith. Walked with her and the dogs in Rock Creek Park – then had lunch. After lunch we dug out one of Beetle's guns for General Marshall which he wanted to borrow.

Monday 2 November 1942

US COS much fussed because Ike has agreed with His Majesty's Government that no notice should be taken of a [possible] Spanish invasion of Morocco as far as the River Sebou [in northern Morocco]. They think we should warn the Spanish we will fight them if they do this! Telegram in from Murphy [US Chargé d'Affaires] saying that the French conspirators [with the Allies] want to postpone TORCH till 20 November! The FM backed the US COS in saying *no* to this. Had a party for all my chaps [in the Secretariat] and Chance, Brand, Hutton, Hart and Archer. After a very cheery meal we discussed the means of improving cooperation. A good evening. News from the Middle East looks pretty good.

Tuesday 3 November 1942

The news from the Middle East is good. It looks as if they have successfully punched a hole in the northern part of the [German] line and will be able to put their armour through.

A fairly quiet day. Deane has let Cooke get away with it again. A US Planners' draft report was prepared in accordance with CCS terms of reference: Cooke then put in a US paper direct to the US COS (which our people had never even seen). The result is to make a complete mockery of the whole Combined Planners' set-up. I shall try and move the FM to make 'an issue' of it with Leahy. Of course if Deane had any guts, he would have stopped such a paper coming up to the US COS – or at least have pointed out that the Combined Planning Staff had been ordered to report on it. But he *has* no guts.

We have been instructed to ask the US COS to give us a provisional line on the 19 US ships, now in British ports loaded for Russia, for a Northern Task Force which is booked for Tangier if the Spaniards go snoky [prowling about –

perhaps in Morocco]. I wonder if they will agree. No sign yet of Axis preparations to meet TORCH. It almost looks as if its real destination has *not* leaked. Admiral Stoeve tells me that the US will not give the Dutch any of the planes which they were holding in trust for them as having been bought before Java collapsed. They [the US] are quite shameless in the way they repudiate agreements.

Wednesday 4 November 1942

Spoke to Deane about the landing craft business. He says that the US COS are fed-up with the subject and will not discuss it any more. I asked him if they wanted to scrap combined planning – if so, why not say so? Every time anything affects the US Navy, Cooke refuses to have any discussion and short-circuits the Combined Planning Staff direct to the CCS. We could have done precisely the same over, for example, the Burma offensive plan, i.e. let the Combined Planners' sub-committee flog away for about a month and then – just before the report was taken by the Combined Planning Staff – whack in a CCS paper saying it was *our* business and we did not propose to discuss it anyway.

Lyttelton and [a Ministry of Production] party arrived from London in the afternoon. News in during the afternoon that we had broken the front in Egypt [at Alamein] and that it looked as if we should make a big killing. *Very* exciting. Called in on the Fields after dinner. The party there were much more excited about the Republican gains in the [mid-term Congressional] election than about Egypt.

Had Richard and Marquis Childs, who writes for a New Orleans paper, to lunch. Childs wanted to know about our system of co-ordination between Services and civil ministries. He expressed the same fear as David Cohn [see 28 October] that there might be a tendency for military fascism to develop in the US. I said I felt that the removal of the Army and Navy heads to the Pentagon was bad, as tending to emphasise their separation from all the civil departments. He struck me as a good chap.

Thursday 5 November 1942

JSM meeting in the morning. I had to leave early to go to a British Supply Council meeting with Lyttelton at 11.00. Lyttelton says he is over here to put across and settle strategic policy and the tactical [negotiating] line is that he can't get ahead till that is done. This is certainly news to us. The awkward thing is that the Cabinet have not yet approved [the latest] COS paper [on future Anglo-American strategy].[38] Asked London to expedite it but Jo says early Cabinet approval is *unlikely*. I can imagine the PM will want to stall on a long-term policy as usual. I am glad myself that our COS do definitely recommend going all-out for the air offensive against the Germans as an essential preliminary to any move on to the Continent. Our [JSM] Planners were told to produce a brief digest of the COS paper.

News in that we have apparently got hold of Giraud all right, and he is on his way to Gibraltar.

Friday 6 November 1942

JSM meeting in the morning to discuss a draft CCS paper which I had prepared yesterday objecting to Cooke's refusal to let the Combined Planning Staff discuss landing craft, though directed to do so by the CCS; and the submission of a very terse paper by the US COS giving us an allotment [of landing craft] and saying they were not prepared to discuss it any more. It was decided *not* to put in a paper, but for Dill to approach Leahy on the matter. At the CCS meeting, after a Navy film unit had done its best for 15 minutes, Leahy reacted very well. Cooke was badly shown up by Grindle and in the end the Combined Planners were ordered to put up for discussion their differences of opinion in a single document. We also got over that, in reviewing Burma offensive plans, the Combined Planning Staff were to correlate with South-West Pacific plans and the Middle East. The Planners' draft of the [British COS] strategy paper was considered immediately after the CCS meeting and a redraft ordered.

Another Lyttelton meeting at 6.00 p.m. After it he had a private chat with the FM and me on [negotiating] tactics. The White House according to Hopkins do not want to become involved at all. Lyttelton is working to get a dinner party at the White House with the President and the US COS and the FM and himself present, and hopes to evolve from it a request from the President for CCS ideas on strategy.

Saturday 7 November 1942

The FM decided after discussing it with Lyttelton to put across our final redraft strategy paper to the US COS 'off the record' [i.e. not as a formal British paper]. He fears and rightly that otherwise they may feel Lyttelton is trying to bounce them through the President. Informed London accordingly. I hope the PM will not blow up![39] News in during the day confirming the zero hour [start] for TORCH [that night]. Information from the Middle East continues to be excellent. It really looks as if we shall bag the whole lot. The timing with TORCH could not have been more perfect. Much telephone discussion with Monnet on the procedure for the Lyttelton mission. He [Monnet] is all for going ahead on production questions as far as possible and leaving the awkward question of long-term assignments till the strategy has been settled. He is only right up to a point – production *will* be affected if our strategic idea of concentrating on the bomber force in Europe goes through.

Got away from the office finally about 8.45 and brought Joan Mainprice back for some food and to listen for radio news of TORCH, which was to be released at 9.00 p.m. It evidently took the news men completely by surprise as it did not come through till about 9.15 – a short news flash sandwiched in among a lot of advertisement stuff. Still it was wonderful at last to know that TORCH was definitely launched after so many tribulations. I pray it may go off well, as it will certainly be *very* difficult with the US if they take a bloody nose! Rang Eleanor [Smith] up to tell her to listen at 9.00 p.m. and that Beetle was in London [not with the landing force].

Sunday 8 November 1942

Called in at the office about 11.30. News in that landings were effected at Oran and Algiers. No news of Patton in the Casablanca area. Giraud had played the shit at Gibraltar – refused to play unless made commander in chief of the whole outfit. However a broadcast in his name had already gone out from Algiers! – though Generals Mast and Berthelot who were working for us have apparently been arrested. They are trying to take Darlan into 'protective custody'. At 6.00 p.m., news was in that Giraud has come round fairly satisfactorily – so he may be an asset after all. Still no news from Patton.

Lunched with Bill Donovan – I wanted particularly to be with him today. It was always his idea for the US to occupy North Africa. He had Buxton, one of his chaps, there too. Went to a football match with him in the afternoon. To the Fields' for supper – a small party only. Heard on the radio that Algeria had asked for an armistice. We are in possession of Algiers and Oran. Some scrapping on the Casablanca front. Spain seems quiet. It looks like a big success. Thank God.

Monday 9 November 1942

The news from North Africa continued good. Algiers has definitely capitulated; we have an airfield at Oran and most of the area. All the west coast landings were effected but there was considerable trouble with the naval forces and coast batteries there. Giraud is moving in to take command of the French forces that come over [to the Allies' side]. It looks as if Darlan is in the bag. Losses seem to have been quite light considering the very large forces involved.

The atmosphere in the War Department is very cordial. Vittrup [US Secretariat] told me he had come to the conclusion that we knew more about German air strengths than they did. He, the poor old thing, has been kept back after all, to be secretary to the new US Strategical Survey Committee, consisting of admirals and generals, which is to work independently of the US Planners. Vittrup very exercised as to how it is all to fit in with the existing committees.

A telegram in from the PM ordering our strategical digest [see 5 November] to be withdrawn. A report from Beetle shows that the PM is thinking of pushing Turkey into the war as a bridge to Russia and as a bridgehead to the

Balkans! No wonder he doesn't want the COS paper put over! However Arnold's reaction is highly favourable – also Deane's. The FM gathers that it is OK with Marshall. King is furious because Lyttelton [a mere civilian] is dabbling with strategy at all. The FM roared off a protest pointing out that the present time was most propitious to put our ideas over. I advised him to send it 'private' to the CIGS who was to decide with the COS whether it would embarrass them or not before delivering it.[40]

Had some talk with Hasler on a Civil Secretariat for the British Supply Council, but we decided nothing.

Tuesday 10 November 1942

News in during the day that Oran had fallen into our hands completely. Lyttelton got a telegram from the PM telling him he was *not* authorised to deal with strategy! No reaction from the COS on the FM's telegram to the PM.

Vittrup came up for a talk about his new job as secretary of the US Joint Strategical Survey Committee, which is to be composed of two admirals and two generals. He realises there will be a lot overlapping between it and the Planners and Strategical Committee. He is a very good straightforward chap. Johnny Grindle had a final bust-up with Cooke over landing craft. Cooke just refuses to discuss amicably at all. I think he realises he was very badly shown up at the CCS meeting last Friday, and is such a common little squirt that he can't extricate himself graciously at all.

Wednesday 11 November 1942

News in during the day that Casablanca and Oran were both in our hands. This gives us all our objectives. Darlan and Giraud are now both at Algiers squabbling as to who should be 'king pin'.[41] Clark is there trying to settle it! But Darlan has told all hands in North Africa to cease resistance which is something. We are going to have trouble with those Frenchmen though. The radio news is that the Germans are occupying unoccupied France and Pétain has therefore released French forces from the Armistice conditions. Things are certainly moving fast! The Germans as expected are flying troops into Tunisia. [Montgomery's] pursuit of Rommel continues.

Marshall has asked the FM to come over and talk to him off the record tomorrow about our future strategy paper – and what he thinks about King and Marshall going over for discussions in London. That is a great tribute to the FM's reputation for straightforwardness. The COS agree that the FM's signal to the PM, pressing for our strategy paper to be handed over officially, should go in to the PM.

News in that Stalin has agreed to receive the Air Mission to fix arrangements for the move of the Allied air force to the south Caucasus.[42]

Dined at the Embassy. Other members of party were Averell Harriman;

Commander Vanderbilt and wife; Mrs Davis, head of US Red Cross; John Foster. I was much cross-examined. We had some interesting reminiscences from Halifax about the black days of 1940.

Thursday 12 November 1942

The FM went over to the War Department and had an off-the-record talk with Marshall about Mediterranean strategy. Arnold, McNarney, Handy, Wedemeyer and Deane there too. He was sorry he did not take me with him as I suggested! I gather from Pope that Wedemeyer is now complaining that the Mediterranean is a blind alley that holds out no prospects of exploitation.

Friday 13 November 1942

CCS meeting in the afternoon. Went to a meeting held by Lyttelton at 6.00. He hopes to have a meeting with the President to get him to settle the points in dispute and confirm the [combined production] agreement during the coming week. Progress in the discussions seems to be fairly good.

We are well beyond Tobruk. Troops have occupied Bône and are pushing eastward hard.

Appendix: The Combined Chiefs
of Staff Organisation

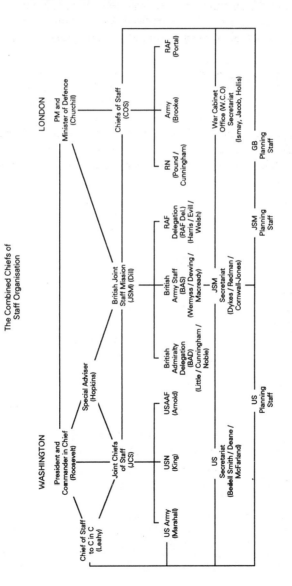

The Combined Chiefs of
Staff Organisation

WASHINGTON

LONDON

Chief of Staff
to C in C
(Leahy)

President and
Commander in Chief
(Roosevelt)

PM and
Minister of Defence
(Churchill)

Special Adviser
(Hopkins)

Joint Chiefs
of Staff
(JCS)

British Joint
Staff Mission
(JSM) (Dill)

Chiefs of Staff
(COS)

US Army
(Marshall)

USN
(King)

USAAF
(Arnold)

British
Admiralty
Delegation
(BAD)
(Little / Cunningham /
Noble)

British
Army Staff
(BAS)
(Wemyss / Dewing /
Macready)

RAF
Delegation
(RAF Del.)
(Harris / Evill /
Welsh)

RN
(Pound /
Cunningham)

Army
(Brooke)

RAF
(Portal)

US
Secretariat
(Bedell Smith / Deane /
McFarland)

JSM
Secretariat
(Dykes / Redman /
Cornwall-Jones)

War Cabinet
Office (W.C.O)
Secretariat
(Ismay, Jacob, Hollis)

US
Planning
Staff

JSM
Planning
Staff

GB
Planning
Staff

Notes

Introduction

1. Macmillan diary, 26 January 1943, in Macmillan, H., *War Diaries*, Macmillan, London, 1984, pp. 7–10.
2. Pendar, K., *Adventure in Diplomacy*, Cassell, London, 1966, p. 135.
3. Jacob diary, 14–18 January 1943, Jacob Papers (privately held).
4. Scott, W., *Heart of Midlothian*, Black, Edinburgh, 1890, pp. 80ff.
5. Jacob diary, 19–23 January 1943; Caraway oral history, US Army Military History Institute, Carlisle Barracks, Pennsylvania.
6. J. J. Dykes to Winifred, July 1943, Dykes Papers; Ismay, General Lord, *Memoirs of Lord Ismay*, Heinemann, London, 1960, p. 291; Kennedy, Major General Sir John, *The Business of War*, Hutchinson, London, 1957, p. 287.
7. Bourne to Winifred Dykes, 7 February 1943, Dykes Papers (privately held).
8. DSM citation, 30 January 1943. Cf. JCS to COS, 4 February 1943. Both in CAB 122/274, PRO.
9. Frankfurter diary, 29 January 1943, in Lash, J. P., ed., *From the Diaries of Felix Frankfurter*, Norton, New York, 1975, p. 173.
10. Ismay to Kingsley Dykes, 9 February 1943, Dykes Papers; Ismay, p. 291.
11. John Dykes letter, 15 November 1982; Davison to Howkins, 6 February 1943, CAB 119/59, PRO.
12. See 26 July 1942.
13. See 27 April, 11 June, 1 October 1942.
14. Dykes diary, 12 December 1933, Dykes Papers.
15. Jacob, obituary of Dykes, *Royal Engineers Journal*, December 1943.
16. See Danchev, A., *Very Special Relationship*, Brassey's, London, 1986, especially pp. 48–55.
17. Cf. Dill to Marshall, 12 November 1941, Marshall Papers, 64/25, Marshall Research Foundation, Lexington, Virginia.
18. See Cline, R. S., *Washington Command Post*, GPO, Washington, 1951, pp. 100ff; Gwyer, J. M. A., *Grand Strategy*, III, i, HMSO, London, 1964, pp. 381ff.
19. Handy oral history, US Army Military History Institute.
20. Lord Broughshane (Patrick Davison) interview, 19 October 1981.
21. Bedell Smith to Winifred Dykes, 30 January 1943, Dykes Papers. Cf. Eleanor Bedell Smith to Coleridge, n.d. [February 1943], CAB 122/274, PRO.
22. See Snyder, W. P., 'Walter Bedell Smith: Eisenhower's Chief of Staff', *Military Affairs* XLVIII, 1 (January 1984), pp. 6–14.
23. See, variously, Lawrence, W. H., 'Tough man for a Tough Job', *New York Times* magazine, 17 March 1946; *New York Times* obituary, 10 August 1961; Ranelagh, J., *The Agency*, Sceptre, London, 1988, pp. 190–202; Bruce Lockhart diary, *passim*, in Young, K., ed., *The Diaries of Sir Robert Bruce Lockhart*, II, Macmillan, London, 1980.
24. Dykes to Mary Ravenshear, 8 March 1942, Dykes Papers.
25. See 20 July, 15 August 1942.
26. Jacob interview, 12 August 1981.
27. Stirling to Dykes, 13 September 1942, CAB 122/1582, PRO; Churchill to Dill (unsent draft), 15 December 1942, PREM 3/217/7, PRO; Pownall diary, 17 June, 8 November 1944, in Bond, B., ed., *Chief of Staff*, II, Cooper, London, 1974, pp. 175, 193.
28. Eisenhower to Handy, 28 January 1943, in Chandler, A. D., ed., *The Papers of Dwight D. Eisenhower*, II, Johns Hopkins, Baltimore, 1970, pp. 927–29. Cf. Eisenhower to Winifred

Dykes, 30 January 1943, Dykes Papers.
29. See 10 October 1942.
30. See 12 October 1942.
31. BUS(J)(41)40, 'The Establishment of a Nucleus British Military Mission', 4 April 1941, CAB 99/5; BOXES 38, Eden to Halifax, 10 May 1941, CAB 122/12, PRO.
32. Vogel to Dykes, 19 October 1941, WO 193/319, PRO.
33. BOXES 92, [amended] COS Directive to JSM, 6 September 1941, CAB 122/23, PRO.
34. UK Treasury Delegation estimates (rounded out), CAB 122/66, PRO.
35. Macready, G., *In the Wake of the Great*, Clowes, London, 1965, p. 194; Halifax, Lord, *Fulness of Days*, Collins, London, 1957, p. 262; Halifax diary, 6 June 1941, and secret diary, 14 May 1942, Halifax Papers, Borthwick Institute of Historical Research, York.
36. Coleridge to Cornwall-Jones, 28 September 1941, CAB 122/1582, PRO.
37. Dykes to Jacob, 7 and 10 December 1942, and correspondence in CAB 109/49, PRO; Lord Inchyra (Derick Hoyer Millar) interview, 30 May 1984.
38. Dykes to Mary Ravenshear, 8 March 1942, Dykes Papers.
39. Jacob memoir, 'Vivian Dykes' (1982); LETOD 64, 4 April 1942, FO 800/410, PRO. The Marshall Memorandum is printed as 'Operations in Western Europe' in *Grand Strategy*, III, ii, pp. 675–81.
40. Carver to Redman, 28 April 1943, CAB 122/1582, PRO.
41. COS(W) 271, 1 September 1942, and correspondence in PREM 3/439/14; Dykes to Stirling, 2 September 1942, CAB 122/1582, PRO. See 1 and 2 September 1942.
42. Stirling to Coleridge and Dykes, 18 February and 3 March 1942, CAB 122/1582; JSM History, III, p. 3, CAB 102/386, PRO.
43. Hodges, A., *Alan Turing*, Unwin, London, 1985, pp. 246–48, 269; Simkins, P., *The Cabinet War Rooms*, Imperial War Museum, London, 1983, p. 58.
44. RAF Delegation History, AIR 45/2, PRO.
45. Churchill, speech to US Congress, 26 December 1941, Kimball, W. F., ed., *Churchill and Roosevelt*, I, Princeton UP, Princeton, 1984, p. 309; Churchill to Roosevelt (unsent first draft), 5 February 1942, PREM 4/17/3, PRO.
46. Donnelly autobiography (unpublished, 1979), pp. 646, 668–69, Donnelly Papers, US Army Military History Institute.
47. Dill to Montgomery-Massingberd, 3 September 1942, Montgomery-Massingberd Papers, 160/21b, Liddell Hart Archive, King's College, London.
48. See for example Gristwood, S., *Recording Angels*, Harrap, London, 1988; Mallon, T., *A Book of One's Own*, Ticknor & Fields, New York, 1985. The categories are Mallon's.
49. Bryant, A., *The Turn of the Tide* and *Triumph in the West*, Collins, London, 1957 and 1959 [hereafter Bryant I and II]. See especially Bryant's 'preludes', pp. 13–44 and 15–26.
50. Hamilton, General Sir Ian, *Gallipoli Diary*, I, Arnold, London, 1920, p. vii.
51. Ibid., p. vi.
52. Dykes to Donovan, covering note with diary, File 940, Box 75B, Donovan Papers, US Army Military History Institute.

Part I: The Donovan Trip
26 December 1940 – 3 March 1941

1. 1608, FO to Lampson, 24 December 1940, FO 371/24263, PRO. Cf. 2875, Lothian to FO, 1 December 1940, ibid.
2. Troy, T. F., *Donovan and the CIA*, University Publications of America, Frederick, MD, 1981, p. 37. 'Bear-leading' was the expression used by the official who briefed Dykes before departure. Mack note, 23 December 1940, FO 371/24263, PRO.
3. The best account of the trip is Smith, B. F., *The Shadow Warriors*, Deutsch, London, 1983, pp. 40–54. See also Cave Brown, A., *The Last Hero*, Joseph, London, 1982, pp. 152–59; Stevenson, W., *A Man Called Intrepid*, Macmillan, London, 1976, pp. 225–29; and Troy, pp. 36–41. For the Dykes–Eden argument see 20 February 1941.
4. Ford, C., *Donovan of OSS*, Little, Brown, Boston, 1970, pp. 13–14. On Donovan's life and times see also Cave Brown, Smith, and Troy.
5. On this earlier trip see Smith, pp. 30–39, and Troy, pp. 29–36.
6. MacVeagh diary, 15 January 1941, in Iatrides, J. O., ed., *Ambassador MacVeagh Reports*,

Princeton UP, Princeton, 1980, p. 283. Cf. Balfour minute, 19 December 1940, FO 371/ 24263, PRO.
7. Colville diary, 14 January 1941, in Colville, p. 400.
8. Retailed by Rendel to Nichols, 24 January 1941, FO 371/29722, PRO.
9. Quoted in Smith, p. 52.
10. See 8 January (Wavell), 11 and 17 February (Marshall-Cornwall), 11 January (Wilson), 9 February (Cunningham) 1941.
11. See 3 and 20 February 1941. Cf. telegrams in 'Colonel Donovan's Mission' File, Box 304, Hopkins Papers, Roosevelt Library, Hyde Park, New York.
12. See 13 January and 5 February 1941.
13. See 20 February 1941.
14. Churchill at War Cabinet, 24 February 1941, WM(41) 20th Confidential Annex, CAB 65/21, PRO; Avon, Lord, *The Eden Memoirs*, II, Cassell, London, 1965, pp. 195, 198; O/43125, Dill to Haining, 21 February 1941, PREM 3/206/3, PRO.
15. See 20 and 25 February 1941. Cf. van Creveld, M., 'Prelude to Disaster', *Journal of Contemporary History* 9, 3 (July 1974), pp. 65–93; Cruikshank, C., *Greece 1940–41*, Davis-Poynter, London, 1976.
16. See 10 January 1941.
17. See for example 15 and 29 January and 1 March 1941.
18. See 30 January and 9 February 1941. It is now known that British Air Attachés in Belgrade had a hand in the coup deposing Paul in March 1941. See Wheeler, M. C., *Britain and the War for Yugoslavia*, Columbia, Boulder, 1980.
19. See 25 January 1941.
20. See 8 January and 24–25 February 1941.
21. Morgenthau diary, 20 March 1941, quoted Troy, p. 40. Cf. General Kennedy's reaction, Kennedy, pp. 87–88.
22. For Donovan's role in the development of the CIA see Ranelagh, Smith and Troy.
23. General (later Field Marshal) Sir John Dill (1881–1944): Commandant, Staff College, Camberley, 1930–33; Director of Military Operations & Intelligence, 1934–36; GOC Palestine & Transjordan, 1936–37; GOC Southern Command, 1938–39; Commander 1st Corps, BEF, 1939–40; CIGS, 1940–41; Head of British Joint Staff Mission, Washington, and senior British member of the Combined Chiefs of Staff, 1942–44.
24. On this earlier trip see Troy, pp. 27–28.
25. Cave Brown (p. 153) claims that the meal, whose date and time he mistakes, came from a birthday hamper provided for Donovan by Lord Mountbatten, containing three bottles of Moselle, a flask of hot turtle soup, fresh lobster, cold pheasant, Stilton cheese and Bath Olivers – all served by an orderly in a white mess jacket with gleaming brass buttons and white gloves!
26. Channon was also on a quasi-official trip around the Mediterranean, recorded in his famous diary, January–February 1941. Rhodes James, pp. 342ff.
27. Cf. Channon diary, 3 January 1941, Rhodes James, p. 343. See Freya Stark's evocative travel writing, *The Southern Gates of Arabia* [1936], *A Winter in Arabia* and *Over the Rim of the World* (selected letters, edited by Caroline Moorehead), Murray, London, 1982, 1940 and 1988.
28. Forerunner of the Special Air Service (SAS).
29. Later Sir Michael Wright (1901–76): 1st Secretary, Washington, 1943–46; Ambassador to Norway, 1951–54; Ambassador to Iraq, 1954–58; delegate to disarmament conferences of early 1960s.
30. O/35174, Dykes to Dill, 13 January 1941, Dykes Papers.
31. Catroux, Note pour le Colonel Donovan, 14 January 1941, ibid.
32. Admiral Sir Andrew (later Lord) Cunningham (1883–1963): C in C Mediterranean, 1939–42, 1943; Naval C in C TORCH Expeditionary Force, 1942; 1st Sea Lord, 1943–46.
33. Harold (later Lord) Caccia (1905–   ): Ambassador to USA, 1956–61; Permanent Under Secretary, Foreign Office, 1962–65.
34. Guy 'Guido' (later Major General Sir Guy) Salisbury-Jones had been a student at the Staff College, Camberley, with Dykes in 1932–33 (when Dill was Commandant). He became Marshal of the Diplomatic Corps (1950–61) and a renowned viticulturist.
35. For a richly detailed, fictionalised account of the society and atmosphere in Athens during this period see Olivia Manning's *Balkan Trilogy*, Penguin, London, 1981.
36. Cf. note of conversation with General Heywood, 16 January 1941, Dykes Papers.

37. For MacVeagh's view of the Donovan trip see Iatrides, pp. 281–93.
38. Donovan to Knox [draft], 18 [?17] January 1941, Dykes Papers. Copies of six Donovan–Knox telegrams, including this one, are in 740.0011 EW 1939, RG 59, Diplomatic Branch, National Archives, Washington, DC. A copy of Knox's 15 February reply to some of them, delivered by hand to London, is in the Dykes Papers.
39. When they were both in Military Intelligence at the War Office.
40. Donovan, memorandum of conversation with the Bulgarian Foreign Minister, 21 January 1941, Dykes Papers.
41. Donovan, memorandum of conversation with the King, 22 January 1941, ibid. Cf. Rendel to Nichols, 24 January 1941, FO 371/29722, PRO.
42. For an ironic and affectionate portrait of the émigrés of Europe in London during the war see Anthony Powell's *The Military Philosophers*, Heinemann, London, 1968. Powell was an Intelligence Corps liaison officer with the Poles, Belgians, Czechs, and Free French, among others.
43. Later Sir Ronald Campbell: Minister, Belgrade, 1939–41; Minister, Washington, 1941–45; Assistant Under Secretary, Foreign Office, 1945–46; Ambassador to Egypt, 1946–50.
44. Later an acclaimed writer, Leigh Fermor was then a daring Intelligence officer. After the fighting in Greece and Crete in 1941, he organised the resistance on Crete, living for over two years in the mountains disguised as a shepherd. He effected the capture and evacuation of the German commander there. See his *A Time of Gifts* and *Between the Woods and the Water*, Murray, London, 1977 and 1986.
45. Nominally Assistant Air Attaché (and pilot for Donovan and Dykes), Forbes seems to have been heavily involved in intelligence work. 'C' was the head of the Secret Intelligence Service, Colonel (later Major General Sir Stewart) Menzies. 'D' may be a reference to Section D of a sabotage organisation subsumed within the newly reorganised SOE. See Foot, M. R. D., *Resistance*, Paladin, London, 1978. See also 9 February 1941.
46. Donovan to Knox, 3 February 1941, Dykes family papers. Repeated to CIGS, 5 February 1941.
47. Dykes to Dill, 5 February 1941, ibid.
48. Cf. Churchill to Roosevelt, 28 January 1941, Churchill, III, p. 24. On Churchill's interest in Donovan's work, see Smith, p. 429, n. 78.
49. See 5 January 1941.
50. Note on conversation with Admiral Cunningham and Air Chief Marshal Longmore in HMS *Warspite* on 9 February 1941, Dykes Papers.
51. Euchre is an American card game for two, three or four persons, with the 32, 28 or 24 highest cards of the pack. If a player fails to make three tricks he is 'euchred', and his adversary scores against him. Cf. Channon diary, 10 February 1941, Rhodes James, p. 356.
52. Donovan to Knox, 20 February 1941, Dykes Papers.
53. Note of conversation with Mr Eden and General Sir John Dill at Cairo on 20 February 1941, ibid. Cf. Eden, p. 198; Dill to Haining, 21 February 1941, PREM 3/206/3, PRO.
54. Donovan to Roosevelt, 21 February 1941, ibid.
55. And later the creator of James Bond. See also 25 February 1941.
56. Special Operations 2, the sabotage and resistance support section of the SOE.
57. Brigadier (later Lieutenant General Sir) Ian Jacob (1899–   ): Assistant Secretary of the War Cabinet, 1940–46; Deputy Secretary, 1950–51; Director General of the BBC, 1952–60.
58. Major General Hastings (later General Lord) Ismay (1887–1965): Assistant Secretary, Committee of Imperial Defence, 1926–30; Staff Officer, War Office, 1933–36; Deputy Secretary, Committee of Imperial Defence, 1936–38; Chief of Staff to Minister of Defence (Churchill) and Deputy Secretary of the War Cabinet, 1940–45; Secretary General, NATO, 1952–57.
59. Major General Sir John Kennedy (1878–1948): Deputy Director and Director of Military Operations, 1938–44; Governor of Southern Rhodesia, 1946–54.

Part II: Washington – Organising for War
12 December 1941 – 5 April 1942

1. 'Washington goes to War', *Life*, 5 January 1942. See also dos Passos, J., *State of the Nation*, Routledge, London, 1945; Nicholas, W. H., 'Wartime Washington', *National Geographic*

Magazine, September 1943.
2. Stimson, H. L. & Bundy, M., *On Active Service in Peace and War*, Hutchinson, London, 1949, p. 281.
3. Dill to Brooke, 3 January 1942, quoted Danchev, p. 57.
4. 'Washington goes to War'.
5. See Danchev, A., 'The Combined Chiefs of Staff and the making of allied strategy in the Second World War', in Freedman, L. & O'Neill, R., eds., essays presented to Sir Michael Howard, OUP, Oxford, forthcoming.
6. See 11 January 1942. On Monnet in Washington see his *Memoirs*, Collins, London, 1978, pp. 150ff.
7. See 11 March, 14 March, 12 May, 18 May 1942.
8. 1930Q/11, Dill to Brooke, 11 March 1942, AIR 8/1072, PRO. See also 11–16 March 1942.
9. Eisenhower to Marshall, 16 March 1942, in Chandler, I, pp. 188–89.
10. See Danchev, *Very Special Relationship*, Brassey's, London, 1986.
11. JSM 305 and 322, Dill to COS, 16 and 27 July 1942, CAB 105/39, PRO.
12. Brooke diary, 9 February 1942, quoted Bryant, I, p. 296.
13. Turner to Gerow, n.d. [?11 January 1942], quoted Danchev, p. 12.
14. See 11 September 1942.
15. Cunningham to Noble, 6 February 1944, quoted Danchev, p. 65.
16. Bedell Smith to Ismay, 20 February 1943, ibid., p. 61.
17. Auxiliary Territorial Service for women, forerunner of the Women's Royal Army Corps (WRAC).
18. See 16 May 1942 for a survivor's account.
19. Commander Charles R. 'Tommy' Thompson RN (retired) and Detective Inspector W. H. Thompson respectively.
20. Major (later Sir) Reginald Macdonald-Buchanan ('Narcissus'), more companion than ADC: a man of a certain age, a whisky magnate, increasingly deaf and ineffectual (see 24 December 1941), devoted to Dill; relinquished his appointment with great reluctance in mid-1942.
21. W.W.1, American–British Strategy, 23 December 1941, printed in *Grand Strategy*, III, ii, appendix 1.
22. Most recently 3rd Army, on manoeuvres in the southern states. Summoned by Marshall to the War Department as Assistant Chief of Staff in the key Operations and Plans Division (OPD), a vital proving ground for his subsequent career. Left for the European Theatre of Operations, and fame and fortune, in June 1942.
23. Thomas T. 'Tom' Handy took over OPD from Eisenhower in the rank of Major General. Later General, he became one of the most trusted of the small circle of 'Marshall men' around the Chief of Staff.
24. The rebarbative Rear Admiral (later Admiral) Richmond Kelly Turner, expelled at length to an active command in the Pacific in 1942.
25. A reference to Coleridge's relatively lowly rank – Commander RN.
26. Son of the Earl of Antrim and sometime Conservative MP for Dartford (1924–29), a gregarious and remarkably effective figure.
27. Knight Grand Cross of the Order of the Bath.
28. Commander of the Order of the British Empire.
29. W.W.8, Post-ARCADIA Collaboration, 8 January 1942, CAB 99/17, PRO. Revised as the combined paper W.W.16, 14 January 1942, printed in *Grand Strategy*, III, ii, pp. 673–74.
30. On the ABC Conversations see Matloff and Snell, pp. 32–43.
31. A response to the suggestion that Dill should represent Churchill in Washington. On the genesis of Dill's appointment, so vital to the Anglo-American alliance, see Danchev, pp. 10ff.
32. GREY 338, Hollis to Stirling, 14 January 1942. Cf. 226, Dykes to Price, 16 January 1942, both CAB 120/29, PRO.
33. The Public Health Building is now the Department of Interior, South.
34. The unpleasantness was carefully muffled in the official record. Cf. C.C.S. 3rd meeting (Item 10), 3 February 1942, CAB 88/1, PRO.
35. At $4 to £1.
36. Dykes to Hollis, 21 November 1942, CAB 12/177, PRO.
37. Both speeches at this prestigious event received extensive publicity. See *New York Times* and *Washington Post*, 27 February 1942.
38. 1930Q/11, Dill to Brooke, 11 March 1942, AIR 8/1072, PRO; extensively used by Marshall at

JCS 6th meeting, 16 March 1942.

39. The quarters at Fort Myer, Virginia, were just outside Washington D.C. The Pentagon (then under construction) occupies adjoining land.

40. This interesting exchange can be followed in JSM 104, Dill to COS; T384/2, Churchill to Dill; and JSM 122, Dill to Churchill. 5, 14 and 15 March 1942, PREM 3/478/6, PRO. See Danchev, p. 22.

41. Bowes-Lyon headed a Political Warfare Executive Mission in Washington, 1942–44. Whitney, an American intenational lawyer, was, according to his entry in Who's Who, engaged in 'various missions for the US Government in liaison with the UK' (i.e. intelligence work) throughout the war.

42. JSM 155, 1 April 1942, CAB 105/38, PRO.

Part III: Washington – Finding a Strategy
6 April 1942 – 14 July 1942

1. Marshall to Dykes, 23 March 1942, Marshall Papers, 58/42, Marshall Research Foundation.
2. Wedemeyer, A. C., Wedemeyer Reports, Holt, New York, 1958, p. 80; interview, 19 August 1982. See also pp. 84, 135–36, 211–12.
3. Franks, O., Britain and the Tide of World Affairs, OUP, Oxford, 1955, p. 35.
4. 'Operations in Western Europe', printed in Grand Strategy, III, ii, pp. 675–81. The Anglo-American strategic debate of April to July is concisely treated in Grand Strategy, IV, pp. xv–xxv.
5. Wedemeyer, p. 135.
6. See 19 June 1942.
7. 107, Churchill to Roosevelt, 8 July 1942, in Kimball, I, pp. 520–21. Amplified in COS(W) 217, COS to JSM, 8 July 1942, CAB 105/54, PRO.
8. See for example 10 July 1942.
9. On suspicion of Churchill see Danchev, pp. 32ff.
10. LETOD 193, Dykes to Stirling, 10 July 1942, CAB 122/302, PRO.
11. Halifax secret diary, 15 July 1942, quoted in Danchev, p. 35.
12. First encountered on the Donovan trip. See 24 January 1941.
13. An isolationist and protectionist pressure group concerned to safeguard American interests first, last and always.
14. Forester was then working for the Ministry of Information. See also 11 June and 1 October 1942.
15. Also the well-connected and wealthy owner of Ditchley Park, near Oxford, Churchill's retreat from the bombers 'when the moon was high'. See Tree's memoir of that title (Macmillan, London, 1975). His connections extended from the social and political into the intelligence sphere (e.g. Donovan).
16. Of especial interest to Dykes the Royal Engineer.
17. Formerly Churchill's Principal Private Secretary (1940–41).
18. In a huge covert operation of immense thoroughness, based in Bermuda, the British were opening and examining thousands of pieces of international mail. The information was used to monitor, e.g. German commercial and intelligence-gathering activities in South America and elsewhere. The operation was shown to Donovan en route to London in December 1940.
19. Inventor of the bulletproof material 'pykerite'. See also 27 May, 19 June and 25 July 1942.
20. For the first time since early December 1941.
21. Stevenson worked under William Stephenson (later Sir William, codename INTREPID, no relation) in the clandestine British Security Coordination offices in New York. See his best-selling but unreliable account of A Man Called Intrepid.
22. Part of an 'exchange' scheme arranged by Dill and Marshall. See Danchev, p. 99.
23. On the Special Information Centre see Joan Bright's own memoir, The Inner Circle, Hutchinson, London, 1971.
24. 'Strategy is none of their godamn business.' Quoted in LETOD 350, Dykes to Jacob, 6 October 1942, CAB 120/173, PRO.
25. Leahy became chief of staff to the US Commander in Chief, that is, the President – referred to only half-jokingly by Roosevelt as his 'leg-man'. See Danchev, p. 58.
26. Knight Grand Cross of the Order of the British Empire.

27. See also 23 June 1942.
28. As a commanding officer, in the substantive rank of Lieutenant Colonel.
29. Nash at one time ran a sweet shop in Kidderminster. I am grateful to Dr Mike Pugh for this information.
30. LETOD 193, Dykes to Stirling, 10 July 1942, CAB 122/302, PRO. See also 11 April 1942.
31. Dill's important JSM 300 to Churchill, 14 July 1942, CAB 105/39; analysed in the Joint Planning Staff's *Aide-Mémoire* on Future Operations, 16 July 1942, AIR 8/1074; discussed with Dykes at COS(42)75th meeting (O), 18 July 1942, CAB 79/56. All PRO. Cf. Brooke diary, 17 July 1942, quoted Bryant, I, pp. 422–23; Churchill, IV, pp. 396–97; Kennedy, pp. 253–55.

Part IV: TORCH – Conception and Birth
15 July 1942 – 15 November 1942

1. CCS 94, 'Operations in 1942–43', 24 July 1942, printed in *Grand Strategy*, IV, pp. xxiii–xxiv.
2. See 30 July 1942.
3. Marshall to Roosevelt, 10 July 1942, OPD Executive Files 10, Item 53, RG 165, National Archives.
4. See Stoler, M. A., 'The "Pacific First" alternative in American World War II strategy', *International History Review*, II, 3 (July 1980), pp. 432–52.
5. Ibid. See also 10–15 July and 15 August 1942.
6. Printed in full in Kimball, I.
7. Slim diary, quoted in Danchev, pp. 39–40.
8. Dykes note, n.d., with JIC daily summary 252, 19 August 1942, CAB 122/1582, PRO.
9. See 8 November 1942.
10. COS(42)75th meeting (O), CAB 79/56; Dykes to Coleridge, n.d. [20 July 1942], CAB 122/302, PRO.
11. *Soldiers and Statesmen*, Cassell, London, I, pp. 73–149. Secretary Stimson, for one, thought history was about to repeat itself. Dill's allusion sparked a run on the book in Whitehall. Churchill was not amused. Stimson diary, 12 and 15 July 1942, Stimson Papers, CUL; Kennedy, p. 254.
12. A suspicion never dispelled. See Brooke diary, 20 and 21 July 1942, 24 May and 23 August 1943, Alanbrooke Papers, KCL.
13. On Ismay's 'dislike' of Dill see also 15 August 1942. For the significance of such attitudes see Danchev, A., 'Dilly-Dally, or Having the Last Word', *Journal of Contemporary History* 22 (1987), pp. 21–44.
14. CCS 94.
15. I.e. a stiff reply.
16. Dykes, Note on the development of American thought in favour of offensive action in the Pacific Theatre, 15 August 1942, Dykes Papers.
17. And Democratic candidate in the 1952 Presidential election, defeated by Eisenhower.
18. IZ 1227, Dykes to Dill, 23 August 1942, AIR 8/1075. Dill's earlier message was COS(W) 261, Dill to Dykes for Marshall, 21 August 1942, CAB 105/54; his response, OZ 1087, Dill to Dykes, 25 August 1942, AIR 8/1075. All PRO.
19. JSM 367, Dykes to Dill for COS, 25 August 1942, CAB 105/39. Dill replied that the COS 'realise that we are not just post offices and at our time of life must have discretion in representing their views . . . [and] that we have done what was possible to counteract the American swing to the Pacific'. 60885, Dill to JSM, 26 August 1942, CAB 122/1061, PRO.
20. Dykes to Stirling, 26 August 1942, CAB 122/1582, PRO.
21. Nancy Furlong (née Charrington), daughter of a brewery owner and widow of a fellow student of Dykes's at the Staff College, was Dill's second wife and many years his junior. They were married in October 1941. See Danchev, p. 5.
22. Dykes to Stirling, 29 August 1942, CAB 122/1582, PRO.
23. Dykes to Stirling, 2 September 1942, CAB 12/1582, PRO.
24. JSM 376, JSM [Dykes] to COS, 3 September 1942, CAB 105/39, PRO. This telegram in effect started the protracted process of strategic review which reached a climax at the Casablanca conference in January 1943. See Danchev, pp. 88–95.

25. Dykes, The present state of combined planning with the USA, 7 September 1942, CAB 122/115, PRO.
26. Later Naval Commander of the Eastern Task Force in the Mediterranean (1943) and Allied Naval Commander-in-Chief of the Expeditionary Force for OVERLORD (1944).
27. Said by Dill to out-King King. JSM 386, Dill to COS, 15 September 1942, CAB 105/39, PRO.
28. Stirling to Dykes, 13 September 1942, CAB 122/1582, PRO.
29. On the persistently vexatious Persian railway question see Dykes to Dill, 21 September 1942, CAB 122/115, and Major E. H. Steele-Baume's diary of events, 22 September 1942, CAB 122/1582, PRO.
30. Dykes to Dill, 21 September 1942, CAB 122/1155, PRO. This memorandum was passed 'off the record' by Dill to Marshall, and by Marshall to Handy.
31. Dykes to Stirling, 23 September 1942, CAB 122/1582, PRO.
32. Dykes to Dill, 26 September 1942, CAB 122/115, PRO.
33. At Bletchley Park. Jocularly known as the Golf, Cheese and Chess Society (GCCS). Forerunner of the present day Government Communications Headquarters (GCHQ).
34. *The Ship* appeared in 1943 (Penguin edition, London, 1949), 'dedicated with the deepest respect to the officers and ship's company of HMS *Penelope*' (HMS *Artemis* in the book).
35. I.e. for Giraud, then in Vichy France, to lead the French forces in North Africa into the Allied camp, a hope substantially fulfilled. After the TORCH landings and the assassination of Admiral Darlan, Giraud became High Commissioner of French North and West Africa; on the formation of the Committee for National Liberation, co-president with the prideful de Gaulle – hence the next sentence in the diary.
36. Dykes, Combined Chiefs of Staff Organisation, 10 October 1942, circulated as a report by Admiral Cunningham, COS(42)319(0), 17 October 1942, PREM 3/465/1, PRO.
37. Cocktails made with whisky (one glass of rye or Canadian), Angostura bitters (two dashes) and sugar (one lump), according to the *Savoy Cocktail Book*.
38. COS(42)345(0)(Final), American–British Strategy, 30 October 1942, PREM 3/499/6 (with Churchill's annotations), PRO.
39. Dill's actions and the Prime Ministerial reaction can be followed in Danchev, pp. 23 and 90–91. See also 9 November 1942.
40. IZ 2151, Dill to Churchill, 11 November 1942, in IZ 2127, Dill to Brooke, 9 November 1942, CAB 122/21, PRO.
41. KINGPIN was Giraud's codename.
42. See 9 October 1942.

Index

ABDA (Australian-British-Dutch-American area) 82, 83, 85, 88, 91, 93, 96, 97, 105, 109, 110, 112, 113
Aircraft allocation 141
Aquitania 114
ARCADIA 7, 69–70
Armistice terms 216
Arnold, General 'Hap' 120, 121
Aspasia, Princess of Greece 35
Atlantic Charter 6
Australia 137, 140, 144, 146
Australian Corps 106

Badoglio, General 24
Bataan 131
Battershill, Governor 49
Beaumont-Nesbitt, Paddy 89, 99, 108, 114, 165, 216
Beaverbrook, Lord 73, 74, 108, 118
Bedell Smith, Brigadier General Walter 7–9, 70, 71, 72, 127, 130, 155, 171, 174, 178, 180, 181, 183, 188, 190, 196, 199, 200
Benghazi 98
Benson, Colonel Rex 83
Berkeley, Major Claud 104
Blunt, Jasper 34
BOLERO 128, 129, 136, 138, 139, 141, 143, 145, 151, 158, 161, 163, 166, 167, 168, 175, 176, 178, 180, 183, 189, 203, 205, 206
Bond, James 23
Boris, King 40
Bourne, Brigadier Geoff (later General Lord Bourne) 91, 93, 127, 174, 188–9
Bowes-Lyon, Hon. David 121
Bowhill 201
Bramwell-Davis, Ronnie 76, 96, 164
Brant, General 148
Bright, Joan 151
Brooke, General Sir Alan (later Field Marshal Lord Alanbrooke), 1, 7, 70, 71, 129
Burgis, Lawrence 150
Burma 138, 158, 207, 211
Burns, General 92, 94, 97
Butler, Harold 208
Butler, Smedley 93

Cairo Conference 14

Campbell, Ronnie 94, 131
Canberra, HMAS 187
Casablanca 188, 225
Catroux, General 27, 54
Censorship 146, 159
Chance, Leslie 91, 98, 114, 131
Chiang Kai-Shek 82, 101, 117
Chinese Army Corps 211
Churchill, Mary 73
Churchill, Winston 1, 73, 78, 129, 172
Civil Missions 87
Clark, Ashley 143
Clarke, Brigadier Dudley 30, 57
Coleridge, Commander Richard (later Captain Lord) 3, 12, 93, 94, 96, 184
Combined Chiefs of Staff 7, 14
Combined Intelligence Committee 136
Combined Munitions Assignment Board 131, 134, 135, 136, 138, 185–6, 202, 210
Combined Planning Staff 130, 203, 205, 221, 222, 223
Combined Production and Resources Board 120, 157, 165, 167, 185, 196, 208
Combined Raw Materials Board 140
Combined War Production Board 140
Commonwealth Munitions Committee 154
Cooke, Admiral 'Savvy' 71–2
Coordinating Council 120
Cornwall, HMS 131
Cornwall-Jones, Brigadier Arthur 14
Cunningham, Admiral 52, 72, 160, 191, 193, 199, 210, 214
Cunningham, General 27

Darlan, Admiral 217
Davenport, John 188
Davidson, General 215–16
Davison, Patrick 114
De Valera 25
Devonshire, HMS 131
Dieppe, raid on 191
Dietrich, Marlene 162
Dill, Field Marshal Sir John 5, 7, 22, 59, 60, 69, 70, 71, 80, 82, 83, 92, 95, 102, 142
Dobbie, General 25
Dominion Missions 97

237

Donovan, Colonel William J. ('Wild Bill') 5–6, 10, 19–65, 79, 81, 86, 99, 131, 199
DOTELs 12–13
Douglas, Sir William 85
Duke of York, HMS 73, 90, 110
Dulwich College 137
Dunbar-Nasmyth, Admiral 24
Dunsany, Lord and Lady 34
Dutch East Indies 121
Dutch representation 98
Dykes, Ada Winifred 4
Dykes, Alfred Herbert 4
Dykes, Brigadier Vivian
  Bedell Smith, Brigadier General Walter, on 7–8; *see also* Bedell Smith
  birth 4
  CBE 5
  children 4
  China, service in (1926–8) 4
  death of (1943) 2–3
  diarist 1, 15–16
  education 4
  Ismay, General on 3; *see also* Ismay, General
  Jacob, Brigadier Ian, on 5; *see also* Jacob, Brigadier Ian
  MBE 4
  marriage (1922) 4
  Monnet, Jean on 3; *see also* Monnet, Jean
  Royal Engineers, adjutant of (1929–31) 4
    commissioned into (1917) 3
    rejoins (1922) 4
  Royal Signals, service with (1918–22) 4
  Second World War, service in
    Atlantic Conference 6, 75
    Casablanca 1–2
    Combined Chiefs of Staff 9, 10, 73; *see also Combined Chiefs of Staff*
    Donovan Trip (1940–41) 5–6, 15, 19–23
      Alexandria 34, 52, 61
      Ankara 45–8
      Athens 34–7, 43–5
      Baghdad 54–5
      Belgrade 40–1
      Cairo 26–34, 51–61
      Cyprus 48–9
      Gibraltar 25, 61–62, 64
      Istanbul 45
      Jannina (Ioánnina, Greece) 42–3
      Jerusalem 49–51
      Koritza (now Korçë, Albania) 41–2
      Lisbon 64
      Madrid 62–4
      Malta 25–6, 61
      Nish (Niš, Yugoslavia) 39
      Salonika 36–8
      Sofia 39–40

Fort Belvior, visit to 143–4
Gander (Newfoundland), impressions of 148, 182
Joint Staff Mission, service with 7, 10–14, pp73ff
Labrador 148
London, visits to 64–5, 149–52, 175–81
Montreal 147–48, 201
Newfoundland 153
Nigeria, HMS, visit to 218–20
Ottawa 201–202
Quonset Airfield, visit to 184–5
Royal Engineers, command in 5
War Cabinet Office 5, 13, 16; *see also* War Cabinet Office
Washington, ARCADIA Conference in 7, 69
  embarks for 74–6
  impressions of 69–70
  working in, 76–123, 130–47, 153–68, 183–201, 203–18, 220–6
US Distinguished Service Medal, awarded 3
War Office, Italian Section of Military Intelligence of (1934–5) 5
  Overseas Defence Committee, secretary of (1935–8) 5
Wedemeyer, Colonel (later General) 'Al', on 127; *see also* Wedemeyer, Colonel

Eagle, HMS 188
Eden, Sir Anthony 22, 58, 59, 60
Egypt 28, 163, 166, 167, 222
Eisenhower, General 8, 70, 76, 80, 91, 102, 117, 119, 127, 133, 135, 139, 147, 150, 151, 160, 177, 178, 192, 199
Elmhirst, Air Marshall 30
Erskine, Brigadier 55
Evatt 146
Evill, Air Marshall 120, 121
EXCESS 33, 36

Far East 80, 102–3, 106
Fish, Bert 28, 63
Fleming, Commander Ian 22, 62
Fleming, Peter 62
Forbes 44, 45, 48, 49, 50, 53
Forester, C. S. 4, 137, 155–6, 210
Formidable, HMS 52
Frankfurter, Mr & Mrs Felix 95
Franks, Oliver 128

Galloway, Brigadier 30
Garforth, Bob 131

Georgoulis, Colonel   42
Gerow, Brigadier-General   82–3, 102
Gifford, General   58
Glassford, Admiral   218–19
Gneisenau   105
Godfrey, Admiral   20
Gort, General   20
Griggs, Margaret   165
Greece   28, 34–7, 43
Guadalcanal   187, 216
GYMNAST   77, 78, 79, 82–4, 87, 128,
   159, 166, 167, 171, 176, 177–9, 180,
   181, 183, 189, 200; *see also* TORCH

Haining, General   58
Halifax, Lord   11, 106
Hall, Noel   99
Hamilton, General Sir Ian   15
Hankey, Sir Maurice   5
Harris, Air Marshal (later 'Bomber')   10
Haverfordwest   2
Hermes, HMS   131
Heywood, General   55–6
Hoare, Sam   62, 63
Hoblin, Miss   164
Hollis, Brigadier Jo   75, 142
Hong Kong   75
Hopkins, Harry   22, 69, 92, 128
Hore-Ruthven, Mrs   29
Hornet, HMS   220
Hoyer Millar, Derick   12, 94
Hutchinson, General   28

Illustrious, HMS   33
India   135
Indiana Ocean   131
Institute of Peace Affairs   166
Intelligence organisation   22
Invasion of the Continent, plans for   119
Iraq   204
Ireland   25
Ismay, General   65, 72, 131

Jacob, Brigadier Ian   15, 64, 75, 82, 142
Java   83, 107, 108, 109, 111, 113
Jefferson, Mike   182
Joint Intelligence Committee,   130, 172
Jowitt, Sir William   208

Kennedy, General   65, 82
Kerr, Reggie   79, 94
King, Admiral Ernest J.   7, 70–2, 90, 91,
   92, 101, 113, 116, 130
King, C. J. S.   73

Knatchbull- Hugessen, Ambassador   45–6
Knox, Captain   131
Knox, Colonel Frank   20, 35
Koritzis, Prime Minister   44
Kremer   86

Lambe, Captain Charles   74, 75, 79, 80, 91,
   93
Lampson, Lady   34, 52
Lampson, Sir Miles (later Lord
   Killearn)   26, 60
Lancaster aircraft   200
Leahy, Admiral   154
Lease and Loan Bill   58
Leggatt, Wing Commander   185
Leigh Fermor, Patrick   22, 42
LETODs   12
Liberator aircraft   175
Libya   156, 160, 163, 164
Little, Admiral Sir Charles 'Tiny'   10, 155
Lomax, Brigadier   32
Longmore, Air Marshal   26–7, 29, 30, 51,
   52, 58, 59
Lyttelton, Oliver   108, 118, 146, 150, 213,
   222, 223, 225

Macdonald, (Air Attache)   41
Macdonald-Buchanan   74, 77, 91
McDonell, Angus   78
McDowell, Major   93, 95, 96
McEnery, Miss   188
MacKay, General   32
MacMichael, High Commissioner   49
Macmillan, Harold   1
MacVeagh, Ambassador Lincoln   20–21, 35
MacNair, Lieutenant General   77
Macready, General   87, 89, 217
Madagascar   140, 141
Mahomed Ali, Prince   56
Mainprice, Joan   104, 105, 112, 113, 116,
   119, 122, 133, 134, 137, 138, 145, 147,
   153, 165, 187, 192, 200, 205, 211, 220,
   223
Malaya   74
Maloney   132
Manor Court Country Club   103
Marrakesh   1
Marshall, General George C.   6, 8, 9, 70,
   71, 81, 128, 135
Marshall Memorandum   128
Marshall-Cornwall, General   29, 56
Marx, Louis   118, 119
Mason-Macfarlane, General   25
Maynard, Air Commodore   25
Metaxas, Prime Minister   35, 44
Middle East   70, 101, 106, 116, 117, 123,
   184, 185, 204, 221

Moats, Miss 209
Monnet, Jean 70, 86, 92, 94, 95, 117, 120,
    133, 209, 214
Monro, Gordon 174
Montgomery, General 225
Montgomery, Paymaster Commander 91
Morgenthau, Henry 23
Morrison, Mr & Mrs 93
Mountbatten, Admiral Lord 128, 152–3,
    158, 181
Munitions Assignment Board 103, 104,
    106, 122
Mussolini 24

Neame, General 49, 50
Nimitz, Admiral 122
North Africa 128, 129, 185, 204, 216, 225
Northern Ireland 100, 101

O'Connor, General 32, 58
Office of Strategic Services 165
Oran (Algeria) 225

Pacific 172
Pacific Command 119
Pacific War Council 121, 133
Palairet, Sir Michael 34
Papagos (Greek Commander-in-Chief) 35–6
Partridge, Miss 151
Paul, Prince 41, 57
Penelope, HMS 210
Pereira, Ambassador 63
Persia 204
Persian Railway 204, 205
Political Warfare Executive 121, 210, 212
Pollock, Brigadier 53
Popoff, Foreign Minister 21
Portal, Air Marshal Sir Charles 217
Pound, Admiral Sir Dudley 134, 135
Price, George 108, 112, 115
Prince Eugen 105
Prince of Wales, HMS 74, 145
Pringle, USS 219
Public Health Buiding 102, 114
Pyke 147, 150, 178, 181

Queen Elizabeth 114
Queen Mary 114

Ramsay, Admiral 200, 203
Repulse HMS 145
RIVIERA 75
Rogers, Group Captain 25

Rommel, Field Marshal 201, 225
Roosevelt, Eleanor 116
Roosevelt, President 1, 172
Ross, Lieutenant Colonel Alick 39, 81
ROUNDUP 128, 149, 150, 153, 171, 176,
    178, 180, 183, 189, 200, 204

St Nazaire 120
Salisbury-Jones, Guy 36, 44
Salter, Sir Arthur 82
Scanlan, General 64
Scharnhorst 105
Scobell, General 26
Second Front 129
Secret Intelligence Service 15, 164, 231
Self, Sir Henry 85, 87, 94, 95, 97, 108,
    118–19, 122, 131, 132, 133, 156
Shearer, Brigadier 22, 29, 53–4
Sherman tank 201
Sherwood, Bob 79
Shipping Priorities Committee 121
Singapore Island 98, 105
Skeet Gallery 148–9
SLEDGEHAMMER 128, 129, 171,
    177–80, 183, 189
Slessor, Wing Commander Jack 4
Slim, Field Marshal 172
Smith, Arthur 33, 54
Smyth, Ada Winifred *see* Dykes, Ada
    Winifred
SNOWPLOUGH 147, 181
Solomon Islands 187, 189
Somerville, Admiral 64
Soong, T.V. 96
Southampton, HMS
Sparkes, Sir Ashley 82
Special Operations Executive 123, 164, 192
Stanley, Oliver 179
Stark, Admiral 81, 101
Stark, Freya 29
Stevenson, Adlai 189
Stewart, Brigadier Guy 2, 73
Stewart, General 202
Stimson, Henry 69
Stirling, William 104
Stoeve, Admiral 212
Stoeve, Mme 136
SUPER-GYMNAST 88, 90

Tedder, Air Marshal Arthur 30, 54
Tobruk 32
Tomlinson, Major General 61
TORCH 171, 180, 181, 183–8, 190–5,
    198–200, 202, 209–11, 216, 217, 220–4
Torr, Brigadier 25, 62
Tulagi 187

Tunisia   225
Turner, Admiral Richmond Kelly   71, 81, 85, 86

US Navy Department   71
USSR   166, 167

Van Mook   101
Van Tetz, Mme   136
Victory Programme   75, 82–4, 86, 133
Vogel, Frank   76, 91

Warspite, HMS   52
Watson, 'Pa'   98
Wavell, General   26, 27, 28, 33, 51, 53, 55, 58, 59, 79, 80, 82, 88, 91, 98, 100, 105, 108, 109
Weddell, Ambassador   62
Wedemeyer, Colonel (later General) 'Al'   135, 205, 206

Wemyss, Lieutenant General Sir Colville 'Chicken'   10, 94, 96, 102
Western Desert   31–3, 179, 184, 213, 218, 220
Weygand, General   27, 40, 44
White, John   132
Whitefoord, Jock   73
Whiteley, Brigadier Jock   30, 33, 52
Whiting, Bill   79
Williams, Brigadier   122
Wilson, Colonel (later General) 'Jumbo'   4, 31
Wilson, Sir Charles (later Lord Moran)   74
Woodford, Mrs   136
WORKSHOP   51
Wright, Michael   33, 52, 55

Yates, Anne   166

Zeebrugge operation   120